RUSSIA'S FUTURE

Photographs by Henry Weaver

RUSSIA'S FUTURE

The Communist Education of Soviet Youth

KITTY WEAVER

PRAEGER

PRAEGER SPECIAL STUDIES • PRAEGER SCIENTIFIC

Library of Congress Cataloging in Publication Data

Weaver, Kitty D
    Russia's future.

    Bibliography: p.
    Includes index.
    1. Communist education—Russia. I. Title.
LA832.W37   370'.947   80-28754
ISBN 0-03-059029-9
ISBN 0-03-059028-0 (pbk.)

Published in 1981 by Praeger Publishers
CBS Educational and Professional Publishing
A Division of CBS, Inc.
521 Fifth Avenue, New York, New York 10175 U.S.A.

123456789 145 987654321

Printed in the United States of America

For Harry

Socialism is built by living people. And these people are raised by Communists. No other political party in history ever took on the task of the re-education and upbringing of such gigantic masses of human beings. The Communists have proved capable of doing so.

Vitaly Korionov
Pravda, January 1, 1968

Preface

The United States, so concerned with the "Soviet threat" and "containing Communism," has largely overlooked an important field of Communism— the Communist education of Soviet children.

Soviet children learn Communism through a vast network of youth organizations, so widespread that few Soviet children are not reached. The Little Octobrists, for children ages seven to ten, the Young Pioneers, for children ages ten to fifteen, and Komsomol, for youth ages 14 to 27, touch every phase of the child's life. The Communist Party hierarchy carefully thinks out each facet of these organizations. No other political party in history has ever carried out so stupendous a task of socialization on such a huge scale.

Soviet leaders are fond of saying that their children are the "future" of the Soviet Union. In this nuclear age, Soviet children may be part of the future of the United States, too. What are they learning? How do they react to what they are taught? To find out, in 1972, I began a study of the Soviet child's first school of political activism on its fiftieth anniversary—the Young Pioneers.

The Russian language and Soviet affairs were not new to me. I had started to study Russian unwillingly in 1961. A Russian-born friend who taught French in the small Virginia town where my husband and I live insisted I take a Russian course she was starting. I said I couldn't think of any subject that interested me less than Russian. She said I could drop out of the class if I found it boring so, reluctantly, I enrolled. Within a few months the other students had dropped out of the class one by one and the teacher herself had moved to Connecticut, leaving me with an interest in Russian and no teacher. I enrolled in a Washington, D.C., university where I broadened my field to include graduate courses in Marxism, Soviet education, and politics (in English) as well as courses in Russian language, history, and literature (in Russian).

To try out my Russian, my husband and I took our first timid trip to the Soviet Union in 1963. Finding the country fascinating and the Russian people not at all intimidating, I spent the next eight years studying the Soviet Union. In 1971 I wrote a book, *Lenin's Grandchildren*, about preschool education in the Soviet Union. Research for the book was done with the aid of a woman named Lyudmila, a Russian official whom I met through a diplomat with the Soviet Embassy in Washington. I traveled all over the Soviet Union, visiting eleven of the fifteen Soviet republics. I found none of the American stereotypes of the sinister Soviet to be true.

U.S. diplomats and journalists live a very restricted life in Moscow, as do Soviet diplomats and journalists in New York and Washington. The former are under continual surveillance by the KGB; the latter by the FBI. Because I was not "official" but could speak Russian I was able to go places and do things not allowed ordinary diplomats, journalists, or tourists. In addition, I had the advantage of Lyudmila, whom I also considered a personal friend and whose help was invaluable.

Lyudmila was enthusiastic about a new book on the Pioneers. She would help me as she had on *Lenin's Grandchildren*. I began with what I already knew about the Pioneers.

Contents

RUSSIA'S FUTURE

1

The Happiest Day

"Do you remember the day you joined the Pioneers?" I ask every Soviet I meet. The answer is usually the same: eyes light up, the voice becomes excited, and most say, "It was the happiest day of my life."

This response comes from those who profess hatred for the Soviet Union as well as from Party activists, from Soviet emigrants in Israel, Soviet dissidents in the United States, and staunch supporters of the Party at the Soviet Embassy in Washington, D.C.

The percentage of children who do not join the Pioneers is exceedingly small. Only one Russian I asked could not remember that day. Since this man is now a high Party official, I could not understand it when he said, puzzled, "I remember the day I joined the Komsomol. I remember the day I joined the Party. I can't remember the day I joined the Pioneers." I was puzzled, too, until I looked up his biography and found that the war years coincided with the years he would have been a Pioneer. Although the Pioneers continued throughout the war, there were undoubtedly interruptions for particular individuals.

Later I heard that the dissident writer Andrei Amalrik had never joined either the Pioneers or Komsomol. That he did not like the Soviet Union was clear from his book, *Will the Soviet Union Survive Until 1984?* Was there some correlation between dissidence and membership or lack of it in the Pioneers and Komsomol? When Amalrik gave a lecture in Washington, I was in the front row, ready with my questions. "Why didn't you join the Pioneers or Komsomol? Do you think you would have been less opposed to the Soviet Union if you had belonged to the Pioneers?" I asked.

My questions were translated into Russian for Amalrik. His answer, in Russian, too low for me to hear, was then translated back into English. The question and answer may have been slightly garbled, but the answer I got was disappointing: "There was more idealism in those days," he said. What that meant I still have no idea.

1

The happiest day is not left to chance. From the time the Soviet child goes to nursery school he hears about the Pioneers. A favorite kindergarten song says:

We are not yet Pioneers
We are not yet Octobrists,
But we know who we are for sure.
We are Lenin's Grandchildren!
We are Lenin's Grandchildren!

The Communist education of Lenin's Grandchildren is "not loud, but constant," as Soviet leaders are fond of saying. The psychological characteristics of each age group are carefully studied, and a program is formulated to appeal to a child of that age. The program, *Orientir* (Orientation), gives concrete advice to the leaders of each stage: Octobrists (seven to ten), Young Pioneers (ten to eleven), Middle Pioneers (eleven to twelve), and Senior Pioneers (thirteen to fifteen).

The youngest group, the Octobrists, is characterized as being very emotional, impressionable, active, and inquisitive, but lacking the ability to concentrate on one thing for any length of time. Play is still their main activity, and as Lenin's wife, Krupskaya, herself advised, play must be used in a didactic way to reach the child.

On the Sunday before the first Monday in September, when school begins, many schools have special programs called "Hello School!" There are games, concerts, plays, singing, and dancing. There are balloons, flags, and banners. Everything is very exciting to the soon-to-be first graders.

On the first day of school the little girls wear clean white pinafores over dark dresses with little white collars. Boys wear a uniform of long grey trousers and a grey jacket, similar to an Eisenhower jacket, which has an emblem of an open book sewn on the sleeve. All of the children carry bouquets of flowers for their teachers, so the streets of the Soviet Union on the first day of school resemble a movable flower market. Teachers are cautioned that these flowers must never be left to wither on a desk but must be put in water. In practice experienced teachers commandeer wash tubs from the school basement, or baby bathtubs from a nearby nursery school. Flowers in the tubs sometimes last a week.

When the children have assembled, the director of the school makes a short welcoming speech, and the First Bell is rung ceremoniously. The Pioneers escort the first graders into the school and deposit them in the proper classroom. A large banner over the front door of the school says *Dobro pozhalovat* (Welcome), and the loudspeaker plays the national anthem as the children march into the school. Teachers and Pioneers are told not to be upset if the children do not sit where they are supposed to sit. That can be straightened out tomorrow.

At each school desk is a postcard. If the first grader knows how to read, he can read it for himself, but for the benefit of those who can't read, the card is read aloud:

Dear little friend!

Today you sit for the first time at a school desk. From the bottom of our hearts we wish you to learn well in order to be of great benefit to our wonderful Motherland!

Your senior comrades.

Each child in turn, is asked to stand beside his desk and say his name in a loud voice so that everyone can hear and become acquainted with him.

A short talk on the Constitution of the Soviet Union follows. The new Constitution, the Soviet Union's third, was adopted in October 1977, at the Seventh (Special) Session of the Supreme Soviet. The teacher explains that the Constitution guarantees equal rights and a happy childhood for every child through one unified system of education. To show the state's further concern for the children, free textbooks are distributed—*Rodnaya Rech* (Native Language), *Russkii Yazyk* (Russian Language), *Bukvar* (Alphabet), *Matematika* (Math), and *Dnevnik Nablyudenii* (Diary of Observations). The *Bukvar* is inscribed, "Happy voyage to you, little friend."

Next the child is asked to do his first independent school work: to write down all the figures he knows, all the words he can spell, and all the letters he knows, to draw squares and other figures, and finally to draw a pretty picture.

At the end of the lesson the Pioneers may take the first graders on a tour of the school, with each Pioneer taking a first grader by the hand, carefully explaining everything, including the Octobrist corner and the Pioneer room. If there is time left, the Pioneers may teach the first graders a game, such as "Tell a friend where you live," in which the child must give directions for getting to his home. It is recommended that, in parting, the Pioneer say something like, "Walk bravely, little one. A valuable life, which your native land cares about very much, lies before you."

The Pioneers are old enough to be looked up to by the first graders but still young enough to understand them. The program *Orientir* helps prepare the Pioneers for work with Octobrists. It sounds ideal, but some teachers disapprove of the system, and there is much argument about the efficiency of Pioneer leadership. Is it easier to do without Pioneer leaders?

"Easier! Of course it's easier," says one teacher. "The teacher, who has a college education, more life experience, and authority over the pupils, knows how to do everything a hundred times better than the Pioneer leaders—little boys and girls no more than four or five years older than the Octobrists, without experience or sufficient knowledge, who are not prepared for this work." Even when the Pioneers have attended leadership seminars some teachers are scornful, saying a short seminar can't compare with the education of a teacher.

In actual practice there is usually some compromise. The Pioneers lead the Octobrists, and the teachers lead the Pioneers. When this is done tactfully, everyone is happy. Most teachers think that Octobrists, unlike Pioneers, need adult help, being too young to be independent. The task of both teacher and Pioneer is to create an emotional response in the Octobrist toward the Motherland, the Revolution, and Lenin, as the foundation of a Communist personality.

The first-grade class of thirty to thirty-five is divided into small groups of from four to six children, called little stars (zvezdochki). Children must not be assigned routinely to a little star just because they sit next to each other. They should be from the same apartment house or have the same interests so that their group activity may continue after school. Usually the Pioneers from one detachment (otryad) lead one particular first grade, with one Pioneer assigned to each little star. A Komsomol or a Senior Pioneer is placed over the whole group.

Once a week the Pioneer leader gathers his little star together for a brief (five- or ten-minute) discussion of the school and courtyard news, how well each child has fulfilled the task set for him that week, and assignment of new tasks, with explanations as to how the new task may be carried out. Then the Pioneer tells the children stories, reads to them, shows them pictures, or plays games with them.

Once or twice a month there is a general assembly (sbor) of all the little stars and their leaders. The assembly begins with a formal roll call, an Octobrist song, a short talk about the Motherland, Lenin, or the Pioneers, and then a talk about the work of grown-ups—drivers, builders, firemen, doctors, and so forth. Each assembly develops its own rituals, and a plan is worked out on a yearly basis so that the programs do not become repetitive and boring.

September and October are devoted to preparing the first grader to become an Octobrist. The teacher is urged to think of the children as "helpers" and not merely "pupils." The goal is to create a friendly, relaxed collective.

This does not mean the teacher should not make demands on the pupils. Svetlana Karklina, who gave advice to parents on the radio, said that parent or teacher should say to the child, "I love you. I respect you. Therefore I make demands of you. If I didn't love you it wouldn't matter to me how you turned out, and I would demand nothing from you."

One of the demands made of the first grader is collective action. Soviet educators believe that the child develops only in a social situation. They are fond of a certain story, "The Most Terrible," about little Vova, who offended everyone so much that none of his friends would play with him. Grown-ups would have nothing to do with him, and even animals would not associate with him. Vova was left all alone. The most terrible of all the terrible things in the world had happened to Vova. After a while Vova became ashamed.

He had learned that he couldn't live without people, that it was boring and bad to be all alone.

The children learn about the Revolution and the storming of the Winter Palace. Although the Revolution took place on October 25, 1917, and is called the October Revolution, it is celebrated on November 7, because the old-style calendar was still in use in 1917, and by today's calendar old-style October 25 falls on November 7.

Teachers and some Pioneer leaders know the history of the Octobrists—how, after the Pioneers were formed in 1922, the younger brothers and sisters of Pioneers wanted to be in the group, too, and Krupskaya suggested that an organization be formed for them. A number of groups were formed, called "Seeds of Communism," "Little Red Stars," "Flowers," or "Bouquets." In Moscow B. Kaidalov suggested that children who had been born in 1917 and so were seven years old in 1924, be called *Octobrists* in honor of the October Revolution. Everyone liked the sociopolitical connotations of the word, and on August 4, 1924, the Central Committee of the Communist Party confirmed the work of the Central Bureau of Pioneers, and a document signed by the secretary of the Central Committee of the Komsomol and the chairman of the Central Bureau of Pioneers became the official founding document of the Octobrists. It was agreed that the Octobrists should be a part of the network of the Pioneer organization and not a new independent organization.

The first graders learn the rules of the Octobrists:

An Octobrist is a future Pioneer.
An Octobrist is a diligent child, loves school, and respects his elders.
Only those who love work are called Octobrists.
An Octobrist is truthful and brave, dextrous and smart.
An Octobrist is a friendly child, reads and draws, plays and sings, lives
  a merry life.

Learning the rules and attending meetings and assemblies are presented as play. At the monthly assembly the children gather in circles, arms entwined, and sing an Octobrist rhyme:

Nashikh pravil rovno pyat
Vse ikh budem vypolnyat

(Our rules are exactly five
We will fulfill them all)

"Octobrists!" the leader calls out.
"Are friendly children, live merrily, play, and sing," the children respond. Then the reports begin, starting with the commander of the little star, then the

flower tender, the child in charge of feeding the birds and animals in the nature corner, and so on. These reports are supposed to last no more than five or six minutes and be followed by approbation from the leader: *"Molodets"* (well done). Tasks are assigned for the next time period and a place and time set for the next assembly so that the children have something definite to look forward to.

If possible, the Pioneer leader and the five children in his little star group live near each other so that they can continue their friendly relations outside Octobrist activities. If there are more Pioneers in the detachment than there are little star groups, the little stars may have two Pioneer leaders. Five Octobrists to a group is considered ideal. If the number of children in first grade is uneven it is better to have four in each little star, rather than six or seven.

In addition to the rules in *Orientir* and the seminars for leaders, Pioneer magazines and newspapers often give actual examples of Pioneer leadership. The October 1971 issue of *Pioner* magazine gave a detailed report on Kostya Emelyanov's experience with one first-grade class during the month of October. Before Kostya met with the children, he talked to their teacher and learned their schedule. He took them to the Pioneer room and showed them a short film. All of the children laughed and talked loudly.

"When everyone is merry, what do they want to do?" Kostya asked.

"Laugh," the children shouted back.

"And then what?"

"Sing. Let's all sing."

Unfortunately the children did not know the words to any song, so Kostya had to teach them a song. One child, Erik, kept interrupting Kostya: "I know." "I'm first." "I'm the best." Another child, Lyusa, would not open her mouth or even stand with the other children. After the first song, Kostya asked Lyusa if she knew an interesting song. Lyusa shook her head silently, but at the end of the meeting she came up to Kostya and shyly offered to bring him a record of her favorite song.

On other days Kostya took the children for walks or read to them. He showed them how to make their beds after their naps. (Erik pulled the covers over his messy blanket, thinking no one would notice.) One day when the children were at recess Kostya examined their desks and left little notes, pointing out spilled ink here, disorder in another desk, and good order in another. At the next meeting, as a surprise to Kostya, all the desks were clean.

Children from another little star group, noticing the fun Kostya's group was having, tried to join in, but his children said, "Go away. This is our leader. This is our little star."

"I came here to play with you, not to fuss," Kostya said. "You waste time arguing when we could be using it to play. Our little star will invite other children to play with us. O.K.?"

By the end of October, first graders have learned the meaning of the symbol of the Octobrists: a little red enameled aluminum star whose five points represent the unity of the workers of the five parts of the world with a picture of Lenin at age three in a circle inside the star. Each first grader receives this emblem at a festive meeting on November 7, Revolution Day.

The Octobrists, proud of the new star they are wearing, begin to notice other stars—the big red stars over the Kremlin in Red Square, the star on Soviet soldiers' uniforms, the star on the chests of Soviet heroes. The first-grade reader asks, "What is the meaning of the Octobrists? What obligations do you owe the red star, and how do you fulfill these obligations?" These questions are answered throughout the years as the children learn about the Soviet Union.

The reader has a map of Moscow and stories about the Motherland. What is the Motherland like? The answers are many: "big," "rich," "strong," "friendly," "good," "ours."

The Motherland has many holidays. Christmas, though still celebrated in many families, is not an official holiday. New Year's is more like our Christmas, with a big decorated fir tree and presents for everyone brought by Grandfather Frost (*Ded Moroz*), sometimes called *Moroz Ivanovich* (the patronymic *Ivanovich* means that Moroz's father was named Ivan). Grandfather Frost has a lovely assistant named the Snow Maiden (*Snegorochka*) who helps him with his work, though she is always in danger of melting.

February 23 is Soviet Army Day. The children learn the insignias of the various branches, identify tanks, rockets, helicopters, and so forth. In one school we visited I was surprised to see that in illustrating "Our Street" many of the children had pictured parachutists drifting down to the sidewalks. I found there was a training station for parachutists nearby so the children really did see parachutists on "The Street Where I Live."

March 8 is International Women's Day and a big Soviet holiday. In each school class the boys bring gifts for the girls in the class. Usually a boy and a girl sit together at each double desk. "My seat mate in the seventh grade brought me lilies of the valley on International Women's Day," said a Soviet woman we know, smiling appreciatively at the memory.

In offices and shops the men bring presents for the women workers and usually a bottle of wine or cognac with which to toast them. Because the festivities take place during working hours March 8 is not very productive, but it is fun.

Women office workers may take time off to visit their child's school, where there is a special program for mothers and grandmothers and, of course, more presents, which the children have made, and flowers and presents for the women teachers as well.

April is a big holiday month with the Day of Cosmonauts (April 12) and Lenin's birthday (April 22). In 1972 Octobrists Week was proclaimed from

April 22 to 28. It is now traditional and either starts or ends on Lenin's birthday. "Seven days and every day a holiday," Octobrists are told.

If it starts on Lenin's birthday, the first day is the Red Necktie Holiday, when the best of the ten-year-old Octobrists are inducted into the Pioneers. There is a festive parade and an exhibition in the school by the Octobrists called "Show What You Know."

The second day is the Toy Holiday with a parade of toys and a special exhibit of toys called "We Made Them Ourselves." Pioneers meet with Octobrists that day and take them to a movie.

The third day is the Book Holiday. The clubs Why? and Guess have contests about books. Sporting events take up the fourth day with an Octobrist "Olympics," races, jumping contests, and games, including *zarnichka*, (little summer lightning) the Octobrist branch of the Pioneer war games, *zarnitsa* (summer lightning).

The Friendship holiday comes next, with drawings, poems, and essays by Octobrists on the theme, "May There Always Be Sunshine." There are stories about Soviet heroes and the various Soviet republics and their respective flags and coats of arms. One day is the Work Holiday, which centers on the theme that Octobrists love work. Another day is called "Octobrists in the Land of October," when children are told about Brezhnev, the Pioneer magazines and newspapers, and the happy childhood Soviet children have. The last day is a day of parties for Octobrists in Pioneer palaces, theaters, workers' clubs, and other places.

The first two years of school have taught the child to live in a collective in friendly fashion as he learns, and tries to follow, the rules of the Octobrists. The third year is aimed at making him want to join the Pioneers. He already knows he must study hard, be honest and truthful, and help older people and look after younger children, but his knowledge of how he fits into the Pioneer organization is much weaker.

Some of the things he heard about in the first and second grades are becoming clearer to him now. Some children who could not answer the first-grade question, What is the meaning of the red star? are relieved to find the answer in the third-grade reader: "The red star is the symbol of the working classes of the whole world." I kept forgetting the meaning of the red star myself and told my husband I was afraid I had failed first-grade Communism.

The meaning of the state emblem of the Soviet Union—the hammer and sickle—is easier to remember. It represents the power of the working classes and the indissoluble union of the worker and peasant.

"What is the Party?" the third-grade child is asked. The answer is given by reciting a poem by Yuri Yakovlev in which a Pioneer gives examples of heroism and the Octobrists reply, "That means the Party is a hero." The leader gives another example, this time of friendship, and the Octobrists say, "The Party is a good friend." Next the leader tells of an expedition into the *taiga* (thick forests), and the children say, "The Party is an explorer." The Party is also part of Lenin's family. Finally to the last question, "What is the Party?" the children answer, "It is the red necktie of our leader. It is our Party."

In the third grade the child begins serious study of the laws of the Pioneers. Some of the early rules of Pioneers have been left out of the current rules. Some that I regret are not still included are:

Pioneers wash themselves carefully, not forgetting to wash neck and ears; clean their teeth, not forgetting that teeth are the friends of the stomach.

Pioneers do not smoke. A smoking Pioneer is already a non-Pioneer.

A Pioneer does not keep his hands in his pockets. A Pioneer with his hands in his pockets is not "always ready."

Some of the laws are difficult for the child to comprehend, like the very first law, "The Pioneer is devoted to the Motherland, the Party, and Communism."

Laws that are similar to Octobrist rules are easier: the Pioneer is persistent in learning, work, and sport, a comrade and leader of Octobrists, and a friend of the Pioneers and children of the workers of the world. Even these more easily understood laws need discussion. How do you show friendship? How do you lead Octobrists? For practice, the third graders go to nursery schools and kindergartens to play with the little children. They take part in group discussions about situations of conflict and how to resolve them with justice and study the biography of Lenin to see how he resolved Russia's problems.

There are three more laws: The Pioneer prepares to become a Komsomol member. The Pioneer is aligned with the heroes of struggle and labor. The Pioneer honors the memory of fallen fighters and prepares to become a defender of the Motherland.

The child must learn to evaluate his own character as well as that of the Octobrists, with whom he works, to see if they are worthy of joining the Pioneers. The teacher's evaluations ("Excellent," "Keeps to himself," "Behaves poorly") give the child some criteria, but he must practice making his own judgments.

Some schools take children into the Pioneers several times a year—November 7, December 5, February 23, or May 9—but the most popular day is Lenin's birthday, April 22. By that time most of the third graders are ten years old. The Pioneer council (*druzhina*) must decide if a particular child is ready to join the Pioneers. This depends not only on age and ability but also on the child's desire to be a Pioneer. Sometimes a nine-year-old meets the qualifications before an older child, and occasionally a child is not taken into the Pioneers

until the fifth, sixth, or seventh grades, although this is unusual, and such a child is considered a problem. Some Baptists refuse to let their children join the Pioneers, and some children do too poorly in school to be admitted.

At a group meeting a Pioneer brings up the name of an Octobrist: "Kolya has some insufficiencies such as. . . . " The insufficiencies are detailed: poor grades, inattentive work, and so forth. Then the Pioneer continues, "On the other hand, Kolya tries very hard. He wants to be a Pioneer. I think he will behave better when he is a Pioneer. He is a very good football player and we could use him to help the football team."

The Octobrists are well aware of their own insufficiencies. We were told of one little girl who said, "When you have insufficiencies you try to correct them, but in order to correct them, you need great strength of character—which I don't have."

One by one, the Octobrists are voted on in open balloting, and the day of induction is set. A council of friends of Pioneers from the parent's committee at the school advises parents of inductees when the ceremony will take place, but since both parents usually work they cannot always attend.

Favorite places for holding the ceremony are the Lenin museum or the Pioneer palace. "Tra-ta-ta-ta-ta-ta!" the bugle sounds the opening of the cere-mony as the children march in, the leaders carrying flags. The drummer beats out a tattoo on the drum. "Attention!" the leader calls out. The Octobrists are trembling with excitement. The reports begin. "The Patrice Lumumba

Detachment [each detachment has its own name] of class 6-B has unanimously elected Kolya Fedosov."

Another leader steps forward: "The Twice the Hero of the Soviet Union Boris Safonov Detachment of Class 5-G takes Lyusya Petukhova and Zhenya Kovalev into the Pioneers. Lyusya and Zhenya remained in the fifth grade for the second year, but the detachment helped them with their school work, and now they don't have a single low mark and participate in all the work."

The detachment of Class 7-A took ten children from the third grade. "Class 7-A believes they will be good Pioneers."

"*Druzhina*, attention!" calls the leader. He begins to recite the solemn oath of the Pioneers. The inductees repeat after him: "I, Kolya (each child says his own name), enrolling in the ranks of the Pioneer organization, in the name of Vladimir Ilich Lenin and in the presence of my comrades, do solemnly swear to love my Motherland, live, study, and fight as the great Lenin bequeathed and as the Communist Party teaches, and always to carry out the laws of the Pioneers of the Soviet Union."

"Present the neckties," the leader says, and the best Pioneers of the detachment step forward. As the bugler plays a salute and the drummer beats his drum, each Pioneer ties the red necktie around the neck of one of the Octobrists.

"Pioneers! For the struggle of the Communist Party, be ready!"

"Always ready!" comes the answer from the new Pioneers, as they give the

Pioneer salute: right hand raised slightly above the head, to show the superiority of the Party.

The New Pioneers are given flowers, usually red carnations, which they then take to Lenin's tomb, if the ceremony is in the Lenin Museum in Moscow, put before a statue of Lenin, or lay on the tomb of the unknown soldier.

The children have paid their first tribute as Pioneers.

2

The Red Necktie

The red necktie is the identifying mark of a Pioneer. A triangle of red cotton or polyester, about twelve inches wide at the point of the triangle and about thirty-nine inches long, it ties in a loose knot in front of the collar. The ties for girls and boys are identical and may be worn with street or school clothes as well as with the Pioneer uniform, which is usually a white or blue shirt with blue or grey skirts for the girls and blue or grey trousers for the boys. Both boys and girls may also wear a grey or blue jacket.

The three-pointed tie symbolizes the unity of the three Communist organizations—Pioneers, Komsomol, and the Communist Party. In early May 1972, every child in Moscow seemed to be wearing the red tie.

I had gone to Moscow a week earlier than my husband, flying from Washington to Paris and then on to Moscow the next day. Lyudmila, who had helped me with my first book, met me at Sheremetyevo Airport, and we drove into Moscow together. As always, I marvelled at the vastness of this country and wondered if Napoleon and Hitler had felt as I did when they stood on the outskirts of Moscow with dreams of conquering it.

Lyudmila went with me to the Rossiya Hotel, an emormous structure of steel and glass just off Red Square. "We call it the *Comrade* Hilton," she smiled.

The next day I went to Lyudmila's office, and we planned my schedule. "I can make suggestions," Lyudmila said, "but you tell me what you want to see, and I'll arrange it."

We decided to watch the Pioneers preparing for their fiftieth anniversary parade and drove out to the Pioneer palace in the Lenin Hills section of Moscow. In the plaza in front of the palace, hundreds of Pioneers were massed as two leaders tried to form them into a semblance of a line.

"There are now twenty-five million Pioneers in the Soviet Union," Lyudmila said. "The best Pioneers from all over the country have been chosen to come here for the anniversary." The Pioneer leaders were having trouble with the "best" Pioneers. "I'm a Pioneer," one of them began singing. The other Pioneers sang, too, but a leader stopped them. "Too weak," she said. "Let the stomach muscles work."

The other leader came up to us: "Americans think we regiment our children. I just wish I knew *how* to regiment them."

"Let me try," said a third leader I had not seen before.

"*Devochki* (girls)," the woman said to the straggling line. "This is the fiftieth anniversary of the founding of the Young Pioneers. We are all going to march in the parade in Red Square. We will be on television. We will have all the leaders of the Soviet Union watching us. All the best Pioneers from all over the Soviet Union will be in the parade. Do we want everyone to say those Pioneers in Moscow are not cultured? They don't know how to march in a parade? Now let's try it again."

She blew a whistle and the children straightened into a line, but as they began to march groups bulged out from place to place. The leader ran back and forth trying to push the stragglers into line. When she was unable to control the bulge, she blew her whistle for everyone to stop and start over.

"I don't know how we're going to get them ready for the parade," the first woman said to me, shaking her head in despair. "May 19 is just a week away. I'm mortified to think that in fifty years of Pioneer activities we haven't learned how to march in a parade."

"They'll probably do better when the real parade begins," I said. "In the United States we say a bad rehearsal may mean a good performance."

"Well, I hope you're right," the lady said, obviously skeptical.

When we left the palace to go back to the hotel the Pioneers were still marching in the square, their lines still bulging hopelessly.

I was excited about all the sights and sounds of Pioneers and Moscow and wanted to talk to someone about my impressions. Lyudmila couldn't have dinner with me and I hated the thought of going down alone to the big hotel dining room, where each large table carried a little flag of a foreign country whose tourists were visiting Russia. I didn't want to explain again that I was not part of a group but entitled to a table by myself.

A friend in New York had given me the name and telephone number of a Russian dissident in Moscow. "Her name is Lena, and her family was important in the Revolution. Her father was a friend of Lenin's, but was purged by Stalin," my New York friend said, adding that I really should get the dissident side too.

On impulse, I called the number, not really expecting to get an answer. When a woman answered, I explained that a friend had given me her name, that I was alone in Moscow and thought perhaps she would have dinner with me.

"Who did you say you were?" Lena asked, then decisively interrupted her own question. "I don't care who you are, I'll have dinner with you anyhow."

In an hour she knocked on my door. She was an attractive woman in her late fifties and spoke excellent English. Lena swept into the dining room like

a queen, and I tagged along apologetically behind her. She chose a table for six with a French flag on it, removing the flag as a waiter came up to say the table was already taken by a French group. She waved him away imperiously, and we sat down. It was the habit in the hotel at that time to put strangers at any table that was not full, but when the waiter brought other Russians up to sit at our table, Lena dismissed them. "I don't want Russians at my table," she said. She refused a proffered Frenchman (from the group whose table it was), a German, and a Scandinavian.

The waiters, who usually lounged around the refrigerator (which was always prominently placed in the dining room) and ignored diners' requests with complete insolence, now hovered around Lena solicitously. She ordered caviar and vodka, and when the waiter brought red cavier instead of black she sent it back to the kitchen. I was amazed at her confidence. When she loudly criticized the hotel, the food, and the Soviet government, I suggested she lower her voice. "I don't care who hears me," she said. "This country is no good." She dug into the black caviar the waiter had brought. She downed her vodka, following it with a mouthful of bread in the Russian manner. When an Indian woman in a sari passed our table looking for a seat, Lena graciously said she could sit at our table. The waiter and the Indian woman, who said her name was Shama, both thanked Lena.

Shama told us that she had been to a kindergarten that morning and had been very impressed with its excellence. "Bosh," said Lena. "You foreigners make me sick. You come to Russia and get starry-eyed at everything you see. I have a grandson, Kolya, in kindergarten. He tried to blow up his school."

"What?" Shama and I exclaimed in unison.

"He didn't succeed," Lena said, taking another helping of caviar. "He put pencil shavings in an electrical outlet, thinking that would cause an explosion. When I took him to school the next day, the school nurse was checking him in."

"Nursery schools and kindergartens always check the children on arrival to see if they have a cold or some communicable disease," I explained to Shama.

"Well, that day as the nurse was checking Kolya, the director of the school came up and said she would like to talk to Kolya privately. She took him aside and said, 'Kolya, I have some very bad news for you. Your plot to blow up the school has fallen through.' "

"The director sounds like a very sympathetic person," Shama said. "She didn't embarrass Kolya in front of the other children."

Lena told us more about her grandson. He lived with her most of the time, since his mother, Lena's daughter-in-law, had run off with one of Lena's son's best friends. This man was part German, and after his mother left Kolya began painting swastikas on his hands and saying, "The Germans weren't so bad."

"Lena and her whole family are crazy" I thought, then corrected myself. "No, that's what we accuse the Russians of saying about their dissidents." My head was whirling.

The rest of the dinner passed pleasantly enough. We spoke of books, music, and the theater, and the three of us shared many likes and dislikes. Some of Lena's comments were interesting and new to me. "Were you a Pioneer?" I asked, and when she said yes I asked if she liked being in the Pioneers. "Of course," she said at once.

"Where you in the Komsomol too?"

"I was opposed to the Komsomol and got a group of girls to refuse to join. The Komsomols worked on the other girls by inviting them to join various outings, and soon I was the only one who hadn't joined. I was very interested in the Young Naturalists group, but they wouldn't let me in that unless I was a Komsomol member, so I joined too."

After dinner Lena went up to my room with me. On every floor there is a woman who keeps the keys to the rooms, and often these women have cigarettes or bottled water to sell. When Lena discovered that the woman on my floor had cigarettes she bought every package the woman had. "This is a windfall," Lena said to me, putting the cartons of cigarettes in her bag.

The next day was Saturday. I waited to hear from Lyudmila, but she didn't call. I called her office, but there was no answer. I didn't hear from her on Sunday either but thought nothing of it. Her office was probably closed for the weekend.

I went to a children's theater, which was crammed with Pioneers, to see a play called "Be Prepared, Your Highness," about a foreign prince who goes to a Pioneer Camp for a vacation. "Do you have an automobile?" one of the Soviet Pioneers asks, and the prince replies, "I have my own private elephant." The children are puzzled when the prince says he lives in a palace. "The Palace of Culture?" they ask. They want to know what his father does. "King," he says. "Is 'King' a Russian name?" they ask. The audience greeted the play with delighted squeals of laughter and I enjoyed both the play and the audience.

When on Monday I still hadn't heard from Lyudmila, I called her office. Lyudmila was out, I was told. "When would she be back?" "Maybe soon. Maybe later."

My husband was to arrive on Tuesday so I went to the airport to meet him. "President Nixon is coming to Moscow," he said. "Have you heard anything about his visit?" I said *Pravda* hadn't mentioned it. I told him what I had been doing, then added, "It's odd that I haven't heard from Lyudmila in several days. She was so cordial at first. Do you think my having dinner with a dissident would have had anything to do with it?"

"That was a foolish thing to do," my husband said. "You may have messed up your whole project."

I called Lyudmila again when we got back to the hotel and was told she had gone for the day. The next day I called continually, insisting that Lyudmila be given a message to call me. "When do you expect her?" I kept asking, but was given evasive answers. Finally, after repeated calls, Lyudmila herself answered the telephone. "I can't help you," she said. "What's wrong?" I asked. Silence. "What about the fiftieth anniversary parade on May 19th? That's Friday. Can we at least go to that?"

"I can't help you," Lyudmila said and hung up.

"Now what do we do?" I said, groping for some plan of action. "I'll have to try Intourist," I realized, wondering how I could face the often stony-faced women in the Intourist office who let you stand expectantly before them as they file their nails in indifferent disregard of tourists. I'm not afraid of the KGB, but some Intourist officials and most Soviet waiters intimidate me. I always feel like a beggar in a king's court.

Summoning all my patience and courage I went down to the Intourist office. I explained our problem in my best Russian, as the women always seemed much more sympathetic to Russian than to English. "It's very hard to get tickets for the parade," the Intourist woman said. "I can't promise you anything." She did not say it unkindly and jotted something down on a slip of paper. I was hopeful.

I checked with her a number of times on Thursday. No word. On Friday morning, when I had almost given up hope, there was a knock on our door, and a young man appeared who said he was from the Institute of Soviet-American Relations (now called USSR-USA Society) and would take us to the parade.

It was a beautiful, sunny day. In front of the Rossiya Hotel red and white tulips were in full bloom, and a lilac bush blossomed in St. Basil's courtyard. We walked over to Red Square, which was roped off, and we had to show our passports to get into the stands to the left of Lenin's tomb.

On top of the tomb, officials were filling their stands. We sat next to a distinguished-looking American couple from California, who said they had won the trip through a contest in the magazine *Soviet Life*, although they had been to the Soviet Union a number of times before.

Red Square really was predominantly red. A huge picture of Lenin against a red background covered the entire front of GUM, the State Department Store, and red banners proclaimed "Long Live the Communist Party of the Soviet Union" and "Glory to the Great Soviet people—the Builders of Communism." The trees along the sidewalk in front of GUM wore the fresh green of new leaves. To the left of the stands the Historical Museum bore a huge sign on a red background, "1922-1972." Red flags waved in the breeze, and the red caps and neckties of the Pioneers added to the overall red.

The stands were filling with people. Pioneers who were not marching in the parade but were still in their holiday blue skirts or trousers, white shirts, and red neckties. Fat grandmothers with kerchiefs tied over their heads, proud mothers and fathers, and veterans poured into the stands to take their seats. There was a man on crutches, one pant-leg neatly pinned up above the absent leg, his chest bright with war medals. A large silver balloon trailing messages on red banners floated over GUM. Everyone was excited and in good humor.

Some of the papers and magazines we read said there were 25 million Young Pioneers, others put the figure at 23 million. When the parade began, with legion after legion of Young Pioneers marching through the Square, I thought 25 million looked like an underestimation. There were floats with banners celebrating the Twenty-Fourth Congress of the Communist Party and one with Brezhnev's picture and the quotation, "The Party firmly believes that our children and grandchildren will carry forward with honor the great banner of the October Revolution."

The marchers stopped to salute in front of the stands. Some groups performed native dances in the various costumes of the fifteen Soviet republics. A fire fighters' brigade climbed fire ladders and football teams played a football game. A whole swimming team competed in a sea of wide strips of blue cloth, which billowed in the children's hands. The Young Border Guards marched with their guard dogs—the dogs as conscientious as the children.

I recognized the group I had seen drilling at the Pioneer palace. There wasn't a straggler in the line, the mass holding its form with concrete rigidity. I waved to the teacher who had said she wished she knew how to regiment the children. "She's done it," I said to my husband, then added, "or maybe the children got the message."

I enjoyed the parade so much that I almost forgot about Lyudmila until the couple from California asked about our plans. They knew Lyudmila, too. She's very busy getting ready for President Nixon's visit," the man said. Maybe that was it, I thought, but it still left me without plans.

"If you need help with the Pioneers," the Californian said, "I know just the person. He's a very interesting man. Still a Pioneer, though he must be fifty-five now—Harry Eisman."

"Harry Eisman doesn't sound like a Russian name."

"No. He's Jewish, born in Moldavia. He was a child agitator in the Bronx, a member of the Young Pioneers in the United States. A Communist hero at sixteen—quite a guy—but you can find out about him when you meet him."

When the parade was over the Pioneers in the stands streamed out into Red Square where they joined some of the marchers in seeking autographs from everyone they met. A number of children held up small autograph books to my husband and me, and we signed our names and added Aldie, Virginia, USA, at the bottom.

The man from the Institute of Soviet-American Relations walked back to the hotel with us but did not suggest seeing us again. We thanked him and went into the hotel restaurant for dinner. After dinner we took the proffered key from our floor clerk and walked to our room. Outside our door, his back against the wall, sat a short man with wiry grey hair. He got up when he saw us, and his lips and eyes crinkled into a smile: "I'm Harry Eisman."

3

The Early Years

"**Y**ou might not want to be seen with me," Harry said, when we had settled into our living room. "I was considered a bad boy in your country." He said he had been orphaned in Moldavia (then part of Romania) at age five and sent to live with a sister in the Bronx. "The passion of my life from the time I was seven years old was roller skating," he said. "The only time I stopped skating was to eat, but one night when I came home to supper, my sister said she hadn't fixed any supper."

" 'I've been to a memorial service.' she said.

" 'Who died?' I asked.

"And she said, 'Lenin.' "

Harry leaned back in his chair. "Well, that was the first I had heard about Lenin. Later on I joined the Young Pioneers in New York, which was started by the Young Communist League, the Komsomol, though at that time it was called the League of Working Youth. We Pioneers felt we were part of the workers' movement. We helped raise money to feed the striking textile workers in Passaic, New Jersey, and of course we worked for the freedom of Sacco and Vanzetti when that came up."

"I'm surprised there were Pioneers in the United States," I said.

"The first Pioneer club was started in Chicago in 1923," Harry said. "The children learned revolutionary songs and studied the history of the workers' movement. There were Pioneer organizations in forty-three cities of the United States."

"Did you wear the red necktie, too?"

"Pioneers were forbidden in school, so of course we couldn't wear the ties there. But we wore them to workers' meetings, and we wore them on May Day. Whenever the authorities learned there was a Pioneer in school we were in for trouble. We were called 'propagandists.' "

"Weren't you?" I asked.

Harry laughed. "Yes. I remember our Pioneer oath: 'I pledge allegiance to the workers' red flag and the cause for which it stands. One goal throughout our lives is the freedom of the working class.' "

"That's something I need to know," I said. "What is the goal of the Pioneers today?"

"This here Communism is not as simple as you folks in the United States think," Harry said. "If you're willing to learn what our Soviet kids are like, I'll be happy to help you. I don't mean to sound immodest, but I do have some influence in the Pioneers."

Harry said he would make some phone calls and line up people for us to see. Sure enough, the next day he called and said we were to meet on Sunday with a friend of his who was a librarian and a collector of Pioneer history. Although the library wasn't normally open on Sunday, Harry's friend would open it just for me. "He loves the history of the Pioneers," Harry said.

Harry volunteered to take my husband on a photographing tour while I worked at the library. "I'll even show him a synagogue, though I don't go myself." Harry said. "Every United States Jew who comes to Moscow immediately says, 'Where's the synagogue?' though he never sees the inside of one in New York. They're very surprised that we have a synagogue in Moscow in operation. Not all Jews in the Soviet Union want to leave it."

The librarian was delighted with my interest. He got down dusty documents from high shelves and showed me books about the Komsomol, the Party, and the Pioneers. I was sorry I couldn't take everything home with me. I could have written a hundred books from the material he showed me.

"The first organizations of proletarian youth were the Young Guard in Belgium in 1886; the socialist unions of youth in Switzerland in 1895; Italy in 1901; Norway, 1902; Spain, 1903; Austria, 1904; Hungary, 1905; and Germany and Finland in 1906," the librarian said. "Of course, Russian youth had been interested in revolutionary ideas as far back as 1825, when the average age of the Decembrists was under twenty-four. Then there was 1905, and what many consider the first Russian Revolution—there were children among those killed on Bloody Sunday."

I had read Father Gapon's account of that Sunday in 1905, when Russian workers protested against the deplorable conditions in factories, where children from the age of six on worked twelve to seventeen hours a day alongside men and women. I could almost feel the cold of that January day, the ice on the Neva River and snow on the streets of St. Petersburg (now Leningrad) as the striking workers assembled with their wives and children to present a petition to the Czar. The marchers carried icons and portraits of the Czar and sang hymns and "God Save the Czar." They were unarmed and led by a priest, Father Gapon, who carried the petition demanding improved working conditions, an eight-hour day, and a Constituent Assembly. The children, dressed in their holiday best, ran alongside the marchers or climbed trees to get a better view of the proceedings.

At 1 PM there was an order to clear the streets. Cavalry troops advanced at a trot, then a gallop. The crowd refused to move. At the sound of a bugle the first ranks of soldiers sank to their knees and fired three volleys, two of blanks, but a third with live shells. Gapon said bodies dropped to earth "like logs of wood," their blood bright red against the snow. A little boy of ten, carrying a lantern, fell with the third volley without relinquishing his hold on the lantern. Children were shot down out of trees. Gapon said that the face of every dead child still bore a "frozen smile, so unexpectedly had death come."

Was Bloody Sunday a revolt or a revolution? Lenin said people generally considered a revolution a successful revolt and a revolt an unsuccessful revolution. Though Bloody Sunday seemed a victory for the Czar, Lenin thought it was "rightly regarded as the beginning of the Russian Revolution."

"Both Lenin and his wife, Krupskaya, were interested in youth movements," the librarian went on. "In 1905 a Union of Working and Student Youth was formed in St. Petersburg under the auspices of Lenin's Russian Social Democratic Labor Party, as the Communist Party was called then, to prepare youth for active work in the Party. The members participated in demonstrations and meetings, which were usually broken up by the police, but the struggle persisted."

The librarian handed me a yellowed copy of *Pravda* for May 17, 1917, with an article by Krupskaya stressing the importance of youth organizations for the future of the movement.

He continued to pile books on my desk as he enthusiastically detailed the youth movement. "You know, of course, the events of 1917. Despite all the talk about revolution, the actual event took everyone by surprise. By the beginning of 1917 the excitement about Rasputin's murder had subsided, and Petrograd—originally St. Petersburg, now Leningrad—seemed almost normal. The Duma, which Czar Nicholas II had established in 1905 as a weak consultative body rather than the representative assembly revolutionaries wanted, met on February 14, 1917.

"On February 23, disturbances broke out in Petrograd, arising over people's dissatisfaction with waiting in lines at food stores. Police were called up, and everything seemed well in hand until new disorders broke out and the Czar ordered in his troops. By February 27 most of the troops had defected to the insurgents. The Duma was ordered to dissolve, but after some hesitation it remained in session. On February 27 it elected a provisional committee.

"On the same day in Taurida Palace, the seat of the Duma, the Soviet (Council) of Workers' and Soldiers' Deputies was organized. Membership was large and chaotic, but its business was transacted by an executive committee of fourteen members, one of whom, Kerensky, was also a member of the Duma. The Duma asked the Czar to abdicate, which he finally did, in favor of his brother Grand Duke Michael, who declined the crown.

"On March 2, after negotiations with the executive committee of the

Soviet, the Duma announced the formation of a Provisional Government, with Prince Lvov as president and Kerensky as minister of justice. The Duma and the executive committee of the Soviet, under a system of dual power, asked for the convocation of a Constituent Assembly, equal rights, and political amnesty.

"New organs of provincial administration paid little attention to the Provisional Government but looked instead to the Soviet for leadership. The first major conflict between the "dual powers" came over the issue of army organization and foreign policy. Order No. 1, prepared by the Petrograd section of the Soviet and published on March 2, called for the formation of soldiers' councils in every military unit and the election of officers by the troops. This led to more confusion and made Russia's continued participation in World War I problematical.

"Lenin, meanwhile, was still in exile in Switzerland. The librarian showed me a letter Lenin had written at the time. 'How could such a "miracle" have happened, that in only eight days . . . a monarchy had collapsed that had maintained itself for centuries?' Lenin was jubilant but warned that the first revolution engendered by the imperialist world war would 'certainly not be the last.'

"Lenin immediately made plans to go to Russia, and through the efforts of Swiss socialist leaders he was able to make the journey through Germany in the so-called sealed railway car, arriving in Petrograd on April 3. Greeted enthusiastically at Petrograd's Finland Station, Lenin proclaimed, 'Long live the socialist revolution!' The next day he presented his 'April Theses' to two meetings of delegates to the All-Russian Conference of the Soviets at the Taurida Palace. Among the ten points Lenin made, nonsupport of the Provisional Government, rejection of defensive war, and transition to the socialist stage of the revolution were rejected by the Petrograd Committee of the Bolshevik Party.

"Also rejected was Lenin's suggestion that the name of the party be changed to the Communist Party. The term *Bolshevik*—which means 'member of the majority' in Russian—was a faction of the Russian Social Democratic Labor Party, which was founded in Minsk in 1895, a step toward the unification of Marxist groups. Lenin had not been able to attend the first congress because he had been arrested and exiled to Siberia. The minority party, or Menshevik group, disagreed with the goals of the Bolsheviks, led by Lenin, who returned to St. Petersburg in 1900. By the third Party congress in 1905, the split led to two separate congresses for Bolsheviks and Mensheviks, but there was a perfunctory reconciliation by the fourth Party congress in Stockholm in 1906. Lenin advocated authoritarian centralism and the dictatorship of the proletariat.

"By May 1917, there was labor unrest, agrarian revolution, and a breakdown of the army as the weak Provisional Government tried to maintain itself in power. The Bolshevik faction, a major threat to the Provisional Government, was still weak in its representation in the soviets. A July uprising failed, and Lenin was forced to go into hiding in Finland.

"In July Prince Lvov resigned and a second coalition government was formed with Kerensky as prime minister. The Russian Social Democratic Labor Party, which held its sixth Party congress in July, was at a low ebb. Lenin guided the congress from the underground. In his pamphlet, 'On Slogans,' he wrote that the slogan, 'All power to the Soviets,' advocating the painless assumption of power by the proletariat, was no longer applicable. The present soviets had failed, Lenin said, because they were dominated by the Socialist Revolutionary and Menshevik parties and at present were like 'sheep brought to the slaughterhouse bleating pitifully under the knife.'

"With some misgivings, the sixth Party congress endorsed Lenin's views. The congress also considered the tasks of creating "youth leagues" of young workers, who would help in the tasks of the Party. It was suggested that the Central Committee of the Party give courses on how to set up youth organizations throughout Russia. The main task of the socialist youth leagues was to educate their members in the spirit of class struggle, proletarian internationalism, and love of the Bolshevik Party.

"Youth organizations multiplied—the Petrograd Socialist Union of Working Youth, the Moscow League of Working Youth /Third International, Leagues of Working Youth in Kiev and Ekaterinburg, Spartak in Georgia, and leagues by other names elsewhere. By October 1917 these organizations had more than 35,000 members.

"In August the Germans attacked the northern sector of the Russian front and occupied Riga. The evacuation of Petrograd seemed imminent. The commander-in-chief of the army, General L. G. Kornilov, believed the survival of Russia depended upon a strong government headed by himself. When told that a Bolshevik demonstration was planned for Petrograd and that cavalry troops were requested, Kornilov set out for Petrograd. After a series of misunderstandings and confusions, the Kornilov 'mutiny' was put down and Kornilov himself dismissed by Kerensky. The incident led to the formation of the Third Coalition Government with Kerensky at its head.

"By the middle of September the Bolsheviks had attained a majority in the Soviets of Workers' and Soldiers' Deputies in Petrograd and Moscow, and Lenin believed that the Bolsheviks must take power. Lenin's views, like his April Theses, were at first strongly resisted in high party circles, where it was felt that an insurrection should be postponed until the convocation of the second All-Russian Congress of Soviets. 'To delay is a crime,' Lenin wrote to the Central Committee early in October.

"In disguise, Lenin attended a meeting of the Central Committee of the Bolshevik Party in Petrograd on October 10. After a long discussion the committee approved Lenin's declaration that 'armed insurrection is inevitable and the time for it fully ripe.' The meeting also elected a political bureau of seven members, including Lenin, Trotsky, Zinovev, Kamenev, and Stalin.

"The direction of the insurrection was in the hands of a military revolutionary committee set up by the Petrograd soviet. Trotsky, chairman of the Petrograd soviet, was also chairman of the military revolutionary committee.

Lenin was still in hiding and did not appear at Smolny, the seat of the Petrograd Soviet and the Bolshevik Central Committee until the evening of October 24. The military revolutionary committee organized the Red Guards, distributed arms, appointed commissars to supervise the activities of army units, and solicited the allegiance of the Petrograd troops. On October 24, the Provisional Government acted to rearrest Bolshevik leaders free on bail and close Bolshevik newspapers. Troops, chiefly cadets from nearby military schools, were brought in from nearby garrisons.

"The Bolshevik-controlled cruiser *Aurora*, which was anchored on the Neva River opposite the Winter Palace, was ordered put out to sea, but the *Aurora* sailors ignored the order and put themselves at the disposal of the military revolutionary committee. On the night of October 24, armed detachments under the orders of the military revolutionary committee, under Lenin and Trotsky, occupied railway terminals, bridges, the State Bank, the telephone exchange, the central post office, and other public buildings. Since most of the troops were on the side of the insurgents there was no resistance and no bloodshed.

"The next morning (October 25) Kerensky left the Winter Palace in an open touring car accompanied by another car carrying the American flag in order to go to Gatchina in an effort to secure loyal troops. The Provisional Government remained in session under the protection of a women's battalion, detachments of cadets, a small number of Cossacks, and a few armored cars. The Bolsheviks besieged the palace and at 6:30 PM issued an ultimatum demanding the surrender of the Provisional Government under threat of bombardment by the *Aurora*. (At 11 PM thirty or thirty-five shells were fired from the Peter-Paul Fortress, but only two of them hit the palace, causing minor damage.) The insurgents entered the palace and arrested all ministers.

"While the uprising was at its height, on the afternoon of October 25, Trotsky presided at a session of the Petrograd Soviet, where Lenin made his first public appearance since July. The Second All-Russian Congress of Soviets was scheduled for the 25th, but was postponed from hour to hour awaiting news of the capture of the Winter Palace. The congress finally met just three hours before the arrest of the Provisional Government, at 10:45 PM on the 25th. After a stormy session in which the Mensheviks and other opposition leaders walked out in protest, the assembly passed the decrees on peace and land and confirmed the Council of People's Commissars, Russia's new chief executive agency. The peace and land decrees, written and sponsored by Lenin, called for peace without annexations or indemnities and abolished private ownership of land.

"Lenin said that winning the Revolution had been as easy as lifting a feather. However, coping with postrevolutionary Russia was not to be so easy. Almost immediately, Russia was attacked by the Germans in the Baltic, Byelorussia, and the Ukraine, by the British in Murmansk, and by the Japanese in the Far East. Internally civil war raged. The Duma refused to recognize the new government. The Union of Railway workers would not recognize the Bolsheviks, and its members said they would take over the railways themselves. The postal and telegraph workers refused to deliver mail or send telegrams for Bolsheviks.

"The new government had little experience to prepare it for the tremendous tasks it faced. John Reed, the American journalist, pictured the confusion in his book, *Ten Days That Shook the World*. The new Commissar of Commerce explained to Reed in a 'sort of humorous panic' that he knew nothing whatsoever about business. Reed saw Menzhinsky, commissar of finance, in a goatskin cape, huddled in a cafe corner, figuring anxiously on a dirty envelope, 'biting his pencil meanwhile.'

"At its seventh congress, in March 1918, the party voted to change its name from the Russian Social Democratic Labor Party (Bolshevik) to the Russian Communist Party (b), the "(b)" still standing for Bolshevik.

"It was not until 1952, at the Nineteenth Party Congress, that the name *Bolshevik* was dropped. Khrushchev reported: 'The Central Committee considers that a need has matured to make the name of our party more precise. It is proposed that the All-Union Communist Party (of Bolsheviks) henceforth be called the Communist Party of the Soviet Union.'

"Khrushchev explained that the words *Communist* and *Bolshevik* expressed the same thing, 'and, Comrades, although all of us have grown used to calling Communists Bolsheviks, there is no longer any need to retain the dual designation in the name of the Party.'

"Khrushchev then gave a short definition of the Communist Party: 'The Communist Party of the Soviet Union is a voluntary, militant union of Communists holding the same views, formed of people of the working class, the working peasantry, and the working intelligentsia' whose chief tasks were to 'build a Communist society by gradual transition from Socialism to Communism, to bring about a constant rise in the living standards and cultural level of society, to educate the members of society in internationalism and establishment of fraternal bonds with the working people of all countries, and to strengthen in every respect the active defense of the Soviet Union against the aggressive action of its enemies.'

"Under Lenin's initiative in July and August 1918, an All-Russian Congress of the League of Working and Peasant Youths was suggested as a first step to creating a unified national youth organization. Sverdlov, secretary of the Central Committee, and Lenin's wife, Krupskaya, were active helpers in this movement. Meeting with some of the youth leaders, Sverdlov suggested that the new organization be called the Communist League of Youth because its goal was to be the Communist education of youth. Sverdlov's suggestion was accepted, and a meeting in Moscow from October 29 to November 4, 1918, created the Communist Youth League (*Kommunisticheskii soyuz molodezhi*)— the *Komsomol*.

"At the end of the Congress, Lenin received a delegation from the Komsomol and asked many questions: How were the youths to be taught? Was there kerosene for the reading room? What was the political mood of the delegates? How was the organization to be financed?

"This last question brought some confusion to the delegates, who until then had not thought about financing. Lenin said the Party must take care of the Youth League, and he gave the delegates a note to Sverdlov telling him to help them.

"Lenin also asked about the name 'Communist' and said the league's actions as well as its name must be Communist. The youths soon had a chance to prove their dedication. Russia needed soldiers to defend the Revolution during the civil war that followed it, and it was said that along with their Party card the Komsomols received a rifle and bullets. Before long there were signs on many of the Komsomol headquarters: 'Closed. Everyone has gone to the Front.'

"The Eighth Congress of the Communist Party, meeting in March 1919, passed a special resolution about youth, who would be a well-prepared reserve for the Party. The Komsomol would train the youth to enter the 'open door' of the Party.

"In Moscow in October 1920, the Third Congress of the Komsomol was addressed by Lenin himself in a historic speech, 'The Tasks of the Youth Leagues.' The first task, Lenin said, was 'Learn.' Learn what? The reply, 'Learn Communism,' Lenin said, was too simple. Communism must not be learned by rote. The entire young generation must be organized and united by the Communists, who must set an example of training and discipline.

" 'What is a Communist?' Lenin continued. '*Communist* is a Latin word. *Communis* is the Latin for *common*. Communist society is a society in which all things—the land, the factories—are owned in common and the people work in common. That is Communism.'

"Building a new Communist society would not be easy, Lenin said. They must take what was good from the past and use it with the new. There was no promise of a land 'flowing with milk and honey.' Instead there must be iron discipline in an arduous struggle. The youth must take upon themselves the task of abolishing illiteracy in Russia. They must help with work in suburban vegetable gardens: 'People are starving; there is hunger in the factories. To save ourselves from starvation, vegetable gardens must be established.'

"The starvation of which Lenin spoke became more widespread. Land had gone unplowed during the Civil War, and the failure of the harvest in the summer of 1920 and the hard winter of 1921-22 increased the hardships. Millions of Russians starved to death. In addition to famine, Russia was decimated by disease, including epidemics of typhus and typhoid.

"The expropriation of banks, the merchant marine, grain dealers, and factories coupled with the disruption of industry caused production to sink to new lows. In March 1921, Lenin set up the New Economic Policy (NEP), which permitted limited private enterprise. Foreign capital and trade was again solicited. Gradually the economy returned to normal, although there was some grumbling among the younger people that NEP was a retreat from Socialist principles. Membership in the Komsomol declined disastrously.

"There was also a noticeable drop in the age level of Komsomol members. During the Civil War the older youths had served at the front, leaving only those too young to serve at home. The eighteen-to-twenty-year-old group was superseded by a fifteen-to-seventeen-year-old group. It was suggested that the age limits for Komsomol membership be lowered to fourteen through sixteen; however, since this new group seemed closer to children than to adults, different educational methods were needed.

"Independent proletarian organizations for younger children had been formed as early as 1917 in Petrograd, called 'Children's Workers Club in the Name of World Revolution,' as well as 'The Children's Proletkult' in Tula in 1918, 'Children's International' in Kiev in 1920, 'Young Worker's Army' in the Ukraine in 1920, and 'Muraveinik' in Kiev. Muraveinik (Anthill) members organized a library and an art circle and published one of the first children's newspapers. The children busied themselves in 'socially useful labor'—electrifying their buildings, repairing dachas, improving sanitation in summer camps, and organizing ball games for children. On the first all-Russian Subbotnik (a Saturday devoted to voluntary community work), the children cleaned yards and constructed a central town square.

"Russian Scouts had been organized in 1914 under the auspices of the Czarist army, and by 1917 there were 50,000 Scouts in Russia. Krupskaya and Lunacharsky (minister of education) were much interested in the form and method of Scout activities. Krupskaya, while disliking the bourgeois goals of the Scouts, was interested in the emotional appeal of Scout rituals and thought some of the methods employed in Scout work might be used in a Communist children's organization.

"A society called 'Young Communists of Scouts,' following the work of the Boy Scouts, had already been denounced at the Second Congress of the Komsomol as were some bourgeois sport organizations. The congress saw in such organizations the bourgeoisie's last attempt to stifle the Communist revolution. An organization of 'Red Scouts' was suggested, but Krupskaya said that, although Scouts understood the psychology of young people, they were dedicated to the defense of the monarchy, the church, and the upper classes.

"In January 1922, the Moscow committee of the Komsomol invited certain left-wing Boy Scout leaders to cooperate with the Komsomol in creating a new organization. In February a group of two Komsomol activists and one Scoutmaster with practical experience in scouting was appointed to set up such organizations in three regions of Moscow—Khamovhiski, Sokolniki, and Krasnopresne. The new groups were soon being called 'detachments of young Pioneers,' and their motto was, 'All proletarian children must be in the ranks of the Pioneers.'

"There were some dissenting voices: 'Why do we need such children's organizations?' 'How can you teach children politics they won't understand?' Nevertheless, at a Komsomol conference in Moscow held from May 16 to

May 19, 1922, it was decided to set up a Pioneer organization throughout the country. The last day of the conference, May 19 became the founding day of the Pioneers.

"In October 1922, the Fifth Congress of the Komsomol passed a special resolution about the Pioneers, confirming the laws and customs of the Pioneers and approving the solemn oath of the Pioneers: "I solemnly swear that I will be true to the working class and will help my fellow workers know and obey the laws of the Pioneers.'

"The Pioneers had seven laws:

1. The Pioneer is true to the working class and Communism.
2. The Pioneer is a friend and brother to every Pioneer and Komsomol.
3. The Pioneer is honest and truthful. His word is like granite.
4. The Pioneer is disciplined.
5. The Pioneer daily helps his fellow workers to build a Communist society.
6. The Pioneer loves work and respects useful labor.
7. The Pioneer is pure in thought, word, and deed.

The iron law of the Pioneers was, 'I will try always, everywhere, and wherever possible to acquire knowledge in order to use it for the good of the workers.' To the slogan, 'To the struggle for worker's rights—be ready!' the reply was 'Always ready!' (The Russian word *gotov* may be translated as either "ready" or "prepared," but since the motto of the Scouts is "Be Prepared," the Soviets prefer "Be Ready" and "Always Ready" for the Pioneers.)

I was so immersed in my work at the library that I listened only absent-mindedly when my husband told me of the days he was spending with Harry. "You're missing a real live Pioneer," my husband said. "Harry is the whole history of the Pioneers in one person." As I began to listen to Harry's story, I grew more and more interested.

4

The Heroes

Harry attended a junior high school in the Bronx that had 3,500 pupils but no cafeteria or lunch room in it's six-story building. Harry's detachment of Young Pioneers decided something should be done about a lunch room. At that time the principal of the school had declared a policy of "self-government," but voting rights were restricted to upper-class students, and Harry's group in the seventh grade was excluded. Harry and the Pioneers formed a "Progressive Party" to fight both the voting exclusion and the lack of lunch facilities. They persuaded another school "party" called "Tempo" to join forces with them in a "united front." Out of seven candidates the united front won five places.

Under the auspices of the Pioneers, a monthly newspaper, *The Young Spark* (after Lenin's paper, *The Spark*—"from the spark the conflagration") was published, and, in addition to articles on school life, there were articles about the Pioneer organization in the Soviet Union. The paper demanded the addition of a cafeteria and the right of all to vote in real self-government as well as abolition of the salute to the flag and the saying of the Lord's Prayer. The Pioneers were also raising money for the hungry children of striking miners in Pennsylvania and Ohio. The principal of the school was opposed to every one of these measures, and Harry and his Pioneers were refused their "rights."

In response, the Pioneers held a mass demonstration in front of the school just before May Day 1928, urging students to skip school and attend meetings to declare their solidarity with the working class. The principal called the police. Harry and his friends were taken to the police station in a "Black Maria" (as Harry called it), where they were lectured and dismissed.

The principal scheduled examinations for May 1 and said that anyone not attending school that day would not be promoted to the next grade. The Pioneers consulted their Komsomol leaders. "If everyone stays away from school that day, the principal won't be able to fail the whole school," the leaders advised. Harry agitated for the May 1 holiday, but secretly worried that the campaign would fail.

May 1 was a sunny, warm day. The Pioneers picketed the school, explaining to all schoolchildren the significance of May Day and urging them to attend a workers' demonstration in Madison Square Garden rather than go to school. Again the principal called the police. "Get in that school!" the police ordered. "Don't touch us!" the Pioneers shouted back. "We have the right to assemble."

Again, Harry and his friends were taken to the police station. The judge, looking at Harry's barely four-foot height, said, "This isn't a kindergarten!" Then, turning to the Pioneers, he asked, "Why didn't you go to school today?"

"This is the worker's holiday, the 1st of May."

"What do we do with them, Your Honor?" a policeman asked.

"Take them back to school."

"I will not go back to school. This is a workers' holiday," Harry insisted.

"I'll show you what kind of school you'll go to," the judge said, losing his temper. "I can send you to a reform school." Ten Pioneers, including Harry, were kept in the station. Some ran about, some sat quietly, some cried. Harry was taken to a cell where he lay on his cot, thinking about the Pioneers and the 1st of May. Suddenly, he heard shouts outside the building: "Free Harry Eisman!" His fellow Pioneers had come to his rescue, but they, too, were dispersed by the police. The next day, the Pioneers returned with $100 bail for Harry, and he was released into the custody of an older brother until his trial on May 4. Before he released them, the judge lectured the boys on their misbehavior and commented that Pioneers were too young to understand the meaning of May Day.

Harry was released into the custody of an older brother, but warned that if he persisted in his bad behavior he would be sent back to Moldavia. The principal took Harry back, reluctantly, but soon afterward, when the principal was vilifying the Pioneers in assembly, Harry rose from his seat and said, "That is slander. I will defend the Pioneers."

Harry's brother was called to the school, and Harry was told to apologize and to stop publishing *The Young Spark*. Harry said he would stop circulating the paper in school but would not stop publishing it. The principal suspended him from school.

"Harry let me borrow his press clippings," my husband said, showing me a big envelope full of mimeographed newspaper articles. "They look genuine," he said. "We can check them at the library when we get home."

The story was neatly put together, including a comment from Harry's principal, who described Harry as a "small unnoticeable boy—a typical child Communist—absolutely sincere."

My husband continued the story, filling in with some of the clippings. "Harry transferred to a new school where he continued his Pioneer activities. He was making street speeches, standing on a milk can so he would be seen.

Parents were warned not to let their children attend pro-Eisman meetings. Harry said some parents urged officials to look up schedules of steamers bound for Russia, 'where Soviet schools already existed for teaching Soviet ideals.' The right of free speech for a child, and a foreigner at that, was questioned."

One article told of a delegation of 250 Boy Scouts who were harassed by Harry and his Pioneers as they were leaving New York for a jamboree in England. Police were called and Harry was again arrested, this time accused of kicking a policeman's horse in the ribs and spitting on the policeman's shoulder. Since Harry was only four feet tall, his lawyer argued, it was unlikely, if not impossible, that Harry would spit seven feet upward, but the judge was quoted as saying:

> Now the offense here is a serious one. It was an assault on the government. You might just as well have gone to Albany or Washington or the City Hall and committed some outrageous assault. The kick and the horse—nobody is going to condone that—but spitting upon a man's person, you know, particularly when he is wearing the uniform that serves you and serves me, is unpardonable.

Harry was sentenced to a reform school at Hawthorne, New York. When he came up for parole in January 1929, he was released on condition that he would not take part in any mass meetings or demonstrations.

To welcome Harry home, 250 Pioneers gathered in front of Children's Court, carrying placards and signs exposing the Boy Scouts as tools of government militarism and condemning the jailing of Harry Eisman. A clipping from the New York *Herald Tribune* reported "a triumphant procession resembling a college celebration with Eisman riding on the marchers' shoulders like a football game hero." In front of Communist Party headquarters at 26 Union Square, two policemen ordered the Pioneers to disperse. They grabbed the children's signs and started destroying them, but the children fought back. A passer-by telephoned police headquarters, and the riot squad was sent out. Harry darted into the building and addressed the crowd from a second-story window. The police herded the other Pioneers into the building, where Harry finished his speech to loud applause.

The next clipping told of a dinner in Harry's honor at Unity Cooperative House. The *Herald Tribune* wrote: "250 Young Reds Jeer Flag After Union Square Riot—Stage Dinner in Honor of Comrade Just out of Jail and Scoff at Lord's Prayer." The New York *Times* reported: "Child Communists Clash with Police."

In March an unemployment demonstration turned into a march toward City Hall. William Z. Foster, the Worker's Party candidate for president of the United States, was arrested, and so was Harry. Foster got a suspended sentence. Harry got a five-and-a-half year sentence to the Hawthorne Reform School.

There were clippings from various Communist papers describing Harry as a "Boy Martyr," a "Child Victim of Capitalism," and the "World's Youngest

Political Prisoner." The Young Pioneers of the Soviet Union invited Harry to visit them when he was freed.

The authorities at Hawthorne told Harry that if he could raise the $125 needed for passage money and if he would not attempt to return to the United States for at least two years, they would waive the rest of his sentence, and he could accept the Soviet invitation. Harry had never been to the Soviet Union, spoke no Russian, and knew little about Soviet affairs, except that he was regarded as a hero. He accepted the offer.

"Prize Bad Boy Gets Free Trip to Red Paradise—Young Pioneers Honor Abuser of Flag, Boy Scouts, Bible, Police and Their Horses—$125 Sends Him to Russia—Arrested Six Times—Expelled by School for Impudence" headlined the *Herald Tribune*, as I read the last clipping in the envelope. "What happened next?" I asked.

"Harry was too excited to notice that his steamship ticket was to Riga, in Latvia, not then a part of the Soviet Union," my husband said. "Harry was in for a surprise."

Harry got off the ship when it docked in Hamburg and sent a telegram to the *Daily Worker* in New York, announcing his arrival. He could already imagine the headline: "Boy Hero Arrives in Europe." After sending the telegram, Harry visited the Bureau of Pioneers in Hamburg, where he was greeted warmly. From Germany he took a steamer for Leningrad, where he arrived on a grey, though not very cold, December evening in 1930.

There was no one there to meet him, though the German Pioneers had sent a telegram to Leningrad announcing his arrival. Harry had the equivalent of thirteen rubles in his pocket. "How much does it cost to go to Moscow?" He asked a friendly interpreter at the Information Bureau. "Twenty-three rubles." she said, then seeing Harry's creatfallen face, she took Harry to the Europa Hotel and introduced him to the director there. Harry explained that he had come to the Soviet Union at the invitation of the Soviet Pioneers.

"Let me see your documents, the man said sternly.

Harry took out his U.S. passport, which was stamped in large letters, "Without the Right of Return," and a letter a friend from the U.S. *Daily Worker* had received from the Leningrad Pioneer Organization asking the *Daily Worker's* help in putting them in touch with the famous New York Pioneer, Harry Eisman. Harry also took out his Komsomol card, wondering if he had to explain how a Pioneer hero happened to have a Komsomol card. He decided the Director would know that Pioneers usually turned into Komsomol members when they reached fifteen.

The hotel director read the note and then telephoned the editor of *Leninskaya Iskra* (Lenin's Spark), the Pioneer newspaper in Leningrad. "Harry Eisman is here," he said.

"That can not be," the editor said. "Today's issue of our paper announces Harry's arrival in Hamburg. He'll arrive in Moscow in a few days, and we're busy preparing a delegation to send to Moscow to meet him."

"He says he is here now," the hotel director said, as Harry listened uneasily.

After some confusion, Harry was at last accepted as being the real Harry Eisman, and that evening he was introduced to a wildly applauding audience of Pioneers at a concert for Pioneers at the Leningrad Philharmonic. For the next three days, from morning to night he was greeted by enthusiastic Pioneers. A packed hall cheered him at a reception in the Leningrad Children's House of Culture, and at one point his admirers pursued him in such numbers that he escaped them by fleeing in a horse-drawn droshky down a street where horses were not allowed.

Then on to Moscow, where he was again greeted as a hero by admiring crowds. He chose to live in the first Pioneer's Commune (today Children's House No. 22 in the Zhdanov District), where both local and foreign Pioneers lived. When Harry first saw the grey building that housed the commune, the large dim halls, the children dressed in drab, dark clothes, and a grey-haired matron with a severe face, he thought, "Oh no! Not Hawthorne again and more 'rules of conduct.'"

The commune was not Hawthorne. It was a fully self-governing body where everyone helped everyone else. They helped Harry to learn Russian. They helped him on his frequent triumphal tours around the Soviet Union. They listened intently as he explained to Maxim Gorky (when he visited the commune) about the Scottsboro case in the United States. Harry was gratified later when Gorky wrote "The Logic of History" and "Capitalist Terrorism Against the Negro Workers of America."

Harry toured the Soviet Union "to tell the Pioneers everywhere of the American Pioneers and to bring them the pledge of international solidarity." He visited Stalingrad, a new Soviet city arising in the midst of thatch-roofed cottages and ox-drawn vehicles. He went to the Pioneer camp, Artek, made speeches to the Red Army, and was given a Red Army uniform as a gift. He met with the president of the Moldavian Soviet Republic and visited the graves of his parents in a Kishenev Jewish cemetery. For nine months he traveled, and then the authorities decided it was time Harry had worker's training.

Harry chose to attend the school connected with the Moscow Automobile Plant, one of the best Party schools in the Soviet Union and entered the factory school in September 1931. The school's goal was the "cultural, political, and technical development of the new Socialist citizen." Upon graduation, the student was ready to serve his factory, his class, and his Party.

By this time Harry was beginning to feel he was infallible. Some of the courses he was asked to take he considered superfluous. Why should he waste his valuable time studying biology, Russian literature, English, physical education, or industrial hygiene? He made out a schedule of his own, "calculated to the second." The authorities rejected Harry's schedule. With the possible exception of English, all the courses were necessary.

Harry was very offended. He refused to attend the courses he considered unnecessary. He felt very sorry for himself, thinking, "Well, here's Harry Eisman. The whole world knows him for his good work. Millions of children in Soviet schools are taught to regard him as an example of international solidarity. What if they knew what has happened to Comrade Harry?"

At the next general assembly, the chairman said, "The first point on the agenda, today, is the question of Harry Eisman."

Comrade Misha was the first to speak. He pictured Harry as a ringleader of disruption, who did not want to study, did not respect the collective will, and was a burden on the group.

Next, Bovka, Harry's best and closest friend, spoke against Harry. One after another the speeches condemned Harry: "Comrade Eisman, what you were and have done, we grant. We are proud to have you among us. You are a Komsomol. You bear the same membership card we do. You live and work with us, so why not really become one of us? Why try to be a law unto yourself? If it comes to comparisons of laurels and desserts, we are not without them ourselves. Only our achievements are on a different front—the tremendous front of Socialist construction. No, Comrade Harry. You are utterly wrong, and we demand a complete change in you. Be a real Komsomol. Study and work. If you need help we'll give it to you, but if you won't go in harmony with the collective body and won't listen to us, then we'll speak in another tone.'

The assembly voted to give Harry a reprimand. He sat on one side of the room feeling miserable. His friend Bovka came over and sat beside him. "I'm still your friend," he said, giving Harry a pat on the shoulder.

"That pat on the shoulder meant a lot to me," Harry said, as he finished telling us the story. "Bovka was right to put the Cause above our friendship."

Harry sighed a little. "I straightened out after that, but I'll never forget what it was like being a boy hero. The girls—the pretty girls. Do you know what it's like to have hundreds of pretty girls looking up to you as a hero when you're still in your teens?"

Some of the Pioneer heroes were not as lucky as Harry. One of the first Pioneer heroes, and still highly regarded, was Pavel Morozov, a contemporary of Harry's who lived during the early days of collectivization, when farm land was being expropriated from rich landowners and even from some of the prosperous peasants, who were called kulaks.

In a Russian book for children I found Pavel's story. It begins in the village of Gerasimovka, at a town meeting called to elect a village chairman. Zoya Aleksandrova, a local teacher, is the first to speak. "Soviet power has given us a great task—to build a new society." She said the village had many limitations: "We don't even have a Pioneer organization here."

"We don't need Pioneers!" someone in the audience shouts, but others are anxious to get on with the election, and Pavel's father, Profim Sergeevich

Morozov, is nominated. "First, he's a poor peasant, second, he's wholly on the side of Soviet power, and third, we know him."

"He drinks!" someone complains.

"He drinks, but that doesn't mean he's a drunkard."

Morozov is elected.

Later a Pioneer organization is begun in the village school. Morozov's two sons, Alyosha and Pavel, are invited to join. "Pioneers are dirty people," Alyosha says, but Pavel declares, "I'll join the Pioneers."

When Morozov hears that Pavel has joined the Pioneers he says, "I won't feed a Communist." In a drunken rage, he beats Pavel so badly that Pavel lies in bed unable to move for three days.

Pavel begins to watch his father. He notices that strange men come in the night and give his father money. When Komsomol members ask Pavel's father if there are still kulaks in the village he lies: "There aren't any kulaks."

Pavel discovers that his father is selling papers to men who come in the night. The papers testify that the men are not kulaks but poor peasants. Pavel realizes that his father is helping the kulaks!

Pavel consults with his teacher: "You said we must fight our enemies."

"You must kill them," the teacher says firmly.

"I can't," Pavel agonizes, "the enemy is my father."

Pavel's mother worries. "You can't testify against your father," she says, but Pavel knows his duty. He goes to the town council with his story, and the police arrest his father.

The town is in an uproar. "*Molodets!*" (Well done!) some say, but others mutter, "Red Devil." The village divides into those for and those against Pavel. "A father is always a father," some say, but others argue, "Pioneers aren't afraid of anything."

"I want to be a real Communist," Pavel says.

"Kill such a son," Pavel's grandfather says.

Not long afterward a crowd of angry villagers (some said, led by Pavel's grandfather) set upon Pavel and kill him. With his death Pavel became one of the first Pioneer heroes.

"I hated Pavel Morozov," the dissident Lena had told me the night we had dinner together. "I couldn't imagine turning *my* father in to the authorities."

Soon there were more powerful enemies for Soviet children to fight, and more heroes. On June 22, 1941, at 4:00 AM, Germany attacked the Soviet Union and seemed destined to overwhelm her. Millions were taken prisoner. Byelorussia, northern Russia, and the Ukraine were overrun and occupied.

When the Germans invaded Byelorussia, a Leningrad Pioneer, Zina Portnova, was visiting her grandmother there. Zina joined a Byelorussian partisan group as a scout. One day while she was on a scouting mission she was captured by two German officers. They took her to a staff room to interrogate her, but Zina grabbed a pistol that was lying on a table and fired, killing one of the officers.

She jumped through a window, firing again as the other Germans pursued her, but her pistol misfired and she was captured and tortured to death.

One out of every four people in Byelorussia died in the Great Patriotic War, as the Soviets call World War II. The Germans herded survivors of invasions into death camps, some composed exclusively of old people, some just for children. One camp for children was located near a German military hospital. The children's blood was drained from their bodies for use in the hospital, and when the children were too weak to give more blood, their bodies were thrown to the dogs. Today at Khatyn, outside Minsk, there is an impressive memorial to the Byelorussian villages and towns that were destroyed in the war.

One niche of the monument commemorates these children, and today's visiting Pioneers take off their Pioneer ties and tie them to the gratings. These fluttering red ties are mute tribute to the children who died in the war. They are even more touching than the gigantic bronze figure of a peasant carrying the body of his dead son, killed when the twenty-six families of the village of Khatyn were herded into a barn and the barn set afire. Those who tried to break out of the barn were shot. One woman, escaping with her son, shielded him with her body. Our guide said, "She gave life to her son twice."

Still, Khatyn's spirit is not one of gloom but of hope—hope that there will never be another such war. The eternal flame is set in a huge marble slab, which also contains three living birch trees symbolizing the three out of every four Byelorussians who lived through the war.

Those who lived do not forget the dead. In Minsk there is a bronze statue to Marat Kazei who was only eleven years old when the Germans invaded Byelorrusia. Marat was small and thin, but he was an excellent horseman and a crack shot so he joined the partisans. One day when Marat and his commander were reconnoitering they were ambushed by some Germans. The commander was killed, but Marat, with a grenade in his hand, went forward to meet the enemy. When the Germans were only a few steps away, Marat threw himself upon them, exploding his grenade and blowing himself up with the Germans.

In Moscow there were bombings every day at seven in the morning and four in the afternoon. Women, old people, and very small children took shelter in the subway, where the trains' current was shut off and the trains turned into dormitories. No youths or grown men were allowed in the subways; they were on the roofs of buildings, catching fire bombs by the tail and throwing them into sand boxes to extinguish them. Boys and girls, too young for the army, soon learned to lift the smoking, foot-long fire bombs by the tails, or "fins." Moscow's anti-aircraft trapped the planes that had dropped the bombs and forced them out to the suburbs, where they were shot down.

"There must never be another war," Soviet children are told constantly while they are learning about the child heroes and heroines. There is Zoya Kosmodemyanskaya, who worked with the partisans, severing German telegraph lines, bombing German bridges, and dynamiting roads. Zoya was captured

and sentenced to be hanged. On her way to the gallows she was taken past some collective farmers and called out: "Comrades! Be brave, fight, beat the fascists! I'm not afraid to die, comrades. It's happiness to die for one's country!" Then turning to her executioners she said, "Now you hang me, but I am not alone. There are two hundred million of us, and you can't hang us all."

There is Lyonya Golikov, who joined the partisans when he was fifteen (and the Komsomol later) and was decorated for his heroism. A story about him in the third-grade reader, *Nasha Rodina* (Our Motherland) ends with the words:

> Thus Pioneer Leonid [Lyonya] Golikov became a Hero of the Soviet Union.
> But Lyonya did not know about his award. He died in an unequal battle in the village of Ostraya Luka on January 24, 1943.

The Soviets have also designated Hero Cities, including Moscow, Kiev, Sevastopol, Leningrad, Stalingrad, Minsk, and others that were battlegrounds during World War II. People who lived through the war remember what war is like, and their children are constantly reminded of it, but today there are new, nonmilitary heroes as well.

In the same reader that tells of Lyonya there is a story written by a modern hero—Yuri Gagarin, the first man in space. Gagarin tells how, before going into orbit, he visited Red Square, the Kremlin, and Lenin's Mausoleum. The day before take-off was spent in complete rest; he had already studied all of the elements of the expedition, including the contents of the cosmic kitchen supplied with juice and pate which he would drink through a tube.

On the day of the flight, dressed in a bright orange spacesuit, Gagarin climbed into the armchair of the spaceship and waited for take-off. He was asked if he were happy. "Of course I'm happy. In all times and epochs the highest happiness of mankind is to participate in new discoveries. I want to dedicate this flight to the people of Communism."

Suddenly Gagarin was alone in the spaceship with only the radio to connect him with the surrounding world, yet there still remained sixteen minutes of "free time" before take-off. What did he think about in those minutes? He said he thought about the day long ago when he became a Pioneer and the red necktie was first put around his neck. He knew that the word *Pioneer* meant reconnoiterer, investigator. "Remarkable word! What a pity that we can't preserve our first Pioneer necktie to the end of our days, as our most precious memento."

The spaceship *Vostok* (East) lifted off the ground, and Gagarin marveled at the beautiful colors he saw around him. He soon became used to his own weightlessness, but inanimate objects played tricks on him. After making a few notes in his ledger he put his pencil down and it floated away. Although fastened with a cord, the pencil somehow got untied, and he lost it entirely, having to make his observations only on the radio after that.

At the end of the story Gagarin advises Soviet school children: "Your task will be easier and harder than ours. Easier because we already know a lot. Harder because each time the task becomes more complicated and so does the apparatus."

There are also more mundane heroes. Heroes of Socialist Labor are rewarded for contributions to their factory or farm. Whatever form a hero takes, he is generous with his time. Almost every apartment house in the Soviet Union has one or two heroes who speak to Pioneer groups and invite children to their apartments to look at their medals and scrapbooks.

Then there are the supreme heroes whose pictures and statues appear everywhere—the first Communist, Karl Marx, his co-worker, Frederick Engels, and the man who put Communism into practice, Vladimir Ilich Lenin.

Soviet children are told that in some countries there is discrimination between rich and poor, white and black. Unlike the Soviet Union, where people say "our" factory and "our" school, in these countries some people say "my" factory, "my" school, and "my" house, while others in these same countries say, "I have nothing." Soviet children learn that the first person to say that such inequalities must end was Karl Marx.

Karl Marx is such a big figure that it is hard for a small child to relate to him. Instead of Marx as a child, most of the stories about him portray Marx as a father of a lively family. One of the family favorites is his daughter Eleanor Marx (1855-98), who was known by the nickname Tussy.

There are many stories about Tussy Marx, but my favorite was in the December 1971 *Pioner*. As a seven-year-old child, Tussy was very much interested in the Civil War in the United States and followed the course of the war with much interest. According to the story, she decided to write a letter to President Lincoln giving him some advice. One suggestion was that he organize one regiment of boys and another of girls ("like me"). She also thought President Lincoln should fire General McClellan as commander and appoint "Uncle Fred" (Frederick Engels) in his place. A postscript to the letter wished Lincoln success and added, "Do you have any children?"

When Marx came home from the British Museum Library where he did research for his books, Tussy ran to meet him and told him about her letter. "What do you think about it Mavr?" (Mavr was her pet name for her father.)

Marx looked over the letter carefully. "You lied about your age," he said, crossing out "eight" years old and substituting "seven." "In my opinion, a very sensible letter. But if Lincoln appoints Engels commander-in-chief, what will we do without him?"

"This is war," Tussy said resolutely.

She insisted that Marx mail the letter immediately, and he went out with the letter as she went to bed. For days she waited impatiently for an answer from President Lincoln. None arrived, and she decided the London postmaster must be a spy for the South who had intercepted her letter. When Marx doubted this, Tussy accused him of being "very naive."

Tussy wrote another letter to Lincoln, this time adding the information that she was followed at every step by agents of the South. Although she didn't receive an answer to this letter either, she persisted, and wrote a number of other letters, as the war unfolded.

She advised Lincoln to make all his soldiers bathe in the Potomac River so he could detect which of his men were spies, explaining that spies wore false mustaches, beards, and wigs, which would come unglued in the water. Another suggestion was to form an all-Negro detachment, which would be used for night duty, since, being black, they could not be detected in the dark.

When, in November 1864, Lincoln was reelected president, the General Council of the International, at the suggestion of Marx and Engels, sent Lincoln a congratulatory telegram as a "true son of the working class." Lincoln wrote Marx a friendly note of thanks, which piqued Tussy, who was still hurt that Lincoln had not answered her letters.

"I didn't send him a personal telegram," Marx explained. "It was from all of us in the International. Lincoln probably doesn't have time to answer personal mail."

"I won't write him any more letters," Tussy said. "Let him get along without my help and we'll see how well he does."

Soviet children are more intimately concerned with the life of Lenin. The Soviet child of every age has a story of Lenin at a comparable age. There is the baby Lenin with his blonde curls pictured on the Octobrist button and the story of Lenin at age eight playing a boisterous game with cousins while visiting an aunt, in the course of which Lenin knocked over and broke a glass carafe belonging to his aunt.

"Who broke my carafe?" the aunt asked, coming into the room after hearing the noise.

"Not I," said one cousin.

"Not I," said another cousin.

"Not I," said Lenin.

The story, as told in a first-grade Russian reader, explains that it is easier to say "Not I," in such a case than to say "I," but, the story goes on to say, Lenin's lie worried him after he returned home. One night he burst into tears and confessed to his mother: "I deceived my aunt. I said I didn't break the carafe, but I really did break it." Lenin's mother consoled him and said that if Lenin wrote his aunt she might forgive him because he had learned how bad it was to lie.

Lenin is pictured growing up in the close, friendly Ulyanov family. (Ulyanov was Lenin's real name, Lenin being his revolutionary name.) "Volodya," as he was called by the family, was a lively boy, fond of playing jokes for which he was sometimes punished by being made to sit in the "black chair" in his father's study while he thought over his misdeeds.

He was a good student, getting all "fives," the top grade on a scale from one to five. At one gymnasium he attended most of the boys were from wealthy families, and they often teased Lenin by asking him how many servants he had. "I have two wonderful servants," Lenin said. "They shine my shoes, wipe my nose, and defend me against blockheads." With that he held up his two fists. "These are my servants."

Lenin was the third of six children. His older brother, Alexander, was hanged for an assassination plot against Czar Alexander III when Lenin was in the eighth grade. This event had a profound effect on him, both personally and politically. When he went to St. Petersburg (now Leningrad) in 1893 he was already beginning his Marxist studies.

At a *Bliny* (pancake) party for a Marxist circle in St. Petersburg, Lenin met Nadezhda Krupskaya, who was later to become his wife. Lenin and Krupskaya (she is never called Mrs. Lenin) had no children of their own, but they are often pictured with nephews or other children, and Soviet children feel that Lenin liked and respected them. The story about New Year's in Sokolniki (a suburb of Moscow) is a favorite, with pictures of Lenin dancing around the New Year's tree with the children.

There are hundreds of stories about Lenin for children. There are stories of Lenin and his cat, Lenin and his dog, Aida, Lenin choosing a national emblem for the Soviet Union. "Why the sword?" Lenin asked, after looking at a proposed emblem showing a rising sun on a red background, a hammer and sickle, and a sword, all surrounded by stalks of . . . wheat, Lenin continued: "The sword is not our emblem. We just hold it in our hands in order to defend our proletarian state while we have enemies who threaten us, but that does not mean this will always be the case." With his pencil Lenin crossed out the sword. When the artist brought a new sketch Lenin said, "It still needs something." The sculptor Andreev, who was sitting with Lenin, redrew the coat of arms. He added a five-pointed star and the words, "Proletarians of All Lands, Unite!" In 1918 this was accepted as the state emblem.

One story I like has Lenin working late night after night in the Kremlin until one snowy afternoon he looks out his window and sees some children having a snowball fight. "I feel like doing something unimportant," Lenin says to his secretary, and out he goes to play in the snow with the children. That story ends with the statement that the lights burned late in Lenin's office again that night.

5

The Leaders

O ne day Harry pointed out a pale green building on the corner of Serov Avenue and Bogdan Khmelnitsky Street in Moscow. "That's the Central Committee of the Komsomol," he explained. "The head of the Pioneers works there." A few days later my husband and I had a free day so I decided to visit the Central Committee. When I asked Intourist for a car and guide I simply said *gorod* (city), which meant I could tell the driver where we wanted to go in town.

Intourist guides for English-speaking tourists are usually attractive young Soviet women (occasionally attractive young Soviet men) who are studying English. They can be extremely useful as well as pleasant companions, and Genya, the guide we drew for the day, seemed above average. "Shall we visit the Tretyakov Gallery?" Genya asked, as we got in the car and the driver looked at us expectantly for directions.

"I want to go to the Central Committee of the Komsomol," I said.

Genya gasped, "We can't go there."

"But I know where it is," I said.

"I know where it is, too." Genya said. "Tourists don't go there."

"Well, you can wait in the car while I go in," I said.

"They won't let you in."

"Well, I'll try. If I can't get in we'll go to the Tretyakov Gallery."

As the driver parked the car across from the Central Committee building Genya huddled down in the seat as though hiding. I got out and walked in the front door of the building and up some steps to the lobby. A man with a sheaf of papers in his hand was starting down the steps as I went up. He paused and looked at me inquiringly. "I want to see the Pioneers," I said.

"Alevtina Vasilievna?" he said, giving a woman's name and patronymic, and before I could answer he directed me out of that building to another building

51

nearby. There I mentioned an approximation of the name I had heard, and was ushered into an office. Alevtina Vasilievna Fedulova was out, but her assistant gave me a huge map of Pioneer activities, some Pioneer pins, and several books on the Pioneers.

Genya was amazed and intrigued. When we told Harry about it he laughed. "You should meet Fedulova though," he said. "I think the House of Friendship can arrange it for you."

We did meet Fedulova. She is a lovely blonde, warm, friendly, and intelligent. She is a secretary of the Central Committee of the Komsomol, chairman of the Central Council of the Pioneers, and the overall head of the Pioneers. Fedulova was active in the Pioneers as a child, attending the Artek and Orlyonok Pioneer camps, which take only the best Pioneers. After graduation from college she taught chemistry and biology at a pedagogical institute, while continuing her work with the Pioneers as head of a *druzhina* (all the Pioneers in one school). She was secretary to the district committee and then secretary to the regional committee of the Komsomol, went on to be a national secretary of the Komsomol and finally, in 1971, the head of the Pioneers.

"The Pioneer organization is an independent organization of children run by children," Fedulova said, adding that it is closely connected with school. "We want a well-rounded personality, though the basic task of the Pioneer organization is to teach the Pioneer devotion to the work of the Communist Party with the accent first of all on political education."

Each eight- or ten-year school has a paid senior Pioneer leader, who must be at least eighteen years old and have completed high school and a special pedagogical institute. There are twenty-four institutions offering special five-year courses as well as one hundred six pedagogical schools for preparing senior Pioneer leaders (sixty in the Russian Republic, thirty in the Ukraine, and sixteen in Kazakhstan.) In 1969 Kostrama Pedagogical Institute started a correspondence course for Pioneer leaders.

A ten-year-old who has just joined the Pioneers becomes part of a team (*zveno*) of from five to eight children, all of whom are close friends, live near each other, or have some common interest, preferably all three. These children are comfortable with each other and feel free to express themselves frankly.

Each team is combined with two or three others into a detachment (*otryad*) consisting of twenty children, usually all from the same grade. All of the detachments in a school form the *druzhina*, which usually consists of seven or eight hundred children. Each detachment has its own assembly (*sbor*), which is planned by a council of the detachment, whose members are chosen from each detachment. There is also a school-wide *druzhina* Council, with at least three Pioneer members elected by the *druzhina* as well as a member of the Komsomol and the senior Pioneer leader.

Every Pioneer participates in the assembly, which is the highest body of the detachment. A few days before the assembly, each team is given a questionnaire:

"Think and answer: how can your team take part in the competition? What interests you most? What don't you like in the work of your detachment?"

The assembly begins with a discussion of each team's answer to these questions and may lead to lively arguments. An assembly may also include discussions on moral themes and even problems of individual members of the team, like drunkenness in the Pioneer's family, or on such themes as "What is a real friend?" "How has the world changed?" or "What will the year 2020 be like?" At the end of the assembly the children sing "Beat the Drum," and "Fate of the Drummer," or some such song.

An assembly is held as often as the children consider necessary. To keep it from being boring, senior Pioneer leaders and members of the detachment council of *otryad* and *druzhina* council give tactful advice on how to make the discussions more lively and less drawn out.

The highest body of the *druzhina* is also an assembly. Since the *druzhina* consists of the whole school its assembly is held less frequently and is more festive and ritualized. An assembly is usually held at the beginning and end of the school year, May 19 (the birthday of the Pioneers), October 2 (the anniversary of Lenin's speech to the Third Congress of the Komsomol, or some other noteworthy day.

Several months before the assembly the *druzhina* council selects the best suggestions from the teams and detachments and makes a plan for the assembly with the help of Pioneer activists, members of the detachment council, and leaders of each team. For example, detachment no. 1 may be given the task of gathering material on the culture and science of the town where the Pioneers live. Team no. 1 will investigate scientific-research institutions; team no. 2, theater; team no. 3 movies and the circus, and so on.

The assembly begins with a festive parade. Then there are reports from each detachment, guest speakers, musical or theatrical performances by the children, and reports from the *druzhina* council. Leaders caution the children over and over not to let the assembly become boring. We have attended many an assembly and have found them very lively and interesting. Once or twice a guest speaker has rambled on too long, but the children have always listened politely. In their own discussion meetings the Pioneers have a rule that, if a speaker is boring, a Pioneer in the group can stand up silently. If more than one Pioneer stands up the speaker must stop speaking. Although the Pioneers use this rule among themselves, they do not apply it to guest speakers.

Fedulova told us that a goal of the Pioneers is to make each child an active member and avoid passivity. She said the profession of Pioneer leader was like a high-flying bird. The leader should make the children want to fly with her. Since the three things children like best are singing, dancing, and playing, the leader must know how to do all three.

The adult Pioneer leader of a school is a member of a regional pedagogical council, which in turn sends a representative to the Central Council, whose members include the minister of education, representatives from trade unions, war veterans, editors of the Pioneer press, and other important people, such as Natalya Sats, the director of the Moscow Children's Musical Theater.

The Central Council also works closely with the Institute of Communist Education of the Academy of Sciences. The Central Council, which has seventy-seven members, elects a bureau of twenty-three members to work out specific programs, which are then referred to the *druzhina* council.

Komsomol leaders are well aware of the importance of concrete work with Pioneers. Long ago at their sixth congress in 1924, the Komsomol said: "Communism does not fall from the sky, does not spring from the heads or desires of good people, but is built with the victories of workers from factories and fields . . . who do not expect fruits of their labor from God but from their own efforts."

From several interviews with Fedulova and other Party officials as well as from congress documents, press reports, and Soviet textbooks, I tried to reconstruct the way a Pioneer program is built and carried out, from the top down.

Although Brezhnev does not make up a specific program for the Pioneers himself, he, along with the Central Committee of the Communist Party and the Council of Ministers, decides on certain goals involving aspects of national life, which are to be discussed at a Party congress. These goals usually cover a period of five years and are included in the five-year plan for the whole country.

The Council of Ministers is elected by the Supreme Soviet of the USSR, which consists of two bodies, the Soviet of the Union, and the Soviet of Nationalities. The word *soviet*, which means council, consultation, or advice, can also mean an exchange of opinion, a conference, or a temporary meeting for solving particular problems. The Soviets were organized in 1905 as organs of local self-government to lead strikes. Lenin regarded the Soviets as rudiments of the revolutionary state power of the workers and peasants. After the revolution of 1905-07, which ended in defeat, the soviets were revived in 1917, and after a period of dual power with the Provisional Government the soviets took power. "The greatest invention in history has been made; a proletarian type of state has been created," Lenin said.

Today the Soviet system comprises the Supreme Soviet of the USSR, the supreme soviets of the fifteen union republics, the supreme soviets of the twenty autonomous republics, and fifty thousand local soviets. Local Soviets of working people's deputies exercise state power in territories, regions, rural districts, municipal districts, towns, and villages and organize people's control committees.

Candidates for election to the soviets are nominated by Communist Party organizations, Komsomol detachments, and trade unions and at various places of employment. These candidates are then discussed on a local level, and one choice is made so that on the actual ballot there is only one candidate for each vacancy since there is only one party—the Communist Party.

Not all deputies of the Supreme Soviet are Communist Party members, although about two-thirds of them are. The Supreme Soviet meets twice a year and elects a Presidium, which functions as the highest body of state authority between sessions of the Supreme Soviet. The Supreme Soviet also elects the Council of Ministers of the USSR, that is, according to the Constitution, "the government of the USSR, the highest executive and administrative body of state authority of the USSR."

The Central Committee of the Communist Party is elected by Party congresses, which meet every five years. The Central Committee also elects the general secretary of the Party and the Politburo. Between congresses, policy questions are discussed by the Central Committee at sessions called plenary meetings.

Before a Party congress opens, a special commission of the Politburo is set up to examine the Central Committee's draft proposals, developed from suggestions put forward at the union republic Party congresses and at Party conferences. These proposals have been published in the press, and comments from the public have been invited. The public responds with thousands of letters to the editors, and some of their suggestions may be incorporated in the draft.

The Twenty-Fifth Congress of the Communist Party met in 1976 at the Kremlin's Palace of Congresses with 4,998 delegates and 103 guests from 96 countries. Among the guests were Gus Hall from the United States and Fidel Castro from Cuba.

The first point on the agenda was a report from Leonid Brezhnev, general secretary of the Central Committee of the Communist Party of the Soviet Union. At present Brezhnev is the highest Soviet leader.

Born in Dneprodzerzhinsk in 1906, Brezhnev has been a Party member since 1931 and a Komsomol member since 1923. After graduation from a land reclamation technical school in 1927, he became a land reclamation worker. From 1932 to 1935 he was a student at Dneprodzerzhinsk Metallurgical Institute, and from 1935 to 1937 an engineer in the Dneprodzerzhinsk steel plant.

Brezhnev was active in Party work during World War II and was promoted to major general in 1943, to first secretary of the Zaporozhe Province Committee (1946-47), first secretary of the Moldavian Communist Party Central Committee (1950-52), and lieutenant general in 1953. In 1955-56 he was first secretary and bureau member of the Kazhakhstan Communist Party Central Committee, and from 1952 a candidate member, then a full member in 1957, of the Presidium (subsequently the Politburo) of the all-union (national) Central Committee. In 1964 he became first secretary of the Central Committee and then, in 1966, general secretary of the Central Committee of the Communist Party.

In his report to the Twenty-Fifth Party Congress, Brezhnev spoke about the immediate tasks in the fields of foreign and domestic policy. He reported some gains for Communism but noted that capitalism still had considerable reserves.

("The Communists are by no means predicting the 'automatic collapse' of capitalism.") He spoke of the results of the Ninth Five-Year Plan just finished and the goals of the new, Tenth Five-Year Plan for 1976-80.

Among these goals was the political education of young people. Brezhnev complimented the Komsomol on its 35 million membership, "a reliable helper of the Party and its immediate combat reserve," but asked them to beware of overly bureaucratic approaches, which extinguish the flames of interest in the hearts of Komsomol members. "But after all our task is not only to preserve this flame but to fan it. We want our people to retain their enthusiasm, lively minds, and youthful energy throughout their lives."

In the discussion of Brezhnev's report, various first secretaries and ministers spoke, among them Yevgeny Mikhailovich Tyazhelnikov, since 1968 the first secretary of the Komsomol and previously the first secretary of the Chelyabinsk Province Party Committee. Tyazhelnikov spoke of the Komsomol work on BAM (the Baikal-Amur MainLine Railway) and in the Non Black Earth Zone and in building the city of Gagarin. He felt it would be desirable to draft a special "Law on Youth," which would further enhance the authority of the Komsomol.

In conclusion he read an article entitled, "He Is a Bolshevik."

> I can't imagine where this man finds so much energy and sheer capacity for work. Himself the son of a worker, he worked as a stoker and fitter for five years. He was transferred from production to Party economic work. The load he carries is a heavy one, but he is also a student at our institute and the best Party organizer of the fifth-year heat and power course. And he has been the best student in that course, defending his thesis with the grade of "excellent." Now, as he leaves production, this young engineer promises to make a great contribution. And so he will, for he is forged of strong material.

Tyazhelnikov concluded his speech by saying that the newspaper clipping he had read had been written forty-one years earlier—about Leonid Brezhnev!

After reports by the inspection committee and credential committee and speeches by foreign guests, Aleksei Nikolaevich Kosygin, chairman of the USSR Council of Ministers since 1964 and member of the Party Politburo since 1960, gave a report on the proposed five-year plan in his capacity as Chairman of the Commission on Basic Guidelines. Among the ninety members of this commission, in addition to Brezhnev, was the man who was later to take Tyazhelnikov's place as first secretary of the Komsomol, Boris Nikolaevich Pastukhov.

The tasks of the Tenth Five-Year Plan (1976-80) for improving the material and cultural standards of the Soviet people involved concrete goals for economic and scientific achievements and called upon the Komsomol to head the movement of young Soviets to fulfill and overfulfill these plans.

The Congress approved and ratified the five-year plan, which the USSR Council of Ministers then elaborated and submitted for the consideration of the Supreme Soviet in September 1976.

The Eighteenth Congress of the Komsomol met in April 1978. This highest Komsomol assembly was also addressed by Brezhnev, who reminded the delegates that Lenin's advice at the Third Komsomol Congress, to "Learn. Learn Communism," was just as applicable today if youth really wanted to justify the name *Communist*.

Efficiency and quality were to be the watchwords for the 1976-80 five-year plan, with development of the oil and gas reserves of the Tyumin region of western Siberia and agricultural upgrading as the two major endeavors. The banning of nuclear weapons, peace, and detente were also major goals. Brezhnev said he knew the Komsomol could be counted on as a reserve for the Party: "After all, the Party and Komsomol have one goal—Communism, and their path is also one—the path of Lenin, the path of serving the people."

In 1979, in an address to the Pioneers, dedicating the International Year of the Child at the Artek conference, Brezhnev again spoke of his wish for peace: "Peace is the happiness of children, the happiness of all people. Without peace, there is no childhood, no future."

Brezhnev sets the tone of the Pioneer program and gives encouragement, but the Central Committee of the Komsomol is more closely concerned with the Pioneers' specific programs. The Central Committee of the Komsomol is elected by the Komsomol congress, and the Central Committee elects the first secretary in a plenary session. Since the Komsomol was first organized in 1918, there have been eleven first secretaries: O. L. Ryvkin (1918-19); L. A. Shatskin (1919-22); P. I. Smorodin (1922-24); N. P. Chaplin (1924-28); A. I. Milchokov (1928-29); A. V. Kosarev (1929-38); N. A. Mikhailov (1938-52); A. N. Shelepin (1952-58); V. E. Semichastnyi (1958-59); S. P. Pavlov (1959-68); E. M. Tyazhelnikov (1968-1978); and B. N. Pastukhov (1978-   ).

The first secretary of the Komsomol is an important person, and his job may also lead to higher office. One of the first secretaries best known in the West, Alexander Shelepin, was even thought by some Kremlin watchers to be a challenger for Brezhnev's job. A former head of the KGB as well as a former first secretary of the Komsomol, he was one of the youngest members of the Politburo. His promising career seemed to end in the 1970s, when he resigned suddenly for reasons unknown in the United States.

At the First Plenary Session of the Komsomol Central Committee, elected by the Eighteenth Komsomol Congress held in April 1978, Pastukhov was elected first secretary, and Fedulova was elected secretary of the Central Committee and a member of the Bureau of Pioneers, along with eight others. Eleven more were elected members of the bureau, and seven were chosen as candidate members.

The bureau draws up a plan for the Pioneers. Though it takes the theme of the current five-year plan as general background, the result of the bureau's work is a specific plan for two years of Pioneer work. A general theme is chosen, such as, "We follow the Communist example" for 1976-78, or "True to the Legacy of Lenin" for 1978-80. Under that, specific programs, called march routes are chosen. These programs remain constant for some years. Lately there have been eight: My Motherland the USSR; In the Land of Knowledge; Peace and Solidarity; Pioneer Building; In the World of Beauty; Strong, Brave and Agile; Timur and His Team; and Little Star (*Zvezdochka*) for Octobrists.

Pioneers also have a rally (*slyot*), which is similar to a Komsomol or Party congress. The children are reminded in the August 1976 issue of *Pioner* magazine that the word *slyot* comes from the verb *sletatsya*, which means to fly together, and, as Fedulova said, it is hoped that they will all fly high. The first rally, held in Moscow in 1929, was addressed by Maxim Gorky, who wore a red necktie. The famous poet Mayakovsky wrote a poem particularly for the Pioneer leaders which ended "We have one leader, Comrade Communist Party."

The next rally was not until 1962, and others were held in 1967 and 1970. Now it is planned to have one every two years, as they are a great boost to the two-year programs.

Pioneer work is regularly considered at plenary sessions of the Komsomol. Pastukhov and others regularly exhort Pioneer leaders to "resolutely eliminate dryness, superficiality, and unsubstantiated statements in mass political work."

When there are changes in the party leadership, Pioneers read about them in their own newspaper, *Pionerskaya Pravda*. On the front page of *Pionerskaya Pravda* for October, 1980, Pioneers read of the resignation, because of ill health, of Alexei Kosygin, chairman of the Council of Ministers of the USSR, and the appointment of Nikolai Alexandrovich Tikhonov to the post.

The paper reported that Brezhnev, on behalf of the Presidium of the Supreme Soviet and the Council of Ministers of the USSR, thanked Kosygin for his many years of fruitful service to the Soviet state. There followed a short biography of Tikhonov, who was born in 1905, a member of the Party since 1940, a Hero of Socialist Labor and a State Prize Laureate.

The closing months of 1980 were important in other ways too. The Tenth Five-Year Plan was ending, with results being evaluated. The country was looking forward to the convening of the twenty-sixth congress in February, 1981, goals for a new five-year plan for 1981-85, and general plans for the whole period of 1980-90. Basic directives for the economic and social development of the USSR for the period 1981-85 and up to 1990 were being drawn up. Brezhnev reported that the overall goal was to raise the material and cultural level of the Soviet people, and to create better conditions for the all around development of the Soviet personality.

There were some problems too. Pioneers were introduced to some of these rather gently. "What is the spirit of Helsinki?" *Pionerskaya Pravda* asked, answering that world conflicts could be settled "not on the field of battle but at the negotiating table."

Members of the Komsomol were given other news in greater political depth. Almost all of the front page of *Komsomolskaya Pravda* for December 6, 1980 was devoted to the Warsaw Pact talks held in Moscow, beginning on December 5, 1980. Leaders of Warsaw Pact nations, including Poland's Communist Party Leader, Stanislaw Kania, were pictured in the paper, gathered around tables arranged in a square.

According to the paper, the dangers of the arms race were discussed, as the socialist countries reiterated their solidarity with each other. The delegates listened to a report on the VII Plenum of the central committee of the Polish Communist Party, and hoped that Poland would continue on the socialist path. "Poland was, is, and will be a socialist state, with solid links to the general family of socialist countries," the article concluded.

The Party is continually trying to improve the training and selection of Pioneer leaders, and a full-time school for leaders is being planned for 1980 either in Moscow or at Artek.

In each school, a Pioneer leader from the *druzhina* council examines the Party and Komsomol documents ("with pencil in hand for serious note-taking" says *Vozhaty)* relevant to Pioneers and reads Brezhnev's speeches, as well as those by Pastukhov and Fedulova. He studies the *Orientir* program and the recommendations from the All-Union Teachers' Congress. From all of this he draws up a day-to-day plan of work, which may be presented to the school's *druzhina* council and then to the entire *druzhina*. He must know his *druzhina* well. What are these children like? If there are twenty detachments in a particular *druzhina*, there will be twenty detachment leaders with which to cope.

In all of this, the leader must not forget that the Pioneer organization is a voluntary organization. The children must want to be Pioneers.

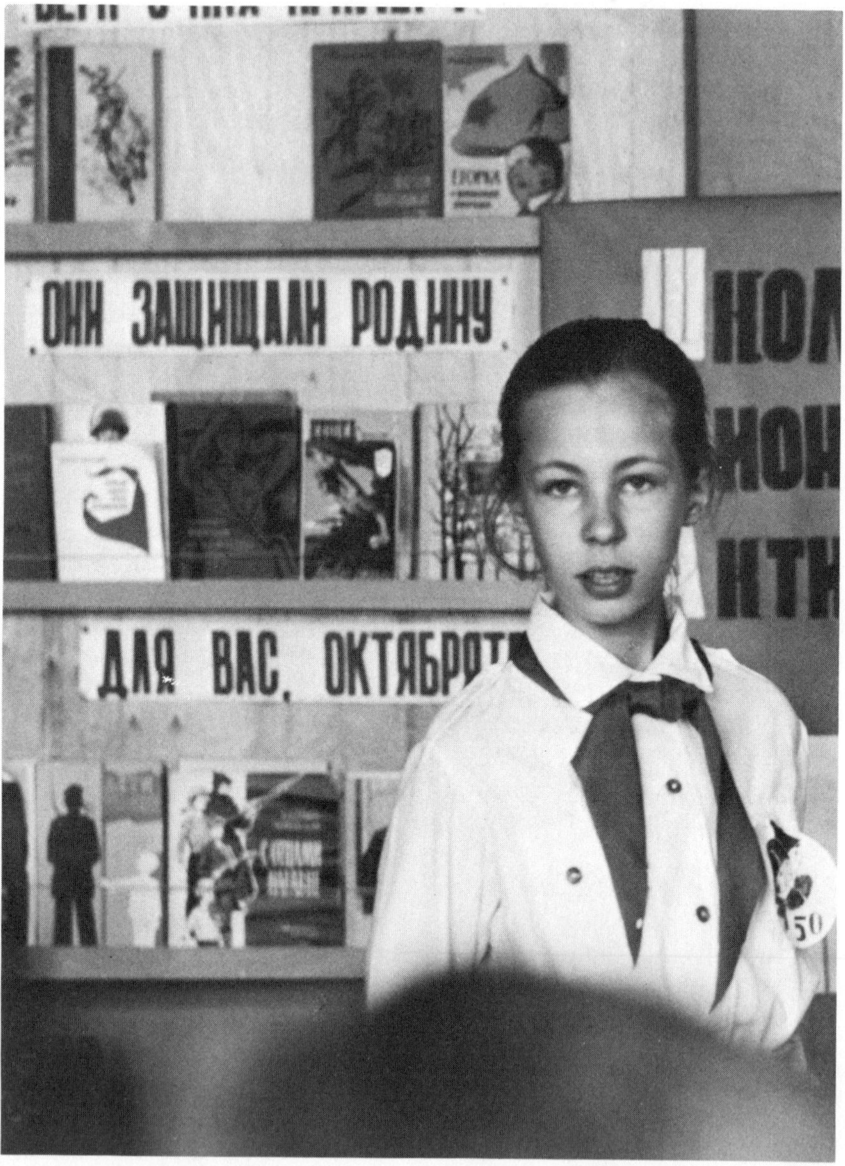
ОНИ ЗАЩИЩАЛИ РОДИНУ
ДЛЯ ВАС, ОКТЯБРЯТ
50

6

The Activists

I first heard about the activist camp at a meeting the Byelorussian Friendship Society arranged for us in Minsk. We met with the local committee for youth organizations, which oversees the work of the Pioneers, and we were introduced to the secretary of the Pioneers, the director of Pioneer organization, a member of the bureau of Pioneers, the assistant director of the Minsk Pioneer Palace, the editor of the local Pioneer newspaper, *Zorka* (Dawn, published in Byelorussian), the secretary of the youth organization, and the chairman of the central committee of the Komsomol for school affairs.

We drank tea and ate cookies and candy as they told us about Pioneer work. The Byelorussian Pioneer organization, one of the first in the Soviet Union, was started in June 1922. Following Lenin's advice, the Pioneers study and take part in the political life of the country through a self-governing, voluntary organization, with programs chosen by the children with the help of teachers who recognize the child's romantic interest in play but also understand the systematic work of the Pioneer organization. Since Byelorussia lost one out of every four of its inhabitants during World War II, the number of Pioneers is still not up to the prewar level. By 1984 Pioneer ranks will swell, though, because children already born will reach Pioneer age by then.

While discussing summer camps, the youth leaders mentioned Zubryonok, a camp outside Minsk where children went all year to learn how to be activists. Each month the campers study a different subject, this month Octobrists, next *zarnitsa*.

The word *zarnitsa* (the title for children's war games) immediately attracted my attention. "Do you think we could visit this camp?" I interrupted.

"Why not?" they said, and several days later we were on our way, traveling some distance outside of Minsk. There was still snow on the fields but the road was clear. The camp's name, *Zubryonok*, means "little auroch" in English. "What is an auroch?" I asked, "I never heard the word before."

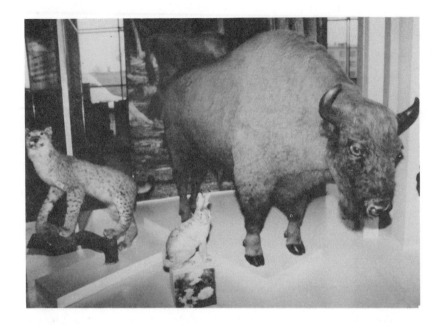

"An auroch is a kind of bison, extinct except here. In western Byelorussia there is a reservation of 90,000 hectares which is a natural wildlife museum. After the war ten aurochs were taken there and bred. Now there are nearly 250 of them. Camp Zubryonok is named for these rare animals."

It seemed the whole camp was waiting for us as we turned in to a wooded area with new buildings. Two girls presented us with a large tray containing a round loaf of freshly baked bread and a small dish of salt. Greeting a guest with bread and salt is a traditional gesture of hospitality. Since I had never been greeted with bread and salt before, I was not sure what I was supposed to do, but I broke off a piece of bread from the loaf, which was still warm from the oven, even on this cold day, and dipped it into the salt before I ate it, and my husband did the same. Then we all went into the building, since our feet were ankle deep in melted snow. (I had started out in high-heeled shoes, but my husband had made me go back and put on boots, and I was glad he did.)

Inside the building was a large stuffed auroch staring at us contemplatively with glassy eyes. I would have called him a buffalo, but I'm not well versed in the species.

There are eleven shifts at the camp, with 760 children in each shift from May to September and 360 the rest of the year, with a possible 60 additional from September to January. From January 12 to February 9, chairmen of the detachment councils and teams learn leadership. In February they are joined by members of the *druzhina* council and representatives of children's homes and boarding schools, and March 15 to April 13 adds the Octobrist group.

The period from April 16 to May 15 is for Young Friends of the Army, Border Guards, *Militsiya* (Police), and Firemen. A rally is held for the Timur and His Team program on May 25 to June 22, and then a shift for activists in clubs for technicals, young mathematicians, physicists, and so on.

The total theme of the 1978-80 program, called "True to the Legacy of Lenin," is surveyed from July 27 to August 27. The shift from September 5 to October 3 is for secretaries of Komsomol organizations; October 5 to October 30 for leaders in sports work and winners of an Olympiad; and November 12 to December 11 for members of the Green and Blue Patrols (Pioneer conservation groups), which includes a competition on nature conservation. The last shift, from December 13 to January 11, is for young correspondents and young artists.

The activists at Zubryonok work out year-long plans for the activities of the Pioneer groups in their own schools based on recommendations from the Central Council of the Pioneers. The plan should be made in May but no later than September. While working on the plan, the children discuss practical problems as well as political theory.

We were invited to join a group of sixth graders who were preparing to lead Octobrists. The little girls looked so sweet, young, and innocent that it was hard to imagine them leading anyone. "Do you get homesick?" I asked.

"Oh, no, they—" one of the Zubryonok directors interrupted, but not before one little girl had said shyly, "I was homesick at first because this is the first time I've ever been away from my Mama, but now I love it here." The director listened to the child's answer intently. We found that all of the grown people connected with Pioneers listened to the children with this same attention and amazement, as though to say, "What is this wonderful thing called a child?"

We joined the children at a roundtable discussion of some of the things a leader of Octobrists needs to know. In addition to articles in *Pioner* (Pioneer), *Pionerskaya Pravda* (Pioneer Truth), *Vozhaty* (Leader), *Vospitanie Shkolnikov* (Education of Schoolchildren), and *Nachalnaya Shkola* (Primary School), the Pioneers study the *Kniga Vozhatovo* (Leader Handbook).

The main task of the Octobrist leader is to convince the child that he is not just a schoolchild but an Octobrist, a future Pioneer, a "grandchild of Lenin." The leaders must know something of the psychological background of the child from seven to nine—he is active, curious, impressionable, and emotional and can't concentrate on anything for very long. The Pioneer visits the Octobrist in the summer before school starts and tells him something about Octobrists' rituals. Now both Octobrist and Pioneer must face the first day of school.

Pioneer leaders must have faith in themselves, says the handbook. So that this faith is not shattered the very first day of school, the leaders are told of some of the problems they might encounter. They may find that many Pioneers are not wearing their neckties. Some Pioneers and many Octobrists will not answer the leaders' salute. They must not let these things upset them. Instead they should see that the Octobrist and Pioneer rooms are open and approach

the children diplomatically: "Hello. I'm the new Pioneer leader. My name is
_____ ." There is no time the first few days for explaining the plans for the
year. Instead, during recess or before and after school the leaders should watch
the children and listen for their names and observe their personalities. They can
suggest games for the children to play, but boy leaders shouldn't be upset if
some of the girls fail to follow their suggestions.

Does the Pioneer leader call the children by their first or last names? First is
better, though the leader may also say "Comrade" Ivan or "Comrade" Nina.
" 'Comrade' is a glorious word."

As a Pioneer leader you go to your first meeting and all of the children
are shouting and running around. Do you ask a teacher to help you, by saying
"Ivan sit down," or "Nina, be quiet"? The handbook says that if you rely on
the teacher you might as well say goodbye to your authority as a Pioneer leader.
Instead suggest a game. Divide the room in half and have a contest to see which
side can be quietest. The handbook says this will quiet the noisiest class in a
few minutes. There are many other concrete suggestions for Pioneer leaders:
never say "You have to"; don't be boring and long-winded; let the children
express themselves independently.

It is not easy to be a leader, says an article in *Pionerskaya Pravda*, recounting the case of Sasha who came to school in a Pioneer necktie before he was a
Pioneer. The other Octobrists made it clear to Sasha what a terrible thing he
had done and he ran home in fright, wondering what awful punishment he might
suffer for his misdeed. When the Pioneer leader heard about Sasha he went to
Sasha's home. Sasha's bright little head appeared around a corner of the door,
his eyes big and frightened. "Come with me," the leader said, and Sasha followed
meekly. They went to the Pioneer room at the school, and the leader explained
the Pioneer necktie to Sasha. "Soon you'll be a Pioneer, and you can wear it
proudly," the leader said. In a short time Sasha was happy again.

We had dinner with the directors of the camp, starting with *zakuski* (hors
d'oeuvres) and toasts with vodka. I cannot drink vodka so I made my toasts in
wine. This is acceptable for a woman, but a male guest must down the vodka.
"*Za vashe zdorovie*" (to your health) is the standard Russian toast, followed by
"bottoms up" of vodka and a bite of Russian bread. Many Russians are able
to drink prodigious amounts of alcohol, alternating vodka, wine, cognac, and
beer at the same sitting. I view drinking with strangers with a certain amount
of fear since I got violently ill from too much champagne on one of our first
trips to the Soviet Union. This puts an extra strain on my husband who must
drink all that I don't.

I thought each course of the dinner was the main one, only to find it followed by still another. The toasts were coming faster, and we were all getting
friendlier and friendlier with each other. Our hosts quoted old Russian proverbs,
and my husband responded with old Virginia proverbs and vodka all around.
We laughed and hugged each other like the dearest of friends. Finally my
husband said, "I'm not only running out of old Virginia proverbs, I'm getting
very drunk."

We were invited to stay at the camp for the next session, which would be about the children's war game, *zarnitsa* (summer lightning). We could hardly bear to part with these fine new friends but my husband had to get back to his law practice in the United States. "Could I have a syllabus of some of the activist lessons?" I asked. "Of course," was the reply. Anything I wanted. We drove back to Minsk somewhat glassy-eyed, clutching a great deal of Communist material which I read the next day.

From all the material I selected a representative syllabus, "How to organize the work of the detachment council, starting with preparations for an assembly."

The work starts with the team of five to eight Pioneers who meet to make suggestions about the work of the assembly, how it could be improved, what should be discussed at the assembly, and which children should be elected to the detachment council.

A Pioneer leader explains the importance of the elections, what an activist is, and who can be an activist. An adult leader may tactfully assist in the evaluations of Pioneer activists but must never make the Pioneer leader feel that his work is not independently important. The children in the team are forming habits that will lead to activism, too.

Each team prepares exhibits and albums of photographs and drawings to show at the assembly. Usually the leaders of each team of a school decide which team will present which exhibit. One team may choose to make a report on art; another to present a "living" newspaper in which children act out the news. The team also decides on the guest list for the assembly parents, grandparents, war heroes, heads of other detachments with whom the team is friendly. The syllabus reminds the children that they must not forget to plan awards for the best students, to be presented at the assembly.

All of the children in the school take part in preparing the Pioneer room, assembly hall, or square for the assembly, putting up decorations and flags and arranging tables and chairs. The children chosen to make reports practice their roles. Everyone practices the *lineika* (line-up or parade), which opens the assembly. On the day of the assembly, the children march in, singing. At the command of the chairman of the detachment to stand at attention the children stand in formation while the chairman calls for reports. The representative of each team steps forward and presents its report. There is another song, and then the children are seated and the assembly begins. The chairman of the detachment council explains the work of the assembly and is followed by a word from the adult leader and reports from members of the detachment council about their work.

Elections for officers of the assembly are held once a year for a detachment of older Pioneers, twice a year for the middle group, and four times a year for the youngest group. Elections are held more frequently in the younger groups so that more children have practice in leadership. When a new detachment council is elected, presents are given to the members of the council and congratulations to the new members. There are a few parting words from the Pioneer leader, and the assembly ends with a song.

Following the assembly an evaluation is conducted. What feature did you like best? What did you find boring or bad? What suggestions do you have for a future assembly? Was the plan of work fulfilled? How did the team participate in the assembly? How can we fulfill the plans of the detachment council? Do you do something new and useful to bring joy to people every day?

These questions are also considered at the first meeting of the detachment when it is planning a future assembly. If there are new activists on the detachment council, they get individual attention from the senior Pioneer leader and the Pioneer leader. This is a critical time in the life of an activist, and the way he is handled now will make a big difference in his attitude later.

Elections in the detachment are handled more informally than elections to the *druzhina* council. The whole school attends the assembly of the *druzhina*, and, if the school auditorium is not large enough to hold all of the pupils at one sitting, a nearby palace of culture or movie theater is commandeered for the occasion. An assembly to which only activists are invited is frowned upon officially, though in practice this sometimes happens. The magazine *Vozhaty* says that an assembly to which only leaders is invited is not an assembly but a seminar or conference.

It is the right of each pioneer, club, detachment, and team to nominate candidates of the council. The names, photographs, and biographies are posted in the Pioneer room or on a special bulletin board headed "Preparation for Elections to the Assembly." The school newspaper and school radio may also carry news of the candidates. All children from the fourth to the eighth grade should participate in the elections, though *Vozhaty* says "first violin" is played by the sixth and seventh graders.

The actual number of members of the *druzhina* council is decided by the assembly. The order of voting depends upon the order of nomination. The names are then put on a blackboard and voted upon in an open election by a show of hands. Between each assembly the council carries out the assembly's orders and keeps the Pioneers advised of any new developments. It also informs the Komsomol committee of the school of Pioneer developments in the school, and the Komsomol committee in turn informs the regional and town staffs of the Komsomol central committee and the central council of Pioneers, which, in turn, relay suggestions and recommendations from the top down.

A new activist must feel that he has the support of adult leaders as well as his peers in the detachment and *druzhina*. The noted Soviet educator, Makarenko, said that every self-governing organization must decide things together and that if they don't lose their authority. They must also formulate a plan of action.

Every member of the detachment council must know what his particular responsibilities are. The duties of the whole council are to organize programs for fulfilling the plans of the assembly, form the Pioneer team and oversee its work, organize the work of the detachment and elections to the detachment and team, and prepare questions to bring up before the general assembly. The council is not responsible for the general theme of the itineraries but is accountable for the concrete tasks of fulfilling the itinerary's goals. They organize *Subbotniks* (Saturday work brigades where work is done without pay) and other clean-up programs and oversee sports and other competitions in the detachment. They must always remember to say "*we* do" rather than "*you* do."

The syllabus details the responsibilities of each officer of the detachment council:

Chairman of the detachment council:

Try to be an example to all your Pioneers.

See that the Pioneers fulfill the laws of the Pioneers.

Be responsible for the regular work of the detachment.

Assign tasks for the team.

Lead the *lineika* (line-up or parade).

Fulfill the detachment's plan and report to the *druzhina* council.

Be responsible for competitions between teams.

Organize checks on the work of Pioneers.

Publicize the decisions of the detachment and *druzhina*.

Organize Octobrist groups.

Control the studies of activists.

Fulfill the tasks set by the *druzhina* council.

Be responsible for visual agitation, such as wall newspapers and exhibits in the detachment corner.

Commissar (assistant to the chairman):

Organize political information in the detachment.

See that all Pioneers read Pioneer newspapers and magazines.

See that all Pioneers know about the major political events in the USSR and organize solidarity groups with workers of the world fighting for democracy and peace.

Strengthen the ties between the work of Pioneers of other Soviet republics and the rest of the world.

Help the *druzhina* council in the international friendship club.

Flag bearer:

Care for the flag, horn, and drum and carry the flag at the assembly.

Head the group of drummers and buglers.

Acquaint the Pioneers with the history and symbols of the Pioneers.

Prepare the detachment to perform these symbols.

Help the flag bearers of the Octobrist group to learn the rituals and symbols.

Organizer for help in studies:

Organize a self-help group for year-round assistance of Pioneers in school and Pioneer activities.

Be interested in what the Pioneers read, establish connections with the library, and recommend new books to the Pioneers.

Organize projects that will interest Pioneers in science, technology, literature, and art.

Help Octobrists and younger schoolchildren with their school work.

Involve all Pioneers in some circle or section.

See that all Pioneers observe the daily routine.

Organizer for work activities:

Synchronize the work between the detachment and the heads of collective and state farms, factories, and offices in town and country.

Acquaint the Pioneers with the work of these organizations.

Organize socially useful labor projects in and out of school.

Create brigades for self-service.

Help the *druzhina* in its work.

Organize work under the Timur and His Team program.

Conserve nature with a green zone of planting.

Organizer for physical training:

Organize sports competitions between teams.

Form sport teams.

Organize trips for the Young Tourist and Tourists of the USSR.

Organize war games.

Plan meetings with interesting sportsmen.

Help Octobrists in sports and mend their equipment.

Organizer for work with Octobrists:

Organize work of the leaders of little stars, and see that they take part in the *druzhina* school of Pioneer activists.

Prepare Octobrists for good work habits.

Editor of the detachment newspaper:

Organize editorial work.

See that the paper comes out regularly.

Keep the material in the detachment corner up to date.

Report on the radio and in the *druzhina* newspapers.

Help the editors of Octobrists newsletters.

Get subscriptions for Pioneer journals.

Arrange readings from Pioneer newspapers and magazines.

Members of the editorial board:

Organize exhibits of wall newspapers.

Form a plan of work for sending congratulatory Pioneer telegrams.

Collect manuscripts, diaries, albums, reports.

Fulfill the tasks set by the detachment council, *druzhina*, leader, teacher, and class leader.

Attend the school of Pioneer activists.

Keep in order such material as crayons and pencils.

Team leader:

Be an example for the Pioneers in the team.

Organize the work of the team. See that they fulfill the tasks. Arbitrate disputes among members of the team and try to keep everyone friendly.

Be present at all assemblies.

Attend seminars of the team.

Follow the activities of the team and take part in them.

Organize self-help in the team.

See that every Pioneer in the team has a task according to his interests and ability.

Check fulfillment of each Pioneer's duties.

Teach each Pioneer how to salute, how to march, etc. and to know how to read road signs and the Morse code.

See that all wear the red necktie correctly.
Know the home conditions of each Pioneer.
Care about the mood of the Pioneers.
Compliment the Pioneers when they do something well.

The first meeting of the detachment council is led by a Pioneer leader, and in case of a tie in the voting the leader casts the deciding vote. There may be songs or speeches at the meeting, but above all the council should think collectively, work effectively, and discuss the conclusions each has drawn.

At the first meeting, the council decides on a ten-day plan for the Pioneers, with tasks and supervisors for each day. Council members must be able to evaluate the most important goal for each day and be able to see their own mistakes and rectify them at later meetings.

The leader handbook gives three secrets for successful Pioneer leaders. Secret One is both simple and complicated. This secret lies within the child leader himself and concerns his attitude toward his work. The book says that if he is indifferent to the work, no amount of books or lectures will help him and no secrets will do him any good, but if he wants to learn he must cultivate his mind, train his memory, strengthen his will power, and refine his emotions. He must never forget the special sense of childhood as a happy time of life, and by his dress and conduct he must be an example to the other Pioneers.

The second secret is to have a plan. Without a plan the leader scrambles around like a squirrel in a wheel getting nowhere. The leader must know "what to do, for whom, and how." A Russian proverb says, "There is no fair wind for someone who does not know where he is sailing." The Pioneers are sailing toward Communism, and although the leader must never forget this goal he is given concrete advice about planning. He should keep a notebook and a calendar of events for each month. In September the month might begin with the ceremony of the "first bell," in which new first graders are welcomed to the school, and go on through excursions, parades, club meetings, and sports, music, art, and so forth.

The third secret is play. Play is considered one of the most important elements in the formation of personality. The leader handbook calls play the eighth wonder of the world. The leader must know all sorts of games and their rules and be able to suggest creative play in which the children act out roles. He also must know how to begin games and how to end them. A game must come to a conclusive end—somebody wins, somebody loses—but it must also end in a friendly fashion, so that even the losers go home in a good mood and with a sense of accomplishment.

To discuss the problems of activist leaders the First All-Union Rally of Pioneer Leaders met in Moscow in 1976. To our surprise and pleasure Fedulova invited us to attend. "You won't hear our praises sung here," she said. "We're here to discuss our problems." I think my husband and I were to be the only foreigners present and we were very excited at the prospect.

7

The Activist Leaders

The First All-Union Rally of Pioneer Leaders met in May 1976, in the beautiful Hall of Columns of the Trade Union House in Moscow. Before the Revolution the building was a noblemen's club, and it is an outstanding example of eighteenth-century Russian architecture. The Hall of Columns, restored in 1968, is a spectacular auditorium of white columns, crystal chandeliers, gilded mirrors, red draperies, and red velvet chairs. On the stage, also flanked with columns and crystal chandeliers, stands a bust of Lenin in the middle behind a table for guests of honor and a lectern on the left for a speaker. We were given seats in a box, on the left, near the speaker's lectern.

The delegates came dancing in. They were young men and women, mostly dressed in blue with white shirts and red neckties. Their mood was merry. They danced in the aisles, singly or by twos. They sang, they skipped, they cheered. They laughed and embraced each other. They sat down for a minute then jumped up to speak to a friend on the other side of the hall.

The guest table on the stage was beginning to fill up as well. Fedulova waved to us from the stage and then said something to the man sitting next to her. Fedulova pointed to us, and the man came over and shook hands with us. Harry, who was with us at the time (like the young people he had been darting in and out, greeting people) was very impressed. "That's Evgenii Mikhailovich Tyazhelnikov, the first secretary of the Komsomol Central Committee," Harry said when the man had gone back to the platform. "He's a very important man."

The auditorium seats kept filling until about twelve hundred or more young people were seated. Suddenly they began to shout in unison: "Lenin! Party! Komsomol! Lenin! Party! Komsomol!" Tyazhelnikov opened the meeting to more applause.

Greetings from Brezhnev were read: "The Party highly values your work and sees in these leaders active workers of the ideological front."

71

"*Slava* (Glory) to the Central Committee of the Communist Party! *Slava, slava, slava!*" the audience chanted.

Fedulova, in high-heeled white shoes, a blue suit, white blouse, and the red necktie was also greeted with applause. She said they were happy that Brezhnev was interested in their meeting, that all of the Pioneer leaders had a warm feeling for the Party, and that everyone looked forward to new victories for the Soviet Union under Communism.

Fedulova said that the Pioneers had gathered enough metal scrap to build 3,200 kilometers of track for BAM and that 16 million children had participated in the *zarnitsa* war games. But, while proud of these accomplishments, she also warned leaders not to think merely in terms of figures. The detachment was the center of Pioneer life, she said, and the assembly held by the detachment was of great interest to the Pioneers.

Fedulova talked about the Pavel Morozov Detachment. All the detachments in the school were supposed to put on a skit, or document in some other ways, the name of their detachment at an assembly. The leaders gave the Pavel Morozov Detachment a two for its performance (failing). Fedulova was outraged at the idea of grading an assembly. She said this also violated the principle of independent action by the Pioneers themselves.

She complimented the many seminars, clubs, and courses for Pioneer leaders and their cooperation with schools, collective and state farms, and industrial enterprises. She also noted that because most of today's parents were Pioneers themselves it was easier for them to understand their children.

Minister of Education M. A. Prokofiev spoke next, emphasizing the need for the unity of word and deed and the task of the moral education of Soviet youth. There was a break for lunch, and everyone surged into the buffet where they ate and drank with hearty, youthful appetites.

There were many distinguished guests: A. A. Leonov, a cosmonaut and Hero of the Soviet Union, reminiscing about his own Pioneer days in Siberia, recalled a girl Pioneer leader named Rimma Leontieva, who was a young parachutist. Rimma knew how to do everything well and wasn't afraid of anything; all of the Pioneers dreamed of being future parachutists and flyers like Rimma. Rimma's greatest contribution to the Pioneers was that she always set a definite goal for them. She didn't just say, "Let's gather scrap metal." She said, "To build a tank with our name on it we must gather twenty tons of metal." Each child had a definite assignment, and Rimma explained just what the task was and why it was necessary. To be a leader was a very demanding profession, Leonov said. Pioneer leaders were teaching the future builders of Communism.

Marshal Bagramyan said that his generation felt that they should give their strength and knowledge, and if necessary their lives, to the work of Lenin and the Soviet Motherland. Viktor Grigorev, a border guard, spoke about the Pioneers who were Young Friends of the Border Guards. S. V. Michalkov, a writer we had met several times, opened his speech with, "I greet you as a comrade in a common cause. Our goal is the same—to build a Communist society."

The delegates spoke briefly of their problems: more material was needed on leadership, the importance of the Revolution, and the psychology of childhood. More symbols were needed, with award pins for various activities. More material was needed on after-school activities, on how to explain the Soviet way of life, and on how to deal with difficult children.

There were also suggestions: involve difficult children in leading younger children, in taking care of school buildings, in sports like wrestling. Don't let the Pioneers become passive.

The delegates were from many republics, including Azerbaidzhan, Uzbekistan, and Turkmenya. There were Tatars, Olympic champions, teachers, students, experienced veteran Pioneer leaders, and inexperienced new leaders. Four hundred nineteen delegates were members of the Communist Party; 159 had awards and medals. One was a member of the regional committee of the Party; one a deputy to the Supreme Soviet of the Tadzhik Republic; 56 were deputies of local soviets; and 614 were members of Party and Komsomol committees. They represented all aspects of Pioneer life.

After every speech there was more or less stormy applause. A pretty blonde girl from Estonia told about the singing holiday during the Republic Week of Music, when thousands of children march and sing. She told of her school with 312 pupils, of which 250 were singers. "I love my work as a Pioneer leader," she said, but added that more material on songs and dances was needed for the leaders. *"Mol-o-dets! Mol-o-dets"* (Well done!), the audience shouted in encouragement.

After the general meetings the rally broke up into smaller group meetings to discuss specific topics. I looked over the list carefully to decide which I wanted to join:

1. The ideological and political upbringing of the Young Pioneer.
2. The development of a Communist attitude toward labor.
3. The role of the Young Pioneer organization in the struggle for basic education.
4. Physical, military, and patriotic education.
5. Moral education of children and their understanding of their rights as citizens.
6. The system and work with Octobrists.
7. Organization of the work of the senior Pioneer leader.
8. The relationship between the Pioneer organization in school and the enterprise that sponsors it.
9. The system and functions of the Pioneer *druzhina*.
10. The functioning of the *druzhina* on a territorial basis.

I chose the ideological and political upbringing section, which was chaired by the editor of *Pionerskaya Pravda*, N. M. Chernova. Political education takes place every minute of the child's life, we were told. The level of political education must be raised so that no child remains passive.

The group discussed various methods of political education such as political museums, the study of Party documents, and participation in the political activity of the country. Some said Party documents were too dull and complicated for children to understand. "Why weren't there more boy Pioneer leaders?" a girl wanted to know, as everyone conceded that there were more girl than boy leaders. There were suggestions that colleges have special courses for Pioneer leaders since the leaders could not expect the Pioneers to understand politics if the leaders themselves did not. The meeting did not achieve solutions to all the problems raised, including the question of how to interest young people in joining the Komsomol and the Party.

There was a discussion of the Communist world outlook and the way children could be involved in international affairs—Soviet children must not be indifferent to human rights violations in Chile, Ireland, and Africa, but at the same time they should work for peace. "Peace is blue skies, happiness without fear," one delegate said.

The rally was not all seriousness. There was an evening of entertainment broadcast on radio and television, an evening at the theater with the stirring war play, "Young Guard," a lively ball at the Pioneer Palace, and a spectacular program of songs and dances at the Grand Kremlin Palace.

The delegates kept notes in red-covered notebooks, and their friends signed their autographs in these books, too. At the end they composed a letter to Brezhnev with their suggestions on how to improve Pioneer work. They listened

as Tyazhelnikov reminded them that Lenin had said that a Socialist society was not a utopia, that they must avoid formalism and continue the struggle to build a better society.

Another speaker pointed out that the children of the 1970s would live and work in a new era—the twenty-first century. The Pioneers have specific programs to prepare them for their voyage into the twenty-first century.

8

The March Routes

The child of ten to eleven is full of the joy of living, friendly (even with strangers) and even-tempered, according to the Leader's Handbook. Children of this age want active, practical projects, which they undertake gladly. However, emotion still plays a major part in their psyches, and failure at a project causes them to lose interest quickly. On the other hand, success spurs them on and nourishes their souls.

Designed specifically for such a child are the Pioneer March Routes, which appeal to all sides of the Pioneer's nature. A march route, from the Russian word *marshrut*, which means a route or itinerary and is a combination of the word *marsh*, or march, and *rut*, or route, is really a program of action—a road map toward a particular goal. To the word route, the word march adds a particular urgency to the program. A *marshrut* is a march toward accomplishment—a series of programs for action.

The programs are grouped under a single theme. In the 1970s the theme was "True to the Legacy of Lenin," and included eight march routes. Before choosing a specific program each child participates in a group discussion on the general theme. What does it mean to be true to the legacy of Lenin? One child said it meant being good at schoolwork. Another agreed that excellence in school was important but if the work were done with a view to personal gain and not for the good of others it was not true to the legacy of Lenin or the Pioneer slogan, "All for one and one for all."

On a specific level one child complained that a boy in his Pioneer group would not help gather pine cones with the group. He preferred to go skating. Another child said that it wasn't the actual gathering of pine cones that was important but the feeling of joint participation in a common task.

One girl said that some children loved to order others around and could find insufficiencies in everyone but themselves. She thought that such leaders should be told that everyone has faults and that it is the leader's duty to help Pioneers correct their faults, not laugh at them.

New Pioneers listen with interest. They are too new to know a great deal about Pioneer life. By next year they may be nominated for a place on the detachment council. Now some of them are preparing to participate in their first assembly as buglers. The opening signal of the assembly is blown by a new bugler and is a sometimes quavering note due to the bugler's inexperience. Then a new drummer beats a tatoo on his drum, which is answered by the old drummer. Finally, old and new drummers play together, the old drummers and buglers nodding encouragement to the new ones. All of the children march into the auditorium in a festive parade, giving the Pioneer salute as they march past the *druzhina* council.

"Third-grade detachment, left! Right shoulder forward—march!" comes the command. The new Pioneers march forward and are given presents by the members of the *druzhina*; then they take their places at the command, "*volno*" (at ease).

The new Pioneers listen to reports of the march routes at the assembly, and later they learn in more detail about the programs and select one particular march route on which to concentrate. Everyone is urged to join one or two circles connected with a march route, though all should be familiar with the general themes. Although the march routes are closely connected with school, the itineraries do not stop when school is not in session but continue all year long in summer camps, Pioneer palaces, and Pioneer rooms. Some of the march routes are new and some are familiar.

The children have discussed the subject of one march route called "My Motherland" since nursery school. Where does a sense of the Motherland begin? It begins with the apartment where the child lives, the street on which the apartment is located, the white birch trees in the countryside, the mushrooms everyone gathers in the woods. The first-grade reader suggests that the center of the Motherland may be the Kremlin, where "the Soviet government and Central Committee of the Communist Party of the Soviet Union work."

The Pioneer has projects related to the Motherland: find all the factories and enterprises in your town that have the name of Lenin. What collective or state farms in your town have been awarded the Order of Lenin? Why? When? In every town there is a street or park named after Lenin. Are there streets named for compatriots of Lenin? Where are they? Take pictures of memorials to Lenin. Write an essay about your experiences with Lenin memorials.

In the "My Motherland" program Pioneers study the fifteen republics that comprise the Soviet Union. They learn the capital of each republic, the local customs, the traditional dress, music, and dances, and may even correspond with a child in another republic. They may include dolls in local costumes and maps of the Soviet Union in the exhibits in the school museum.

The children join Young Tourist groups to tour the Soviet Union. One of the first of these groups toured Kazakhstan on camels in 1932, gathering valuable

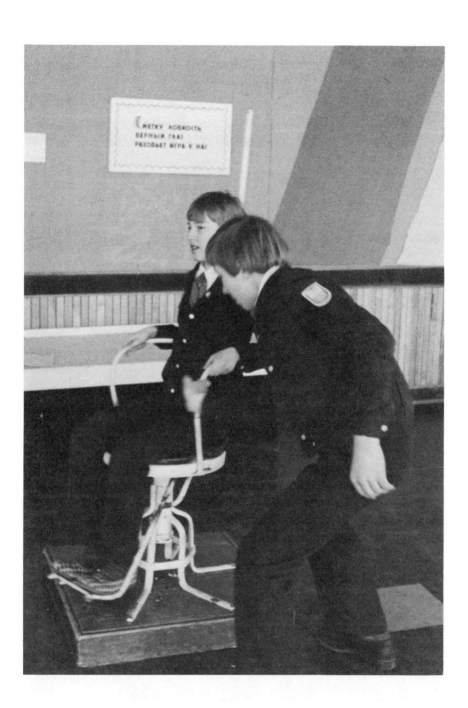

medicinal herbs along the way. Today the Young Tourist with a knapsack on his back is a familiar sight. These boys and girls may stop along the way to help a collective farm gather its hay or work on a conservation project. They still gather medicinal herbs. During the Vietnam War herbs were sent to hospitals in Hanoi. Young Tourists also watch new developments, like the train without wheels, planned for Alma Ata, which will travel at 120 kilometers an hour, powered by electromagnets.

The itinerary, "In the Land of Knowledge," follows Lenin's precept to "study, study, study" or "learn, learn, learn" (In Russian, *learn* and *study* are the same word.) There are many circles included in this march route such as Book Lovers, Collectors, Young Naturalists, Young Technicians, and Young Builders. Pioneer Palaces offer courses in everything from astronomy to playing the zither.

The circles of Young Astronauts and Young Astronomers had a contest called "Expedition to Mars," in which children presented their ideas of life on Mars in tracings on globes and drawings of the childrens' conceptions of life on Mars. Adult members of the Institute of Cosmic Investigation were intrigued by some of the children's suggestions. The majority of the children said that the main scientific problem was to find life on Mars.

Fantasies of the future are encouraged. The Pioneer Council of Young Fantasists wondered what the school of the future would be like, and many Pioneers sent *Pioner* magazine their versions of the school of the twenty-first century. A girl named Lena said she hurried to school one day, afraid she would be late. When she got there the classroom was empty, but another teacher told

her the class had flown off "on an excursion in the Stone Age." Her next lesson, in geography, took place on the banks of the Amazon River.

Some children visualized the school of the future as a box where children would be placed for a short time and come out educated. Other children objected to this concept, saying that children should not be deprived of the joy of their school years.

An adult science fiction writer thought there might be machines that could compress all knowledge of chemistry, physics, and so forth into a few weeks' training course and other machines to program all of the world's learning into a child's mind, but, he asked, "Where is the course on intellect, feeling, kindness, and understanding of people?" He said these spiritual characteristics are learned by working together, not through machines.

The school of the future has its beginnings in the present, the article said. The present depends on adults. The future depends on the schoolchildren.

The Pioneers are interested in the way the rest of the world lives. They study the "political map of the world" and the struggles of people in Vietnam, Kampuchea, Dominica, Nicaragua, and Cuba as well as the struggles of the American Indians and the revolution in Afghanistan. *Pioner* magazine had an article in May 1979 that told of the long struggle backward Afghanistan had with the English and how Afghanistan signed its first friendship treaty with the Soviet Union in 1921. Then, after the Afghan Revolution in April 1977, and the victory of the People's Democratic Party, the new government had been helped by the Soviet Union. The article told of the Afghans who had studied in the Soviet Union and of Soviet engineers and technicians who were in Afghanistan helping to build roads, factories and electric stations.

Whenever we visited schools the children asked about life in the United States, too. What did we think of President Carter? How did we feel about the Chinese sending troops into Vietnam right after we had recognized them? Could we leave the United States?

Knowledge must be presented in an interesting way, say Soviet educators. There are Weeks of Science, Olympiads of Math, and technical clubs like "Integral" in the town of Khimka and "The Future" in Kishenev.

The "Peace and Solidarity" itinerary has had various themes over the years; 1972 was the year of Angela Davis and the Vietnam War. Harry was giving a talk on both topics to some Pioneers in a town outside of Moscow and invited us to go along. He was excited about the trip since the principal of the school was a friend he had not seen for forty years. He told us what a beautiful girl she had been.

On the train Harry and my husband sat together, next to a Russian who listened intently as Harry and my husband spoke English. Finally the man stood up and said to Harry in Russian, "Comrade, it is very *nekulturny* (ill-mannered) to speak in a language the person sitting next to you does not understand." In disgust, he walked to the back of the train.

The principal was at the station to meet us. Harry took one look at her and whispered to my husband, in English, "She looks just like a Russian grand-

mother." Overcoming his disappointment that such a beautiful girl had turned into a grandmother in forty years, Harry made small talk as we visited the school. There were huge banners everywhere with "Free Angela Davis" written on them.

In the school's small auditorium, which looked more like a hallway, the principal introduced Harry as a famous Pioneer and the author of the book, *The Young Pioneers in the Land of the Dollar*. Harry then introduced us, his "friends from the United States, who are not Communists but are still friends of the Soviet Union."

Harry made a rousing speech about Angela Davis's imprisonment in the United States. Next he took out a copy of *Life* magazine showing pictures of young Americans who had been killed in Vietnam. He read out the captions—name, age when killed. It was a long list. "This is not a Communist magazine," Harry said. "This is an American magazine listing these deaths." The children listened, entranced. When the speech was over the children applauded vigorously and gave me some flowers, apparently showing no ill will toward my husband and myself for being from the country that imprisoned Angela Davis and sent its youth to die in Vietnam.

The principal invited us back to her apartment for a sumptuous tea. I thought it was a very good day, but Harry was glum on the way home. "I always try to personalize my talks," he said, "so when I saw that we were huddled into that narrow hall, I said, 'You are in this little hall because you have sent the money for a big auditorium to Vietnam.' I knew something was wrong the minute I said it. The principal said, 'Harry, we have a beautiful new auditorium. We didn't send the money to Vietnam. We like this little hall.'"

"The part about Angela Davis was well received," I said, trying to cheer him up, but Harry was inconsolable. "Angela Davis is going to be acquitted."

"Doesn't that prove that our system in the United States is fair and that it works?" I asked.

"It has nothing to do with your system," Harry said. "I've been following that case carefully. The prosecutor is no good, and I've had experience with prosecutors."

In 1973 the theme was protest against the junta in Chile. That year the Pioneers' demand was: "Free Louis Korvalan" (leader of the Chilean Communist Party who was imprisoned by the junta). In one school the Pioneers were determined to communicate with a political prisoner in Chile. They called Chile long distance and actually did get to speak to a prisoner.

In 1974 Pioneers met with the general secretary of the Communist Party of Portugal, Alvaro Kunyalo. In other years they went to an international children's festival at Artek called "May There Always Be Sunshine" and met Dr. Benjamin Spock, who told them that in the United States there was one country but various childhoods. They attended children's festivals in Berlin and Cuba, sent a Pioneer ship to the children of Angola with toys from members of the Club of International Friendship, or KID, and asked the children of Peru from the Mariategi Club why they didn't call themselves Pioneers.

"The word *Pioneer* sounds like a Communist term to the world," one Peruvian child explained.

"But José Karlos Mariategi founded the Communist Party of Peru in 1928. Don't people know that?"

"They know," the Peruvian child says, explaining that it was a tactic to ensure the uninterrupted success of the children's organization.

At a Moscow school we heard a teacher say that the truly bad people in the world were those who stood aside and said that what was happening in the world wasn't their business. People must be involved, she said, and Pioneer leaders do all they can to see that Pioneers are involved.

Soviet children wonder why the West uses the phrase "Soviet threat." Their newspapers say, "Who is threatening whom?" when they report on prospects for NATO arms in Western Europe and the failure of the Salt II talks. Pioneers answer the question What is peace and solidarity? in various ways: "Peace is life without war." "Peace is a bright sky with happy people under it." "Solidarity is friendship, unity, readiness to speak out for all the suffering in the land." "Solidarity is friendship, help, encouragement. Money in the Fund for Peace, a bag of friendship, trade fairs, meetings, signatures on resolutions— it is our unity with those who fight for peace."

The aesthetic side of the Motherland is covered by the march route "In the World of Beauty." A teacher from Yerevan says much attention is given to aesthetic education in the Soviet Union, "Because beauty is the path to the moral perfection of man, and a man of high morality is the ideal of our education."

In the first days of the Revolution the Soviet of Workers' and Soldiers' Deputies decreed that the art of imperial Russia should be preserved: "Citizens! The old masters have left, leaving behind them a great inheritance. Now this

belongs to all the people." The people were asked to protect the paintings, the statues, the historic buildings. Today old churches, and even whole villages like Vladimir and Suzdal, are being restored.

"In the World of Beauty" is a program for Pioneers to participate in festivals of dance and music and join the Young Friends of Books, Theater, and Music. They enter their drawings in the "I See the World" contest which is sent on exhibit all over the world, and participate in all-union weeks of music, books, children's films, and theater, with all the resources of the Soviet Union going into making these various weeks successful.

Particularly talented children attend special music, dance, or art schools, but for the ordinary child there are classes at Pioneer palaces in dance, art, music, photography, sewing—almost any form of creative work.

The children are also encouraged to see the beauty of nature, and they realize it is their duty to preserve nature, to conserve and protect it. A pleasant landscape littered with trash is not pretty. Soviet educators want children to be in harmony with nature, both plants and animals.

The Harmony Club, started by *Pioner* magazine in 1977, brings the children the comments of some of the top creative people in the Soviet Union. The well-rounded aesthetic development that is the Pioneer ideal is summed up in the phrase from Sukhomlinski: "Musical education is not the education of a musician, but the education of a person." Before attending a concert or an art exhibition Pioneer leaders should tell the children what to look for in music and art; the more they understand, the more they will enjoy.

There are children's art galleries as well as theaters especially for children. Children perform on the radio and television and in major theaters. In Tashkent we saw a very impressive rose festival with a huge symphony orchestra composed entirely of children, some as young as age six or seven.

Octobrists are included in all these aesthetic endeavors because it is thought that the earlier children learn the more appreciative they will become.

"In the Land of October" is a program for Octobrists and their Pioneer leaders. The work of the Octobrist group is planned by the Octobrists' council, which consist of a commander, an Octobrist leader, a Pioneer instructor, and an Octobrist teacher. The council holds weekly meetings and makes concrete plans for Octobrist programs. A general staff, called the council of friends of Octobrists is responsible for specific tasks, such as publishing Octobrist newspapers and creating Octobrist corners and clubs.

The Pioneers, recently Octobrists themselves, work regularly with the Octobrists. The Pioneers study ways of influencing Octobrists and are told that play must be the major medium of education. Even the slogan, "Octobrists love work," is illustrated with games. The Pioneer greets the first grader in the "First Bell" ceremony and introduces him to other ceremonies such as "Octobrist in the Land of October" and "Up the Magic Staircase from the Town of Octobrists to the Land of Pioneers."

The goal of the Pioneer is to make the Octobrist want to join the Pioneers. Octobrists are invited as guests to their first Pioneer assembly in order to increase their desire to become Pioneers. Pioneers also help Octobrists to learn the rules of both Octobrists and Pioneers, but their main activity is play. One of the favorite games is a trip on a "merry train," wherein the children pretend they are on a train with various stops along the way. At each station they meet the hero of one of their favorite books, who gives them a task to fulfill, and only when this task has been fulfilled can the train move to the next station. The task may be to guess a riddle, play a game, or tell a fairy tale.

One of the favorite books of Soviet children, *Timur and His Team*, by Arkady Gaidar, is the basis for another march route also called *Timur and His Team*. The book was the most frequent response whenever I asked Soviet Pioneers to name a favorite book. The book is charming, with sympathetic dogs and stubborn goats and an air of secrecy and excitement. The author, a hero himself, was born in 1904 and joined the Red Army when he was fourteen (he told the authorities he was sixteen). He served in the army for six years, amidst the smoke, fire, and death at the front. In 1923 he became very ill as a result of an old concussion, and the next year, at age twenty, he was put in the reserves. From that time Gaidar began to write, first the autobiographical story of his war years, called *Shkola* (School), then *R. V. S.*, *A Far Away Land*, *War Secrets, Chuk and Gek*, and *Timur and His Team*.

His most popular book, *Timur and His Team*, "revealed the hero in every child," Gaidar said. In the story, Timur is a Young Pioneer who helps the families of those serving in the armed forces. The goal of Timur and his team is to bring joy to the people around them, and today the word *timurovets* is recognized as a synonym for "kind, faithful, grateful, and unselfish." Timur is a kind of Robin Hood whose men usually do their good deeds in secret. The tasks are not necessarily heroic. They include such things as finding a lost goat, consoling a crying five-year-old, picking apples for a farmer. Gaidar was once asked why Soviet children played Timur instead of cops and robbers, as children throughout the ages have done. He answered that the game of robbers was a protest against a slave society and that Soviet children were on the side of the revolutionaries against the robbers.

Pioner magazine told of the formation of one Timur brigade during World War II. Fifteen-year-old Lev Tolstoy Norik was walking past a cinema in Kiev one day at the beginning of the war. He looked at the billboard to see what was playing and saw a sign: "Children! We are starting a Timur team tomorrow at 10 AM." Norik was at the theater by eight the next morning, but there was already a long line of children waiting.

Mariya Teofilovna Boyarskaya, the director of the theater, addressed the children: "Children! You have all seen the film *Timur and His Team*. Now it is your turn to help the heroic Red Army. It will be difficult. Anyone who does not believe in himself had better leave now rather than let us down later." She began taking registrations but reminded the children, "You are still not a team yet. You must prove yourselves in action."

The children began their work—carrying water to apartments, finding and helping families of soldiers at the front, arranging bomb shelters, carrying pails of sand for extinguishing fire bombs. Some children thought their work should be more publicized, but others said, "Without secrets it isn't interesting. We

aren't Scouts who carry huge staffs in their hands and wear wide-brimmed hats so everyone in the world can see Scouts coming to do their good deeds."

In August 1941, Gaidar himself came to Kiev and told Norik and his friends how proud he was of the work they were doing. Kiev fell to the Germans in September 1941. The Gestapo shot Norik's mother, and his father was killed at the front. The director of the cinema, Mariya Boyarskaya was hanged by the Germans with a sign around her neck saying, "Leader of Timur's Team."

In the fall of 1941, Gaidar, who had been a correspondent for *Komsomolskaya Pravda* during the first months of the war, joined the partisans. In October of that year he and four other parisans were on an exploratory raid when they ran into a German ambush. Gaidar, who was in front, was shot. The Germans stripped his body of his notebooks, letters, and records. After the war Gaidar's remains were brought to the town of Kenev and buried under a bronze bust of him mounted on a tall pedestal.

In 1972 the editors of *Pioner* created an all-union staff to advise Timur teams, and in 1973 the First All-Union Timur Rally was held at Artek, with 3,460 delegates. A Timur flag was unveiled at the rally—a steering wheel enclosing a red star within its circle on a blue background. To the slogan, "Joy to the People," the rally delegates worked in nearby fields, gathered medicinal herbs, and gave concerts in kindergartens, collective and state farms, and sanitariums.

The Second All-Union Timur Rally opened in Lenin Square in Cherkass in July 1979, with five hundred delegates from each of the fifteen Soviet republics. The delegates again visited nearby farms where they helped the farmers after the traditional greeting of bread and salt. Money the Timur teams had earned during the year was donated to the Fund for Peace.

9

Fun and War Games

Although the new generation of Soviet children has never heard a bomb explode or seen the destruction of war for themselves, their leaders tell them that life is a relay race from the past to the future. A peaceful tomorrow depends upon preparations made today. The GTO (*gotov k trudu i oborone—* preparation for labor and defense) program is a general program for developing physically fit Pioneers. It covers a wide field.

There are skiing contests in cross-country, racing, and relay racing. By the late 1970s there were fifteen thousand Pioneer detachments participating. Hockey is so popular that a New Year's 1980 game between the Soviet Union and Canada, which began its broadcast on TV at 3 AM kept most Soviet fans up all night watching. For Pioneers *Pionerskaya Pravda* awards a Golden Puck to the best Pioneer hockey team. An equally popular club, Leather Ball, for football enthusiasts has about three million Pioneer members and seventy-two teams.

Each Pioneer chooses the sport that interests him or her most. Every sport has a sponsoring club or a prize donated by a magazine, newspaper, or department. Skaters have a Silver Skates award, swimmers a prize from the Neptune Club, fencers a prize from the Wonder-Fencers. There are also prizes for horseback riders. Most of these sports are available in the child's neighborhood, though for some the child must travel to a Pioneer palace or a riding academy.

Chess is also considered a sport and as such has its own club and prize, known as the White Castle. Adult chess champions frequently come to Pioneer palaces where they play games with the children, sometimes playing several children at the same time. We watched a number of these matches, which all seemed to involve long, motionless sessions of staring at a chess board with intense concentration.

Spartakiads are held for all these sports and gymnastics from time to time. These begin with a festive parade of the sportsmen through the host city and end

at the Lenin memorial or a war monument, where wreaths and flowers are placed. At the Second All-Union Spartakiad of Middle Special Schools held in 1977-78, there were competitions in light athletics, swimming, and shooting. The program was coordinated by the secretary of the All-Union Central Council of Trade Unions, the Secretariat of the Central Committee of the Komsomol, the Sports Committee of the Soviet Union, and the Ministry of Special Education. Preliminaries took place in physical training courses in technical and junior colleges throughout the country. Sports champions often visit schools and Pioneer meetings and answer children's questions.

"Who will be the champion of the world this time?" hockey champion, Alexander Maltsev, was asked.

"What can I say?" Maltsev replied. "The ball is round, anything is possible."

Another child said that hockey seemed to have changed in the last few years, since the Canadians seemed to be winning more often. Maltsev said that the Canadians had begun to play "Russian style," as a collective, which had improved their game.

To a child who said he wanted to be like him, Maltsev advised the child to be himself. "A copy is always worse than the original and is not necessary. You must thrive on your own." Maltsev also took this opportunity to warn against smoking: "If you smoke there is simply no sense in trying out for sports."

Pioneers trying to win the Golden Puck have some problems grown-ups like Maltsev do not have—they must have good grades to be on the team. One such child was written up in *Pioner* when his literature teacher said he could not play unless his work improved. To ensure his success, the teacher, the boy's trainer, the mother of the goalkeeper, his own mother and father, and the parents' committee of the school all joined to help the boy. "Don't give up," they counseled, and with this collective backing he made the team.

Preparations for the Olympics began as early as 1974, with a Pioneer program called Five Times Five (five groups, five stages). In each class the five groups competed with each other in a game called "Catch Up and Run Away."

"You already know how to run and jump," the children are told at the start of the competition. This is a beginning, but only a beginning. The child must practice to keep improving. Without practice he may even regress. "One day you don't do well," the teacher says, warning the children. Is this discouraging? "Let's say right away, in our game there is no place for despondency."

For encouragement the children are told the story of runner Valery Borzov, beginning with his first championship at age twelve at a Pioneer camp. At thirteen Borzov began his first real training. At fourteen he was the champion runner in his town of New Kakhkovka. At fifteen he ran the 100 meters in 10.5 seconds and became champion of his region. At seventeen he received the title Master of Sport of the Soviet Union, and at eighteen he was the European champion and a candidate for the Soviet Olympic team.

Pioneers all over the Soviet Union hope to be good enough for the Olympics some day, if not for the Olympics held in Moscow the summer of 1980. Pioneer newspapers and magazines were full of Olympic news, including the boycott of the Olympics by the United States ("Politics against sport") and an account of "doping," which told of athletes who took drugs to improve their records. For the Olympics, Moscow built a special anti-Drug Center for the scientific investigation of drugging not only in Moscow but for the other centers of Olympic games in Kiev, Tallin, and Minsk.

There were fairy tales for the children about the birth of the 1980 Olympic mascot, Mishka the bear, also called "Olimp." For three weeks Mishka's mother rocked him in his cradle and sang songs of strength, quickness, bravery, ease, and persistance. When he was three the earth taught him strength; brooks, bravery, the wind, speed; the sun, deftness; and the snow, persistence. With all these attributes the world proclaimed him ready to be an Olympic champion.

Another story about Mishka was not so heroic. This Mishka also wanted to be an Olympic champion so he went to a hare to learn running. The hare said, "You'll never be a runner. Better try gymnastics." Mishka went to a monkey to learn gymnastics, but the monkey, too, was discouraging: "Better try boxing." Mishka got some boxing gloves and fought with a bulldog but could not conquer him. Mishka was very sad. "I will never be a champion in the Olympics." Then an artist came along and drew a picture of Mishka as a merry little bear cub with a smiling face and an Olympic belt around his waist. "But I'm not a champion," Mishka said. "You will make up for that by having your portrait on every sportsman and champion," the artist said. And so the little bear began to be called Olympic.

Like the bear cub, Pioneers from Pioneer palaces and clubs, hoping to be good enough for the Olympics, go to sports schools to try out. One such little girl did the required skating school figures with grace and suppleness, and she and her mother were shocked when the coach said he could not admit her to the sports school. "She will never be a first-class figure skater." The coach said, advising the girl to enjoy skating but not in competition.

The Soviets are devising tests to separate future champions from the merely capable. First a "sportogram" is drawn up, taking into account the child's anthropomorphic characteristics, including height, weight, body structure, and proportions, his health and the level of development of his physical abilities, such as speed, strength, and endurance as well as his mental characteristics. These qualities are all determined by means of scientific instruments.

Next, the child's abilities are assessed in line with a specific sport. Should he take up gymnastics, swimming, weight lifting? Scientists have determined that speed and quickness are genetically determined along with height and body proportions. Muscular strength and general endurance are least dependent on heredity and can be built up in training.

The Soviets want champions but do not discourage the average child. Tests show which sport will give a child the most personal satisfaction even though he will never be a champion.

Despite the GTO programs, universities are still complaining that entering students do not meet GTO standards. Kiev University found that a majority of entering women students ran the hundred meters in 18 to 20 seconds, although the norm of third- and fourth-level GTO was 16.2 to 16.0 seconds, respectively. Young men averaged 8.2 pull-ups on a horizontal bar, whereas GTO requirements were 9.

How extensively the Pioneers exercise outside of school depends considerably on the attitude and work of the Pioneer leaders and the relationship of the children to the physical education teacher. The leader handbook says that too often the teacher and the Pioneer leader lead separate lives. Together they can see that there are sports facilities in the school, and if necessary the Pioneers can build sports centers themselves and earn money for the needed equipment. A "wall newspaper" (on a bulletin board) can give a calendar of events and results of competitions. Children are offered a choice of sports, including football, hockey (two varieties), basketball, volleyball, lapta (a game with a bat), badminton, handball, gorodki (skittles), and shooting. The handbook offers a system whereby each team plays another according to a formula. If the letter n represents the number of teams wishing to take part in a particular game and x equals the draw, the formula is $x = n (n - 1) /2$. If six teams are entered for volleyball, you must draw fifteen meetings: $6 (6 - 1) /2 = 15$.

GTO is sometimes called, "Brave, Strong, and Able." I was never quite sure whether GTO was a part of the *zarnitsa* program or whether both GTO and *zarnitsa* were a part of the "Brave, Strong, and Able." At any rate, *zarnitsa*, which in Russian means "summer lightning," has it's own symbol: a red star in a triangle and within the red star an arrow pointing upward and a bayonet. *Zarnitsa* is a program of children's war games.

"In spite of the fact that the name of the march route is associated primarily with war games," the Central Council of Pioneers says, "its contents are considerably broader." In December 1973, the Central Committee of the Komsomol, the minister of education, the Central Council of the Voluntary Society for Assisting the Army, Air Force, and Navy (DOSAAF), the Committee for Physical Training and Sport of the Council of Ministers, the Staff of the Civil Defense of the Soviet Union, the Executive Committee of the Red Cross, and Red Fortnightly met to discuss the development of the war games.

The main task of *zarnitsa*, they concluded, was ideological and political work among Pioneers. This included knowledge of the life and work of Lenin and his circle, the history of the Communist Party, and the revolutionary background of the Soviet people. It should teach patriotism and a love for the Motherland as well as knowledge of the symbols, flags, and national songs of the Soviet Union and the various republics and the Pioneer symbols and rituals.

It should develop in the child an interest in civil defense and a willingness to serve in the Soviet military. To encourage this interest, the child should become acquainted with war veterans and those serving in the armed forces. There are organizations of Young Friends of the Army, Young Friends of the Navy, Young Friends of the Border Guards, as well as Young Friends of Tank Drivers and Flyers. It is thought that the closer the child's ties with the armed forces, the deeper his understanding of what it means to defend his country. "The way to courage leads through the Land of Knowledge," says the magazine for Pioneer leaders.

There are also Young Friends of the Police and Firemen. Every child's life involves close contact with one or more of these organizations. In the hero city of Sevastopol, for example, first graders meet with sailors from the Black Sea fleet. In parades, little children are carried on the shoulders of marching soldiers and sailors, and they are taught that everyone shares a common goal.

Young Friends of the Border Guards help train dogs for guard duty and become acquainted with border guards and their work. Pioneers who have had this training may later attend the KGB school Voroshilov, which celebrated its fiftieth anniversary in November, 1980. *Izvestiya*, recounting the illustrious history of the school, remarked, "A glorious past is a hopeful bridge to the future."

The earlier the children begin *zarnitsa* the better, most Soviet officials say. In the past there have been war heroes who were ten, eleven, and twelve years old. Some died for their country. "The defense of the achievements of socialism against attacks from without always was and remains the bloody business of the Soviet people," says an article in *Nachalnaya Shkola* (Primary School).

The children must be taught courage. The early Soviet educator, Makarenko, said that the only way to teach courage was to put the child in a situation demanding courage. This involved some deprivation and patience as well as courage. The war games show the child why war takes courage.

In 1972, when we met with Fedulova, the head of all the Pioneers, I asked if we could go to *zarnitsa*. She did not say no, but, looking back on it, she did not say yes either. I realized I would have to find out when the next *zarnitsa* was and start working on it far enough in advance so that arrangements could be made. I read all of the Pioneer publications avidly throughout 1972 but could not find a word about *zarnitsa* finals. "They surely would have some mention of the finals in one of the Pioneer publications," I said. "I doubt if the CIA reads *Pioner* or *Pionerskaya Pravda* so they wouldn't be revealing any war secrets."

Then in 1973 I saw that the finals would be held at the Orlyonok Pioneer Camp two weeks later. I called a friend at the Soviet Embassy in Washington, but he was not very encouraging. "We don't have much time to arrange it," he said, though he promised to telephone Moscow and see what he could do. It was impossible to make arrangements, but I did learn one thing. I hadn't been able to find anything about the 1972 finals because there weren't any. For some reason the finals were now biannual rather than annual events.

Since I could not go to the finals in person I asked every Soviet I knew if they had attended the war games. I found some rueful memories. One prominent Soviet told me he had lost his detachment's flag; another said she had revealed her company's war secrets under "torture" (the other children twisted her arm). Although many years had passed since these disgraces, both seemed to feel ashamed that they had let their country down. Most of the people we talked to had enjoyed the war games. Harry said, "We didn't have *zarnitsa* when I was young, but we had something like it. We called it 'war games.' "

It wasn't until 1974 that I found an article in *Vozhaty* (Leader) magazine assessing the 1973 games at Orlonok. The article found many pluses, but there were also some insufficiencies. The author thought some participants defined *zarnitsa* too narrowly, in terms of drill and ceremony alone, instead of seeing it as encompassing the moral and physical attributes of a many-sided patriotic education. Some of the units were created in too much of a hurry, without region-wide competitions.

The author criticized some of the children for heartlessly rushing past their "fallen" comrades without compassion, in a desire to win "at any price." There was also the problem of what to do with the girls. Should they be limited to jobs as messengers, sanitation workers, and cooks? The author concluded that more grown people should be used as advisors and that these should include engineers, radiologists, and agriculturalists, in addition to military men.

From Soviet magazines and newspapers I began to get a fairly clear picture of the training of a member of *zarnitsa*. Youth Army members wear the *zarnitsa* emblem of red star, arrow, and bayonet on their left sleeve. The commander of the detachment wears three stars under the emblem, and the assistant commander for political activities wears two stars. In shooting there are two groups for boys and girls aged ten to thirteen called Young Shooters, and for those aged thirteen to fifteen called Good Shots, with norms for each group. The Good Shots used a low-caliber rifle at 25 m. No. 6 and at 50 m. No. 7.

The children learn to shoot, but they also study theory under the following themes: (1) defense of the socialist Fatherland and service in the Soviet armed forces; (2) shooting and the tasks of the DOSAAF, norms for Young Shooter and Good Shot, the all-union GTO physical education program and classifications for the sport of shooting; (3) acquaintance with construction and use of air-powered and low-caliber rifles; (4) acquaintance with the theoretical basis of shooting; and (5) safety measures in shooting and rules of treatment of weapons, rules and duties of a shooter, and rules of shooting competitions.

Retired army officers are assigned to schools to help in organizing the daily work of *zarnitsa*. According to some young Soviets, these officers are often ineffective and are made fun of by the students, although in other cases they are efficient and well liked. The course itself is fairly uniform, and the desire to enter *zarnitsa* finals is a stimulant to many children.

One of the most interesting divisions of *zarnitsa* is that of intelligence (secret service man, intelligence officer, scout, or reconnoiterer). Young scouts are often successful at seemingly impossible tasks. For example, someone would find an old photograph of a group of partisans, and the children would undertake to find out what had happened to them. A family who had been separated during the war would ask a Pioneer group to locate a missing brother or father; there were frequent pictures in the papers of families who had been reunited through the efforts of some Pioneer scout. These expeditions started with a simple game, "Find the War Heroes in Your Apartment Building," in which the children knocked on apartment doors and asked about heroic deeds.

In the Young Army School the signal man (or woman) is also an important post. The signal man has to know Morse code, orientation by compass, how to overcome obstacles such as radio interference, and such simple signals as "Attention," "Stop," and "Lie down" in hand, flag, and radio signals.

Signal men must know how to unwind cable from a spool quickly and make telephone connections in the field. At the finals, teams receive messages from a commander to see which team can transmit messages fastest (and sometimes break a code as well).

The hospital attendant, orderly, or stretcher bearer (*sanitar*) has to know how to acquire needed medicine quickly and understand the uses of various medicines, including herbs and grasses that can be gathered in the field. They learn how to travel over difficult terrain, change a tire, treat wounds on themselves, and transport the wounded.

To support the army there are secretaries, cooks, people to put up tents, reconnoiterers, translators, and all the people associated with regular army maneuvers.

The Young Army detachments are formed from only one school grade for each detachment. Each unit consists of a commander, an assistant political officer, three signal men, two scouts, four orderlies, five firemen, two inspectors of the movement, and two sharpshooters. There are also flag bearers, buglers, drummers, and an editor of the war list. In each city and region the best teams are chosen to go to the finals, which have been held in Sevastopol (1967), Vladivostok and Narva (1968), Pskov (1969), Brest (1971), Orlyonok (1973), Leningrad (1975), Ulyanovsk (1977), and Tula (1979).

Each school has a seventy-two-hour course in *zarnitsa*, but there are complaints that not all schools follow the program. Participants for the finals should not be taken from any grade past the seventh, but there were complaints that some ninth and tenth graders were used in 1979.

Are war games needed? I thought of a story I quoted in *Lenin's Grandchildren* about a writer who came upon some Soviet children playing war. "Why don't you play Peace?" he asked. The children gave him a puzzled look and asked, "How do you play Peace?" One contemporary Soviet writer suggested children might play more "vegetarian" games than War, but Soviet officials seem to feel there is a need for *zarnitsa*.

War games for the Komsomol groups were organized after the Pioneer war games. In 1980 the Komsomol held the fourth all-union finals of their war games at Sverdlovsk. The Komsomol games called *orlyonok* (not to be confused with the Pioneer camp by the same name) had a useful addition to their games—tanks. *Orlyonok* (Little Eagle), like *zarnitsa* gives a practical beginning to compulsory military training, which starts at age eighteen.

Pioner magazine had a humorous story about the fun the Pioneers have getting ready for *zarnitsa*. It concerned Agent 13, who was always getting into trouble. When the unit goes through a vineyard, Agent 13 seems to be lost. He reappears after an hour, licking his lips. The unit infiltrates a neighboring village, and they disappear "like sugar in a glass of tea." Agent 13 is missing again—sick from eating too many grapes.

I wanted to see the fun for myself, so when in early 1975 I saw a notice that *zarnitsa* would be held in Leningrad that summer, I alerted Harry and a friend at the Soviet Embassy in Washington.

At that time my husband's ninety-two-year-old mother was living with us, and my husband said, "What will we do with Mother?" She, hearing about the trip, said she wanted to go with us. "I've always dreamed of going to Russia," she said. Since we would not be using the car and guide our "deluxe" class entitled us to, Mrs. Weaver could use our time and with hers would have a full day of Intourist care while we attended *zarnitsa*. We had already taken my mother-in-law with us on trips to Spain, Bermuda, California, and other places around the world, and despite her age and the fact that she ate and drank anything wherever she was, she had never had an upset stomach or jet lag (she had never even heard of jet lag). It sounded implausible, but I thought it would work. I called our travel agent and asked him to make three reservations for Leningrad.

A few weeks before *zarnitsa* was to begin, we had a cable from Harry. "Contact friend in Washington for news." I showed the cable to our friend at the Soviet Embassy. "Harry is a great spy. Everything has to be in code." He laughed, then added, "You have your invitation to *zarnitsa*."

My mother-in-law began packing, and I brushed up on my Russian. "It's a good thing you made advance reservations with our travel agent," my husband said. "Everything seems in order."

A week before we were to leave the travel agent called. "I'm having trouble with your reservations, Mrs. Weaver. Now they say there are no hotel rooms to be had in Leningrad."

"But we have our invitation to *zarnitsa*. Why can't we stay in a tent with the Pioneers?"

"That's impossible. You must stay in a hotel and visit the games during the day."

I called Harry in Moscow. I called my friend at the Soviet Embassy, who called officials in Moscow. We could not accept the invitation without a hotel room. There were no hotel rooms to be had in Leningrad. I was bitterly disappointed.

On our next trip to the Soviet Union I talked to one of the officials our friend in Washington had called about our trip. "I found out why you couldn't go to *zarnitsa*." He said. "It seems that Intourist was told that a group of American workers wanted to come to Leningrad. At the time the worker's group wanted to come, most of the hotels were full of guests for *zarnitsa*. Intourist thought the American worker's group could visit some other cities and come back to Leningrad later."

"What kind of workers were they?" I asked.

"Weavers!" he laughed.

10

BAM:
The Pioneer's Train

Having failed at my attempt to see the *zarnitsa* finals, I turned my attention to another Pioneer program—also a sensitive one—the new trans-Siberian railroad, known as BAM because of its route from Lake Baikal to the Amur River (Baikal-Amur Mainline).

Operation BAM became a Pioneer program in September 1976. The main task for the Pioneers is to gather scrap metal, and there are contests to see which detachment of Pioneers can collect the most scrap. The Pioneers are asked to visualize each load of scrap as being a rail on the BAM line or even a whole engine or freight car. Each car weighs 2,500 tons.

The leaders want each Pioneer to feel that he is contributing to a major building project of the Soviet Union. Builders of BAM come to Pioneer palaces and tell the children about their work, and the best and most active of the Pioneers visit the BAM sites and make friends with metallurgists, machine workers, and transport scientists.

Pioneers are vitally involved in all BAM operations. They learn about the first trans-Siberian railway as well as the new one, and they study the map of Siberia, which extends from the Arctic Sea to the Chinese Mongolian border, and from the Urals to the Pacific. Siberia is not an area to be dismissed lightly or conquered easily. It contains most of the mineral wealth of the Soviet Union in addition to great reserves of oil and natural gas, coal, and iron ore. The vast forests (*taiga*) of Siberia would cover all of Western Europe twice. Lake Baikal, while not the largest lake in surface area, is the largest body of fresh water in the world, with 5,518 cubic miles of water at a depth of 5,314 feet. Baikal contains one-fifth of all the potable water in the world. To the Soviets BAM is chiefly economic in nature—opening the riches of Siberia to practical transportation. Some Western analysts see BAM as a Soviet defense measure, ensuring movements of supplies away from the Chinese border, which the present trans-Siberian railway skirts too dangerously.

101

The first trans-Siberian railway was first discussed in the second half of the nineteenth century, when a Colonel Romanov drew up a project for transforming a carriage road into the first railroad in the East. Then an English engineer named Doole proposed a horse-drawn railroad from Nizhni Novgorod to the Pacific. An American named Collins applied to the Russian government for permission to found the Amur Company Railroad Society to join Irkutsk and Chita by rail.

These projects were debated at length, but it was not until 1891 that a railway was actually begun, by peasant teams, Cossacks, soldiers, and convicts using spades and wheelbarrows for most of the work. By 1899 the Irkutsk-Baikal branch was finished, with a special ice breaker to carry trains over Lake Baikal. By 1904 the railway was largely complete, though it was deemed advisable to reroute one section which ran through Manchuria, and rerouting that line took until 1916.

In the 1920s the planning commission of the Council of Labor and Defense drew up a map of a route for a new railway to be built north of the trans-Siberian, and surveying was begun of a Tashet-Ust Kut-Kirensk-Bodaibo-Tynda route. In 1933 the first railway builders began laying track from Oldai (now called Bam) toward Tynda. In 1937 a single-track railway of a simplified type was built between Bam and Tynda, but in 1942 this section was dismantled and the tracks used during the advance of Soviet troops at Stalingrad.

In 1945 a 468-kilometer section between Komsomolsk-on-the-Amur and Sovetskaya Gavan was completed, as was 315 kilometers between Taishet and Bratsk in 1947. Planning and surveying continued as large copper deposits were discovered in the Udokan range and reserves of fibrous asbestos in the upper reaches of the Muya River. In 1972 reconstruction of the Bam-Tynda line was begun northwards from the trans-Siberian railway, with the railway bed one meter wider than the old line.

In the spring of 1974 Leonid Brezhnev addressed the Seventeenth Komsomol Congress: "The Komsomol has always been and remains the Party's militant reserve and reliable assistant," Brezhnev said, telling the Komsomols that he had a task for his assistants: help build the Baikal-Amur Mainline.

The Komsomol, with a membership of 34 million young people, pledged to sponsor the railway, declaring BAM to be an all-union Komsomol shock project.

"This construction is of tremendous importance," said Brezhnev. "The Baikal-Amur railroad will cut through primeval *taiga* and pass through places where tremendous wealth lies, which must be put to the service of the Motherland. A new large industrial area of the country will be created there, and new cities and settlements built. We are firmly convinced that the Komsomols and young people will make a worthy contribution to this great construction project."

The first Komsomol workers to volunteer were given vouchers and set out for Siberia straight from the Komsomol Congress in the Kremlin in Moscow. The young Komsomols were pictured in *Soviet Life*, smilingly waving banners which *Soviet Life* translated as "Komsomol Shock Project" and "Right on, Baikal-Amur Railroad."

Soon afterwards the airport at Ust-Kut, a small town on the Lena River, was busy with passengers who crowded into helicopters taking off for destinations deep into the *taiga*. A ten-hour trip by plane, with a change in Irkutsk, had taken them to Ust-Kut, the last section on the existing railroad. The same trip by train would have taken almost a week. The Komsomol members wore green overalls, with badges on their chests, a stripe on their sleeves, and the BAM emblem. They carried signs representing the cities and republics from which they came: Leningrad, Voronezh, Kazakhstan, Armenia.

Branching off from the Trans-Siberian at Taishet, the BAM line will run north of Lake Baikal, cross eastern Siberia, and terminate in the Far East, reaching the Pacific via Komsomolsk-on-the-Amur. It joins the Trans-Siberian by the Tynda-Bam route, running north-south. Experts claim that the railroad goes through the most difficult route in the history of transport construction—abrupt mountain ranges, hills, valleys, and cliffs, and swift Siberian rivers. Temperatures in winter go to sixty or seventy degrees below zero, but in summer the frozen tundra thaws into marshy plains. The thick coniferous forests (*taiga*) are difficult to penetrate, and for the first shock workers there were few comforts or facilities.

Everything had improved considerably by the time my husband and I flew to Siberia in April 1979, but I was just as excited as the Komsomol workers must have been. We wore our warmest clothes, heavy coats, lined boots, and alpaca-lined caps with ear flaps. We left Moscow's Vnukhovo Airport at 11:30 PM and arrived at Bratsk at 11:30 AM local time (five hours later than Moscow), with a one-hour stop in Omsk on the way. Our plane was full of East Germans who were very loud and uncouth. They pushed ahead of us, kicking us in the shins or elbowing us in the ribs.

Olga, a nice guide from Intourist, met us at the steps of our plane and took us to a waiting car where we chatted with the driver for a few minutes as Olga got our luggage. On the way to the hotel we were surprised to see very little snow. The sun was shining with dazzling brightness, which made us blink after the greyness of Moscow. Our hotel, the Taiga, was a new building to the left of a public square flanked in the back by a building which housed a cinema. We were given a small sitting room and a small bedroom with bath. Olga did not think it was good enough for us, and she complained to the hotel manager, who suggested giving us *two* suites, which pleased us until he told us the suites were on different floors. We took the first small suite, noting that we had the usual deluxe class refrigerator and television set. Several Taiga suites could have been put into one room of our National Hotel suite in Moscow. The elevator, although self-service, had a sign on it stating that it took a lunch break from two to three.

Bratsk, until recently a tiny village of native Siberians, nomadic Buryats and Eskimos, was originally called Buryat, which meant brotherly (in Russian, *bratskii*). When the Russians came in the seventeenth century they began calling Buryat Bratsk, and the name stuck. Under the Czar, Siberia was a place of exile for such advocates of revolution as the eighteenth-century philosopher Radishchev, and later Lenin and Krupskaya. Both Radishchev and Lenin admired the beauty of Siberia, and Radishchev wrote: "What a rich and mighty land this Siberia is—when it is settled it is destined to play a big part in the annals of the world."

"Communism is Soviet power plus electrification of the whole country," said Lenin, and on his initiative engineers searched for favorable places to put dams to produce hydroelectric power. The Angara River was mentioned in the 1920s as a favorable dam site because of its uniform water level throughout the year. Sixty percent of the Angara River's water comes from Lake Baikal. Around the river were natural bluffs of hard rock and a narrow river channel of rock. No foundation was needed. The rock banks were safe, too.

In 1954, when the decision was made to build the dam, the nearest village, fifty kilometers away, was old Bratsk. There were no roads and the nearest communication center was Irkutsk. The first twelve men to come set up tents, heated by stoves which had to be stoked once every hour. When one stoker slept through his turn, the hair of the men had already frozen to their beds—it was seventy degrees below zero.

The summer before, someone had climbed out on a boulder by the river and inscribed: "Here will be built the Bratsk GES [Hydroelectric Power Station]." The builders' optimism was sorely tested. In winter the concrete had to be mixed with boiling water and carried on heated truck beds. Machines broke like glass in the cold, and the men had to start with shovels and axes, changing shifts every twenty minutes to keep from freezing.

In one year after the first twelve workers came to the Angara there were five thousand workers, and in two years there were sixteen thousand, chiefly young Komsomols who had answered the call for help. Millions in the eighteen-to-thirty-year-old group volunteered—more than needed, but they were inexperienced and the task was immense.

On June 21 millions of midges appeared. They swarmed into eyes, ears, and noses, got into shoes and boots, and were impossible to wave away. Chemicals were sprayed over the *taiga* but provided only momentary relief. The midges bred in stones on the river in the rapids and rose to the surface of the water in a bubble of air. The productivity of the men, which had not suffered in the cold, now went down by 30 percent. People wore nets, but the tiny midges penetrated the finest net. Livestock were tormented by them, too. Cows wore dressing gowns with buttons on their bellies to save them from the midges.

In addition to the midges, in the summer frost-free period of eighty-four days mosquitoes appeared—large, vicious, bloodsuckers.

There were ninety-five men to every woman at first. Whole train loads of girls were invited to come from Ivanova, and two years after their arrival Bratsk had the country's highest birth rate. (Today there are 70,000 children out of a population of 230,000, with 38 schools and 120 kindergartens). For ten years after the girls came there was a baby boom which has only recently subsided.

The first year was spent in preliminary work for the dam—stone cracking plants and so forth. The dam was started in 1955. The land had to be cleared, and 40 million cubic meters of wood was cut. The local inhabitants had to be relocated to make room for the lake. It was difficult to move the people. There were many Old Believers who refused to leave. They were offered a house or apartment and money to settle in Moscow or Leningrad, but most stayed near their original homes.

In 1961 the first generating unit was installed. In 1963 the man-made lake (so big it is called the Inland Sea) flooded the midges and solved that problem, leaving mosquitoes and cold as the major problems. In 1967 the completed dam was put into operation, with eighteen generating units.

We passed the Bratsk Inland Sea on our way to the dam the next day. It was a vast expanse of solid ice with a large ship frozen into it near the shore. There was a blue luster to the whole landscape, the blue sky reflecting back the blueness of the deep ice. We drove into a Pioneer camp with picturesque log houses by the lake. There was still snow on the ground here as we left our warm car to walk around. Olga said it was - 9° C. (about 19 F.). The camp, called *Sokolyonok* (Baby Falcon), run by the Union of Transport of the Bratsk Dam, is used as a Pioneer camp for children in the summer and as a rest home for adults in the winter.

We visited another camp—*Krilyatyi* (One Who Has Wings)—which had an indoor swimming pool, and is used by the children of Bratsk, who come out on buses from the city. In a cage on the grounds was a large bear and in another cage were two roe deer. Krilyatyi is run by the aluminum factory.

The dam was enormous. Olga said it was the biggest in the world when it was built, but now the one at Krasnoyarsk was bigger. Bratsk has a capacity of 4.5 million kilowatts, and the Bratsk resevoir is 570 kilometers long. The Bratsk forestry complex processes some seven million cubic meters of timber a year. We were shown through giant rooms with enormous valves and myriads of switches. In one of the huge rooms was a large vigorous oleander in full pink bloom. I had expected to see dams in Siberia. I had not expected to see the healthiest oleander I had ever seen.

"Some of our scientists are talking of building a whole Arctic city under glass," Olga said. "Until then we all have house plants in sunny windows."

"This is very interesting," I said, "but we really wanted to see BAM."

"To really see BAM you would have to go out in a helicopter and then bounce around in a truck to a construction site. There would be no place for you to stay. It would be muddy, cold, and unpleasant, and what would you see? Steam shovels, bulldozers, cranes, men pulling tracks into place with crowbars and by hand, as well as by machine, snow and ice, snow and ice, and thick forests," Olga thought a minute. "I'll show you the railway line to Bratsk."

A little later Olga asked our driver to stop the car. "There it is," she said, pointing ahead of us where there was the familiar black-and-white crossed boards. Black-and-white striped poles stood on either side of the road, with red-and-white striped barriers in raised position. Fencing off the roadway by the tracks was a white board fence, its palings patterned in Williamsburg fashion, which seemed incongruous to the rough setting of tall, straight evergreens thick on either side of the tracks.

The track stretched off into the distance like a lesson in perspective, and in my mind I saw the snowy train scene in the movie, *Dr. Zhivago*. All the Soviet articles I had read had spoken of the romanticism of BAM and here it was before me. Romanticism and realism merged. On one side of the tracks a rough dirt road was collecting wet mud in its ruts. A snow bank to the left of the tracks was covered with a thick forest of tall evergreens at the top of the bank, their straight, erect trunks bare and white in the sunlight, while on the lower slope were smaller Christmas tree-size evergreens.

As I watched, a large round disk hanging over the middle of the road ahead of us began swinging back and forth, and a tinny ding-dong, ding-dong sounded nervously as the red and white crossing gates descended in front of us. On the other side of the tracks a white delivery van stopped. Behind it was a large khaki-colored army supply truck and behind that several Soviet-made cars.

In a few minutes there was a puffing noise on the left, and a black engine with red bands across its square front passed by us. There were no cars behind it. I waved at the engineer and he waved back. The swinging disk stopped swinging. The red lights stopped flashing. The crossing gates returned to their upright position and the traffic resumed. I got back into our car and the driver started the engine.

"BAM is people, really," Olga said, after a pause. "Those I can show you."

The next day we walked a few blocks from the hotel to a school that had some English classes. The principal took us to the tenth-grade class and introduced us. Did we have any questions? I asked the children to tell us about their hobbies.

"My hobby is basketball," one boy said. "I like very much this play."

"Game," the teacher corrected. "Why play?"

The boy misinterpreted the teacher's "Why play?" and continued, "Because this game is quick, active, mobile. I must think when I play. Our team is the first in our region."

"Do you know the history of the game?" the teacher asked, and the boy answered, "Basketball was born in an American university in the last years of the eighteenth century."

"I collect records." another boy said. "I like rock music. I like Uriah Heap, and the Negro group Boney M."

The children were eager to tell me their hobbies—reading, theater, music, athletics, and club work, both Pioneer and Komsomol. "Komsomol gives me much satisfaction," one boy said. "I work on our staff, helping the Pioneers in meetings and class discussions. This work gives me very big enjoyment. I can give to other people all my knowledge. The institute which I shall enter admits only pupils whose hobby is Komsomol."

"My hobby is eating and sleeping, no?" A girl said mischievously, then added more seriously, "I love to read. I like Jack London, Melville, our Russian writers, historical novels. I have read *Ivanhoe*, and *Old Man of the Sea.*"

A few students were whispering together at the back of the room, and when the teacher asked what the trouble was a girl stood up and said politely, "We have been struggling to speak English. Now we would like Mrs. Weaver to tell us *in Russian* what she thinks of Bratsk."

I said, in Russian, that often when I spoke Russian to a Russian he would answer, "I don't speak *German*!" The class laughed, and from then on we began a more intimate conversation in mixed Russian and English.

The children wanted to know what I thought of our president ("If we don't like him we can get rid of him."), what we thought of the Chinese invasion of Vietnam ("Since we had just recognized them, we thought it was very insulting."), what the Chinese thought of the Soviet Union ("They are afraid of you."), why would the Chinese be afraid of Russia ("The Chinese say, 'Take the Soviet soldiers away from our borders and we will believe they are not a threat!'").

We had a thoughtful conversation about fear and peace, the reasons for fear and the apparent but conflicting desire of all the peoples of the world for peace. The class was very bright. It was an interesting, nonbiased discussion.

The parents of these children were engineers, scientists, or workers with a sense of adventure. They had come to Siberia with one trait in common—courage. Not everyone who came to Siberia kept that trait, as a Soviet booklet on Siberia pointed out. Four Siberians were interviewed in a small village of trailer houses on the BAM line. The author had to push the doors open hard because they were frozen shut. Then the icy air from outdoors, meeting the warm air inside, produced a cloud of steam which took a few minutes to clear before he could see the faces of the men.

One man said he had come because of the campaign for workers; "You could hear nothing except BAM, BAM, BAM—the radio, the newspapers, TV." The campaign brought a work force of one hundred thousand as diverse as the four interviewed. Another man said he came because he wanted to be in on something from the beginning. He had worked on the dam at Bratsk when they were already doing the asphalting, and at Kamaz after they had put up the town, but he saw the beginning of BAM.

Another man said he had been the chief engineer on the board of management directing the wineries of the Crimea when he was asked to come in to the district Party committee headquarters. He was told that people of his background were needed at BAM: "Of course the whole thing is entirely voluntary. But the need is great, and urgent. Think it over."

"Why did I come here?" the other man asked. "What do you think—romance of course! The project of the century, the conquest of Siberia—and extra good money." This man was going home. Siberia was too hard for him.

There were too many like this man at first, and the labor turnover was large. The dissatisfied ones left and new recruits were more carefully screened, but still the harsh conditions of Siberia are not easy to bear. Too many of the recruits who had come because the project sounded romantic were disillusioned.

"Romance. I'm bored to death with that word," says a BAM worker quoted in an article on BAM in *Pioner* magazine. "What is needed for those who come to BAM? I'll tell you: courage is needed."

The article in *Pioner* gives young Pioneers a chance to see what BAM is like. The author and the artist who illustrated the article flew in an MI-2 helicopter to the Irkutsk region at the beginning of the BAM construction. They flew low over the *taiga*, landing on the soft bank of the Tayura River, with tree-lined hills to the right and left. There were no tracks for BAM. In fact, there was no town either. The BAM workers were trying to build something to live in before winter came with its harsh winds and cold. The town they were starting to build in 1974 is now *Zvezdnyi* (Starry), but then the electric light poles had been forest trees only a few weeks before. In the "street" were children and dogs, particularly the useful huskies. The people in the town were mostly young. In the nearby forests the cuckoos sang, undisturbed by the roar of bulldozers.

The author continued his journey by helicopter over more *taiga*. *Taiga, taiga, taiga*—nothing but forests, though from place to place he could see round grey spots. "People have been here," the pilot said, and when the author looked more closely he found that the grey spots were forest fires. Some fires are started by storms, but the pilot said that seven or eight of every ten are started by men. He spoke of the Green Patrol, also a concern of Pioneers, which protects and conserves nature. Forest fire fighters are dropped in by parachute to fight the fires.

Other problems involve the drilling into the core of the earth—sometimes as deep as three kilometers to bed rock. Special bulldozers are required to move the red Siberian earth. Intermontane basins are characterized by extreme cold, air stagnation, and temperature inversions in which emissions from smokestacks fall to the ground level and stagnate there instead of rising.

Air pollution is only one of the problems. Seismic action distorts house frames and foundations; there are few roads between settlements; and transportation of workers and local inhabitants is often by caterpillar tractor, which takes hours to go a short distance and jolts its passengers to the point of exhaustion.

In the mountains there are sharp transitions from monolithic rock to friable and aquiferous rock, and as a result tunnel builders have a frustrating time changing equipment. Underneath the region are large reservoirs of hot water and thermal springs, which the BAM builders are already optimistically planning to put to use in heating houses and greenhouses that could grow food year round.

Some of the drinking water has been found to lack essential minerals, and the cold weather requires a different diet for its inhabitants than do more temperate weather conditions. More fat is needed in the diet, and scientists are studying the diets of Eskimos to determine what man needs in this unusual environment.

To all these natural problems are added the man-made ones of inefficient workers, lack of coordination for programs, unrealistic estimates, shortage of supplies, and harsh living conditions. "It is not a picnic," wrote a *Pravda* correspondent, noting that some of the people had not seen a barber or a recent copy of a newspaper since they arrived.

"We build BAM. BAM builds us," says an article in the Pioneer magazine *Vozhaty* (Leader), describing Special Train No. 46, which carried the detachment of the Eighteenth Komsomol Congress to Siberia in April 1978. On the platform fifteen hundred Komsomol members are arriving, with knapsacks on their shoulders, some carrying guitars or accordians.

They are going to BAM, or, more specifically, to Ulan Udz where they will get a helicopter for Nizhni-Angarsk, and then to a small settlement on the Kicher River. The small village on the Kicher, explains the article, does not exist as yet. The passengers on Train No. 46 will have to build it. They will have to clear one hundred kilometers through the wilderness, put up electric poles, and clear a roadway before they can build the village on the river.

In one detachment of 300 people, 264 are Komsomol members, and 34 are candidates and members of the Communist Party. Fifty-seven have higher and special education, 219 have finished secondary school, and 24 have not finished secondary school. By profession there are bricklayers, carpenters, cement workers, foresters, log rollers, drivers, welders, bulldozer operators, locksmiths, and joiners.

To journalists who are seeing them off they say that the detachment was formed from a group on the Neva River who were connected with the Buryat section of BAM. Their region had already sent more than a thousand Komsomol

volunteers to BAM in the last four years. They had ten applicants for every one place available. In a cartridge case they carried a bit of soil from the hero city of Leningrad, and they were already planning the report they would make at the Nineteenth Komsomol Congress.

The pictures in the magazine show the Komsomols marching to the train, connecting the electric wires to the electric poles, and then a circle of Komsomols around a campfire, which blazes inside a star drawn on the ground. The last picture shows a teacher pointing to neatly written words on a blackboard: "Our parents build BAM."

Another article in *Pioner* tells more of life in the BAM area. It is evening in a BAM tent city, and the workers are going home. Before they cross the mud sills of their tents, they take off their wet, frozen shoes and put on slippers and "Keds," as all sneakers are called. "Why bother?" some ask. "What difference if you go into a tent with muddy shoes? These tents are only temporary homes."

Temporary, yes, says the author, but homes too. Towns like Magnitogorsk, Komsomolsk-on-the-Amur, and Bratsk began with such temporary tents. Inside the tents there are two rows of bunk beds and a big stove.

Someone gets out a guitar, another an accordian. As the musicians begin to play, the girls from the next tent come in, and some of the girls and boys link arms and go outside to dance to the music. The story ends with the comment that BAM is being built by people who are building their own characters at the same time.

BAM will continue as a program into the 1980s, but the Pioneers will contribute to building bridges on the BAM line in order to give them a new goal. Participation in BAM is one way the Pioneers keep in step with the Komsomol and Communists. In addition they look forward with equal anticipation to the Twenty-Sixth Congress of the Communist Party of the Soviet Union to be held in February 1981.

What can Pioneers do to prepare for the congress? "Don't waste time," urges *Pionerskaya Pravda*. "Think what you as a Pioneer can contribute to the success of the congress." Pioneers must study the plenary session held in the summer of 1980, and know the goals of the congress, the new five-year plans, and the elections of delegates to the congress.

One of the goals of the congress is food for the people of the Soviet Union in an effort to increase the standard of living while working against unfavorable climatic conditions, Western embargos, and economic problems. For 1980 to 1985 a new program for Pioneers was announced in *Pionerskaya Pravda* in June 1980.

"I am a signal! I am a signal!" says the paper, and Pioneers read about a new program. Everyone is to raise rabbits for food.

"That won't work," my husband said pessimistically, when I told him of the new program. "The children will get attached to the rabbits and never let them be killed and eaten. In five years the Soviet Union will simply be overrun with rabbits. They will have to be fed and the whole project will be a mess."

Pionerskaya Pravda was more optimistic. There were pictures of the "White Giant," a rabbit that weighed six kilograms, and stories about Pioneers raising tons and tons of carrots, grasses, and corn to feed the rabbits. Everything seemed to be going well until July when a child wrote *Pionerskaya Pravda* that toward the end of the school year his school had decided to raise rabbits. They built nice cages, gathered a supply of carrots and grass, and built watering troughs. They took good care of the rabbits at first, then a few Pioneers forgot to take care of their rabbits. The other children got bored with rabbits. The rabbit project was turned over to a collective farm.

"Just what you would expect," my husband said. "That's the way children are."

This explanation was not good enough for Pioneers. "Let's consider the problem together," the leaders said. From one rabbit and its progeny we can get no less than seventy-five kilograms of meat and twenty-five skins a year. The skins will make three fur coats for children or twenty fur hats." The children of

Moldavia have organized 875 rabbit farms and raised 52,000 rabbits for the state. It can be done."

The Soviets do not expect the children to spend all their summers at work. They are entitled to their vacations, just like the grown-ups, and these vacations are spent in summer camps for three or four weeks each summer.

11

A Pass to Artek

The Soviet Union has 50,949 Pioneer camps, which more than 14.5 million children attend each summer for sessions of three or four weeks. The camps range from simple clusters of tents in the suburbs to elaborate seaside resorts with modern buildings and broad plazas.

The showcase camp is probably Artek. We visited Artek quite by chance before I became interested in the Pioneers. We had been staying in Yalta, and our guide, Olga, had taken us to see the usual tourist sights, including Chekhov's house and the bench at Livadia Palace where Roosevelt, Stalin, and Churchill sat during breaks in the talks at the Yalta Conference. "Would you like to see a children's camp?" Olga suggested one day, and soon we were on our way to Artek on the Black Sea.

The glass-walled camp buildings between the towns of Gurzuf and Ayu-Dag began at the water's edge along a curving beach and climbed up the slopes of a forested mountain. Two huge rocks perched romantically in the sea in front of the camp, and on the left a large mountain reminded me of Diamond Head in Hawaii.

The grounds were beautifully planted along paved walks and playing fields, and in the amphitheater a wall of mosaics depicted white, brown, and yellow children united in friendship. As we walked around we saw some campers busy with shovels and wheelbarrows building a new road. Others were swimming in the sea, marching in drills, playing hopscotch on the plaza squares, or simply sitting in the sun reading. Everyone seemed to be doing exactly what he or she pleased.

When I became interested in the Pioneers I immediately remembered our visit to Artek and wanted to visit there again. Perversely, this time I had trouble. Tamara, our guide in Yalta, announced that we would visit Chekhov's house and the Livadia Palace.

115

"We've already seen them," I said. "We made arrangements in Moscow to visit Artek."

"We have no authorization for such a visit," Tamara said. "That's impossible."

I argued. My husband argued. "Impossible," Tamara said. "We might as well go back to the United States," I said, running up to my room tears welling up in my eyes.

"You don't really want to go home without seeing Artek again, do you?" my husband asked. Feeling completely frustrated, we talked for several hours about how we could salvage the trip by changing our itinerary. Suddenly we heard a noise at the door. When we opened it there was no one outside, but we found a letter on the threshold:

Dear Mr. and Mrs. Weaver:

I have the pleasure to inform you that tomorrow you'll have a visit to the Artek Pioneer Camp where you'll be able to take pictures and you'll also be shown around the camp.

Please be ready for the trip at 9:30, in the lobby of the hotel.

Yours truly,

Tamara

P.S. On Monday you'll visit an ordinary Pioneer camp in a place called Alushta (30 km. north-east from Yalta).

When we arrived at Artek a delegation of children welcomed us with bouquets of fresh flowers. A little boy named Kolya, about ten or eleven years old, gently took my arm and escorted me around the camp. We went first to the director's office. Aelita Sakhatskaya, the director, said she knew Harry well: "Every Pioneer knows Harry Eisman."

Sakhatskaya told me that Artek had a budget of 7 million rubles a year, plus 3 million rubles a year for new building projects. There was never any trouble getting all the money they needed from the government, she said.

"Our main problem," she continued, "is that we can't accept all the children who want to come here. We hope to double our capacity, but now, in 1972, we can take only 4,500 children at each session. We have to limit the children we take to the best in the country. The Komsomol assigned a specific number of "passes" to each section of the country, and then there are contests of various sorts to determine who comes. We have the best young artists, students, sports winners, young technicians, activists, and so on. The *druzhina* decides who will come, on the recommendation of the *druzhina* council. A few of the children pay a fee to come here, based on family income. Fifty percent pay nothing, 10 percent pay 120 rubles; 20 percent, 60 rubles; and 20 percent, 36 rubles. Our cost for each child is about 150 rubles for 30 days, which covers uniforms, cultural activities, sea trips, and excursions to Yalta and Sevastopol."

When we left the director's office a different little boy took my arm. Kolya gently disengaged him and took my arm himself, with a proprietary air. He showed me the camp's power station, laundry and cleaning plant, dormitories, library, and dining hall and explained everything in the purest Russian I had ever heard. When we visited the polyclinic Kolya told me about a boy from the United States who had appendicitis. Many foreign children visit Artek. During the international session, from July 15 to August 15, there were 888 children from 59 foreign countries. War veterans, Komsomol, and friendship societies invite these children. The American-USSR Friendship Society sent six children from the United States that year, and other campers included African children from diplomatic families, a child from Rome, and five children from India.

Kolya said that four years earlier a prince from Laos attended the camp. I told him I had seen a play in Moscow about a Prince visiting a camp, and Kolya said that that was based on the prince from Laos. We laughed about the prince in the play having his own elephant. "He didn't bring his elephant to Artek," Kolya said, regretfully.

The majority of children at Artek are Pioneers, although some older and younger children also attend. From September to May children chosen from among the brightest students go to school here. Since they learn very quickly, they only attend school five days a week, instead of the usual six, and have no homework. Twenty-five hundred people, including teachers, and four hundred Pioneer leaders work at Artek.

We visited the seaside camp, which Kolya said contained four "brigades" of five hundred children each. Each brigade is divided into detachments of thirty children each, which are further subdivided into teams of ten children each. There are two Pioneer leaders for each detachment.

"Every day at Artek is different," Kolya said, telling us about some of the children's activities. A major event at the seaside camp is the initiation of the children by King Neptune, who wears a crown, a grass skirt, and little else. With his long white beard, he resembles a summer Santa Claus.

An important yearly ritual connected with the sea took place on Peace Day. The children woke up to the signal of the bugle and selected their own neckerchiefs from the ones on the table. There were ties from many countries—blue, green, red and white, yellow—but all represented the Pioneer organization.

After breakfast each Pioneer presented a glimpse of his own country through a program of songs and dances. At the end of the program a girl from Vietnam

held a huge mirror up to catch the sun's rays as the children all sang, "May there always be sunshine. May there always be blue skies. May there always be Mama. May there always be me." A campfire of friendship was lit, and various children stood watch to see that the fire continued to burn.

Next the children wrote letters of peace and friendship in English, French, German, and all the other languages they knew. The letters contained a plea for peace to all the people of the world from all the children at Artek. The children studied the wording carefully, and argued over the exact message to be sent. They expressed the hope that all the children of the world might live happily in friendship like that at Artek. The message ends: "When the people of the world wake up each morning, we hope they will say, 'Hello, sun, Hello, friend, Hello, peace!' "

The messages were put into the "Bottle Post Office," and that evening, as all the children of Artek watched, the bottle was thrown into the water, where it was caught by a current and drifted out to the open sea, carrying its messages of peace. The children returned to the campfire of friendship to tell stories and sing songs.

Artek covers 750 acres in all, 250 acres in park; there is a forest camp and a mountain camp, in addition to the seaside camp.

We were invited to have lunch with the children in the large, glass-enclosed dining room, where we were waited on by Pioneers on duty. Dessert was watermelon, of which there were vast amounts. Many of the children in the dining room were reading letters from home; the mail had apparently just arrived, and the children read and ate at the same time.

After lunch we visited the House of Friendship, headquarters of the International Friendship Club (*Klub Internatsionalnoi Druzhby*). KIDS clubs are formed in schools and camps all over the Soviet Union. By promoting social and political exchanges among children in various parts of the world, the club works to further its goal of peace and solidarity. Club members exchange letters with children from capitalist countries as well as other Socialist countries, and many cities in the Soviet Union have "sister" cities in various parts of the world.

These cities form particularly close ties, as the children study the history and ways of the "sister."

Club members also study class struggles around the world, anti-imperialist struggles for independence of countries in Asia, Africa, and Latin America, and the activities of such international children's organizations as the Federation of Democratic Youth, the International Union of Students, and the International Committee of Children's and Youth Organizations.

Members of KID are children from the fourth through the tenth grades. They are expected to propagandize constantly the international traditions of the Communist Party of the Soviet Union, the Komsomol, and Pioneers by making speeches, preparing exhibitions, and attending seminars and conventions in order to increase further their own knowledge and understanding as well as to instruct others. Sections of the club are devoted to particular topics, including "My Motherland," "Friends with Various Colored Neckties," "Brother Countries of Socialism," "The International Youth Movement," and "Post Office of Peace and Solidarity." The club is self-governing, though it works under the direction of a Komsomol committee and the council of the Pioneer organization.

I later read that *Pionerskaya Pravda* was urging its KID club members to write a book on the aims of their organization. The newspaper suggested five chapter headings: Solidarity, Letters, Campfires of Friendship, Together—A Friendly Family, and Brotherhood. The book will be called *MIR* (Peace).

There were many children from foreign countries in the KID club room at Artek, and some gave short speeches welcoming us, including a boy from Yugoslavia, a girl from Vietnam, and several children from East Germany. In one of the dormitories I had seen only blacks; Kolya said children could room wherever they wanted, but these preferred to be with their other friends since all were from Africa.

There was still much to see, but it was getting late, so we parted regretfully from Kolya and his friends. Kolya kept my arm to the last, his touch as soft as butterfly wings.

On Monday, as Tamara had promised, we visited Cyprus Camp outside Alushta, the last town on the southern coast of the Crimea. Tamara said this Pioneer camp, founded in 1961, was chiefly for truck drivers' children, about four hundred of whom attend each twenty-six-day session. One-third of the children were from Alushta itself, and two-thirds from the region; all were Ukrainian.

Each year on May 1, local parents bring their children to the Central Children's Park, which has benches around a circular plaza. Parents sit with their children on the bench appropriate to the child's age and class, and a member of the Truck Drivers' Trade Union comes to escort each child to the center of the circle, where he or she is given a pass to the camp. The children are then examined by a doctor, who signs their passes and sends them to a Pioneer leader, who then assigns them to a detachment. Octobrist children, ages seven to nine, are put into groups of twenty-five to thirty, while Pioneers are in larger groups of thirty-five to forty.

Since Cyprus Camp is also a convalescent camp, children who are not well may stay for two sessions instead of the usual one. When the child arrives at camp, additional notations are put on the passport he received in May: his name, teacher's name, leader's name, class, room number, and what group he is in. The child is also given a key to the camp. The cost of the camp is 70 rubles, 50 kopeks, of which parents pay 9 rubles, 60 kopeks and the trade union pays the rest. Transportation to and from the camp is included in the rate.

In the month between the children's receipt of their passports and their arrival at camp, teachers and Pioneer leaders from the camp visit the children's homes, invite children for a walk, and find out their individual interests and abilities. The camp leader should know the child's birthday, parents' names, address, telephone number, and professions, what Pioneer work the child has had in school, which children sing, dance, or play a musical instrument, and what each one hopes to accomplish in camp. Camp leaders also attend parent's meetings to explain the work of the camp and give the parents detailed lists of things the child should bring to camp, from clothes to fishing rods, soap, toothpaste, and knapsack, not forgetting shoelaces, buttons, needle and thread, and writing paper and stamps.

The head of a Soviet children's camp must have had teacher's training and experience with children. The senior Pioneer leader must be at least eighteen years old and a Komsomol member, although he or she may be either a student in a teacher's college or a teacher. Each camp must have a doctor, a nurse, and a physical education instructor in addition to the housekeeper, cook, and kitchen workers. A pedagogical council composed of teachers, pioneer leaders, a physical education teacher, and doctor draw up the plan of work for the camp. Each child, in turn, is asked to be on duty for two hours at a time as the "right hand" of the camp director. These children raise and lower the flag, help in the kitchen, set the table, answer the telephone, and so forth.

The daily schedule usually follows a set plan:

7:00	Get up
7:05 - 7:20	Exercises
7:20 - 7:50	Clean room and dress for breakfast
7:50 - 8:00	Parade and raising of flag
8:00 - 8:30	Breakfast
8:30 - 9:00	Free time
9:00 -10:30	Work in art, nature, technical clubs
10:30 -12:00	Sun bathe, swimming, sports
12:00 -13:00	Free time

13:00 -14:00	Dinner (the main meal of the day)
14:00 -16:00	Rest
16:00 -16:30	Tea
16:30 -18:30	Socially useful labor, games, competitions
18:30 -19:30	Free time
19:30 -20:00	Supper
20:00 -21:30	Club activities, campfire, entertainment
21:30 -21:40	Parade and lowering of flag
21:40 -22:00	Get ready for bed
22:00	Lights out and sleep

The campfire is a Pioneer tradition as well as a favorite nighttime activity at camp.

Most of the directors we talked with said they had very little trouble with discipline since the tone of the camp is set by the peer group itself. One year several boys were sent home from the camp at Alushta because they destroyed some trees; the *druzhina* council decided on the punishment, after listening to the excuses the boys gave and finding them inadequate.

I came across a story in a children's magazine about a "Pioneer Camp Princess" named Lidusha. In typical manner, the story attempts to discourage undesirable behavior that falls short of being truly bad. Everyone thought

Lidusha a little odd. She was twelve years old but afraid of storms, afraid of worms and frogs, and afraid of water, too. One day when she was sitting on the bank of a stream, another camper pushed her in. The water was not deep, but Lidusha coughed and coughed and seemed terribly frightened.

The other girls teased her quite a bit. When Lidusha, proud of catching a tiny fish, put it in a can under her bed and fed it every day, the girls threw out the fish and substituted a frog, which scared Lidusha so badly that she started screaming. On Parent's Day Lidusha begged her mother to take her home.

"Lidusha, my one and only," her mother said, "you really don't like it? You see how fine it is. What air! The birds sing and there are so many games! It is real happiness to be in such a camp." Lidusha did not tell her mother about the tricks the girls played on her, and she stayed in the camp.

All the girls were in love with a certain Pioneer leader named Yasha. He had been a sailor and now was a student in a teacher's college and a Pioneer camp leader for the summer. Lidusha was in love with Yasha, too, and she scratched his name on her arm with a piece of glass.

At night around the campfire, Yasha told the children stories of noble knights who defended the weak and punished evil people. The children particularly liked the story about a knight who saved a princess from an evil sorceress who had turned the princess into a homely girl. When the knight saved her, the girl turned into the beautiful princess she really was.

Lidusha's love for Yasha gave the girls a new idea. They told Lidusha Yasha liked her and wanted her to meet him by the bridge at seven o'clock one night. Lidusha was very excited and put on her best red dress and red slippers. One of the girls who was in on the joke even gave her a red bow for her hair.

The girls told Yasha that someone wanted to see him on the bridge; then they hid under the bridge to see what would happen. Lidusha came first, proud, in her red dress. When Yasha arrived, he was surprised to see Lidusha, "Why are you here?"

As Lidusha stammered in embarrassment, the other children jumped out from under the bridge laughing. Stepping back quickly, Lidusha fell off of the bridge. Yasha jumped down after Lidusha and lifted her out of the water, wiping her face and arms with her handkerchief. "Beasts," he shouted to the other children. "March back to camp."

That night Lidusha was not at the campfire. Yasha sent for her, but Lidusha would not come. So Yasha went to get Lidusha himself, gave her a seat next to him at the campfire, and sang some sea songs especially for her. After that Yasha took Lidusha everywhere with him, and all of the girls were envious. Yasha found that Lidusha knew a great many poems, and he encouraged her to recite. Lidusha bloomed. At the end of the camp Lidusha's mother said, "Just look what fresh air and good food can do."

The author ends the story by saying, "We knew that fresh air and good food

were not all. It was just what Lidusha's fairy tale showed: the noble prince, defender of the weak, could not bear injustice."

The son-in-law of a Soviet friend had been a counselor at a Pioneer camp one summer. He slept in the same barrack with the children, and he said they kept him awake all night. There were always two or three boys having a pillow fight, whispering, or arguing with each other. Sometimes they would drop off to sleep with a pillow in mid-air in the sudden way children relax, but then some other boys would wake up and start roughhousing. "I had to drink fifteen cups of coffee a day to keep awake during the day," the young man said. "I was completely exhausted. I don't think I slept more than a few hours all summer." He paused, remembering, then said, "It was the happiest summer of my life."

We saw the joyous anticipation and nervous apprehension of children and parents one day in June as we were crossing Red Square. The square was lined with big tour buses and trucks, and on the sidewalk hundreds of mothers, grandmothers (and a few fathers and grandfathers), and children were surrounded by suitcases, bags, boxes, and sports equipment. I tried to talk to a few mothers and children, but they were too preoccupied with the task at hand. "Now don't forget to write to us," one mother said. A child suddenly slapped his forehead, "I forgot my Keds." His mother ran in to GUM (the State Depart-

ment Store) to call the child's grandmother: "If she can get a taxi, she can bring your Keds before the bus leaves." A few children were tearful, but most were smiling, delighted and excited; some affected sophistication and pulled away from clinging mothers. It was a typical scene of "Going Away to Camp."

There are a number of camps around Moscow as well as some day camps in the city itself. Dawn Camp, about twenty-five miles from Moscow, is run by an oil industry union and takes children from Siberian oil fields as well as children from Moscow whose parents work for the oil ministry or in research institutes for the oil industry.

Artek and Orlyonok are called Pioneer "republics" and are on a slightly higher level than the ordinary Pioneer camp. A third major camp, called *Okean* (Ocean) was started in the late 1970s on the Pacific Ocean, near Vladivostok. Okean was designed by the Leningrad Zone Scientific-Research Institute of Experimental Planning, which also designed Orlyonok. Planned to be finished by 1980, Okean will have two *druzhinas*, called Brigantine and Sail. Komsomol members have answered the call for help and gone in great numbers to construct the camp for Pioneers. Some of these workers had experience; some had none. The slogan was for those with experience to "Teach a comrade."

Suddenly one day a group of Pioneers from the neighboring Pioneer camp, *Yunga* (Ship's Boy), appeared and said they wanted to help the Komsomols build the new camp, and soon after that another delegation also wanted to help.

This kind of socially useful labor is encouraged in all camps, especially on what is called the Third Shift, which has many older children, some of Komsomol age. It is hoped that these older children will volunteer to go to neighboring collective farms and help the farmers for several hours a day. Experience has shown that when the children are told to help they often do so grudgingly, and the whole experiment seems a failure. But if the *druzhina* council decides independently to help with the work, and especially if they take on a particular project, like building a playing field, the children are glad to work and just as gladly contribute their earnings toward the playing field's construction. One teacher said it was like planting rye or millet. If you planted rye, you didn't expect millet to come up, so you had to "sow" the children's minds psychologically to get the crop you wanted.

The Central Committee of the Communist Party has instructed the union-republic Communist Party central committees, the territory and province Party committees, the Central Council of Trade Unions, the Komsomol Central Committee, the Ministry of Education, the Ministry of Public Health, the Council of Ministers Committee on Physical Culture and Sports, the Ministry of Culture, the Ministry of Trade, and the Central Union of Consumers Cooperatives, to improve the selection of counselors, physicians, physical education instructors, cooks, and other workers in Pioneer camps.

With all these bodies interested in the education of the Soviet child at camp, the children are assured of concerned care. In turn, each child is expected to be a well-rounded personality with politically oriented ideas. Because the child is in camp a comparatively short time and is cut off from his usual sources of information, such as newspapers, radio, television and the dinner table conversation of his family, there are special political information sessions at camp.

The camp library has newspapers and magazines, but the camp leaders do not rely on the child seeking them out. Important local, Soviet, or world news is broadcast over the camp radio or explained at the morning or evening parade. A Program of Peace in Action is discussed on June 22, the day the Soviets entered World War II. Relations between France and the Soviet Union are discussed on July 14, France's national holiday. The children hear stories of the fall of the Bastille, the Paris Commune, and other French events. Five-year plans are discussed on July 2 (Day of Metallurgists) and August 25 (Miner's Day).

Other themes are taken from newspapers and magazines: "Komsomols fulfill the decisions of the Komsomol congress." "Happy is the person who lives in the Soviet century" [In Russian *person* (*chelovek*) and *century* (*vek*) rhyme]. "Live not as you like but according to your country's needs"; "Victory in work strengthens peace"; and "Peace and Solidarity."

"Peace and Solidarity" was a particular theme in the summer of 1978 before the Eleventh World Festival of Youth and Students, held in Havana, Cuba.

12

The KIDS in Havana

For months Pioneer members of the Club of International Friendship, KID, had been writing letters to each other from all over the world. They were excited about the Eleventh World Festival of Youth and Students, to be held in Havana, Cuba, from July 28 to August 6, 1978. The Soviet children's press was full of articles about worldwide preparations for the festival, and there were even occasional articles about it in *Pravda* and *Izvestiya*.

The January 1978 issue of *Pioner* featured the symbol of the festival—a flower surrounded by concentric circles around a globe of the world—on its cover and contained several articles about the festival, including a story entitled "Buenas Días, Ricardo" and a letter from the head of the Pioneer Council of Cuba saying, "Welcome, our hearts are open to you."

"I want to go, too," I said.

"Since you are neither Cuban nor Communist, and, more particularly, not a youth, I don't think you should get your heart set on it," my husband said.

I called the travel agent in New York who handles our Soviet trips. "You have to talk to the American preparatory committee," he said, giving me a New York telephone number. I called the number repeatedly but kept getting either a busy signal or no answer. Again I appealed to my travel agent, who gave me a new number to call.

This time there was an answer on the first ring. "Yes," a lady said. She was in charge of selecting delegates from the United States for the conference. She had hundreds and hundreds of applications, and the number of delegates was limited. Delegates had to be between ten and thirty-five years of age and represent some organization in the United States. "No," she said, with some asperity, they were not all Communist organizations. She wanted a representative assortment of American delegates. No, they did not accept observers.

"Could we go as press?" I suggested, telling her about my previous book, *Lenin's Grandchildren* and my proposed book on the Pioneers, for which my husband was the official photographer.

"It's possible," she said. "I'll send you a press application blank."

In January my husband and I sent in the application. In February I called to see if we had been accepted. "The proposed press list has to be approved in Havana," I was told. I called again in March, April, May, and June. "The press list has been sent to Havana for approval," I was told. "Are we on it?" I asked. "You are on it," the woman said, promising nothing more.

In July I started calling more often. The preparatory committee telephone was always busy. The only way to reach them was to call systematically every five minutes all day long. If I was lucky I got through by late afternoon. The people who answered sounded harried, exhausted, and confused. "We'll let you know as soon as we hear anything," they said. "No, none of the press have been accepted yet."

On Thursday, July 20, the preparatory committee called me. "Can you leave for Havana on Saturday, July 22?" I had planned a dinner party for Saturday, but, remembering Chairman Mao's statement that "a Revolution is not a dinner party," I didn't mention it. "Yes, we can go Saturday," I said. I was told to pick up our visas at the Czechoslovakian Embassy in Washington (Cuba is not recognized by the United States). We then had to fly to Montreal, where an Air Cubana flight would be waiting to take us to Havana. "Bring cash," I was told. "Cuba does not take personal checks or U.S. traveler's checks."

At the Czech Embassy I learned that Cuba now had its own building, and visas were issued there. The Cuban Mission was a new, modern building with a locked door and a guard outside. Inside I found a room full of people, all talking excitedly in Spanish. There was a festival poster on the wall bearing the now familiar flower symbol of converging worlds around a central globe. I was given our visas and a copy of the Constitution of Cuba. "Take cash," the visa man reminded me. "Your hotel will be the Havana Libre."

On Saturday morning we set out. We had no airplane tickets from Montreal, no confirmation of hotel in Havana, no registration slip for the festival. The smog was so thick in Washington we could hardly see the sun. "My son thinks the world will end by the year 2000," our taxi driver said gloomily, adding, "My son won't go to church either."

At the Washington airport we saw a group of very unattractive young people, all of whom seemed to know each other. "Are these our fellow travelers?" we wondered, feeling relieved when they all got off the plane in New York. In Montreal we had to transfer to Mirobel Airport, and only one other person from our plane got on the bus with us. He was a pleasant looking young black man with a moustache and beard. "Going to Havana?" he asked, introducing himself as Tom Allen, a college dean from the Midwest; he had been a delegate to the Tenth World Festival held five years before in East Germany. "I'm thirty-six now," Tom said, "too old to be a delegate, so I'm writing an article for a magazine about the festival."

Someone from the preparatory committee was supposed to meet us at the airport and sell us our tickets to Havana, but there was no sign of any such person. One by one, other people appeared, also looking for their tickets to Havana. These included a group of bright attractive young people who said they were activists who had not been accepted as delegates but who had managed to get a sightseeing tour to Havana so that they could observe the festival at any rate. "I'm not going to Havana to lie on a beach," one said. "I can do that in California where I live."

We all watched nervously for the person from the preparatory committee, rushing up to several people we thought looked official, only to find they had never heard of the festival. Finally Tom said, "There they are," and we joined a crowd around a woman who was handing out airplane tickets, taking U.S. money in exchange. Our bags were checked, and we got on the plane—a brand-new-looking Russian-made Ilushin 62M. The pilot, who had a Russian accent, explained our flight plan as we took off smoothly.

We had a pleasant flight to the José Marti International Airport in Havana. The customs and immigration people were courteous, friendly, and relaxed. We apparently did not have some paper we were supposed to have (not knowing Spanish, I wasn't sure what it was they were talking about), but we were given a blank paper to fill out and then waved through like old friends. A young man asked if we were the Weavers and said he was Olban Santana and would take us to our hotel and be our guide during our stay. We loaded our luggage into a small bus, already occupied by a cameraman from Argentina who was surrounded by huge wooden crates of camera equipment. Tom Allen also came with us.

The Havana Libre turned out to be the former Havana Hilton. When we got into the elevator the operator, a friendly middle-aged woman, shook hands with us, and the bell boy who took our bags refused the proffered tip. My husband patted him on the arm in thanks, and he laughed appreciatively. Our room was comfortable, with a balcony overlooking the harbor and Morro Castle bathed in pale, luminous light, like a fairy tale castle. A soft breeze blew into our room through the open sliding glass doors, but such luxuries as bedspreads, soft pillows, and air conditioning had either been used up or dispensed with.

From our balcony we could see neon signs that said, "Youth of the World, Cuba is your home." The tall building next door lit up with a big arm and fist alternating with the slogan, "Workers of the World Unite!"

The next morning we met Tom in the lobby, and the three of us walked out into the sunshine of Havana. The sidewalks were strewn with pink and white blossoms which dropped from plumeria trees, while overhead were the flaming red flowers of the flamboyant. Yellow alamanda vines climbed around doorways of large, once elaborate facades, and there were sea grape trees, banyans, and palm trees rustling in the constant breeze. Everywhere streets and houses were decorated with brightly colored bunting and the globes of the festival.

On one street corner we saw two young Cuban Pioneer girls watching critically as the policeman directing traffic left the center of the street to speak to a friend on the sidewalk. "Comrade!" one girl called out in Spanish. "Comrade!" The policeman looked around at the ten-year-old who was addressing him with such authority. "You, comrade," the girl said, "get back to your post."

"A police state," Tom laughed, as we watched the policeman go back to directing traffic, while the two little girls walked on down the street with a satisfied air.

"What were the other U.S. delegates like at the Tenth Festival?" I asked Tom.

"Some arrived thinking everything about Communism was terrible and didn't change their minds. Some came thinking everything about Communism was perfect and didn't change *their* minds," Tom said. "Then there were a lot of us who came with open minds to see what we could learn. Communism is not a simple subject."

As we were walking back to the hotel, our guide, Olban, came running out to meet us. "I've arranged for you to see a Pioneer camp this afternoon," he announced. The lobby continued to fill up with people—blacks wearing blue tee shirts with a map of South Africa in white on the front, young Americans with red buttons that said, "Stop SWAT," or "End the Blockade," and more blacks with "Get out of South Africa" printed on their shirts—a very international melange of people.

We took a taxi to the José Martí Pioneer Camp at Tarara, ten or fifteen miles outside of Havana on the beach. The camp had a huge complex of central buildings surrounded by what looked like a resort subdivision of expensive Spanish-style houses, some with swimming pools. Olban said the houses had previously been owned by rich people, including rich Americans, but the state had taken them over, and now the houses were used as dormitories for the children. A central plaza contained a large fountain with an inscription running around its four sides:

Para los niños trabajamos
Porque los niños son los que saben querer
Porque los niños son la esperanza del mundo
Asi queremos que los niños de America sean

For the children we work
Because it is the children who know how to love
Because the children are the hope of the world
And this is the way we want the children of America to be

The children who were the hope of the world were lining up even now in the square to practice their marches for the festival. All of the children who passed us waved in friendly fashion and smiled their greetings; even those running to catch up with their brigade managed a quick wave to us. We watched for a while as the sun beat down. A sudden hard shower began across the street, a quick tropical curtain of rain that did not disturb the sun on our side of the street, and was soon over. Huge black clouds continued to dominate the sky, and I suggested we go inside.

A guide from the camp showed us around the special camps for asthmatics and diabetics. We talked to the doctors in the clinic, who said they felt that asthma attacks were in large part caused by family overprotectiveness and that in camp the child had an opportunity to get away from his family as well as to receive treatment. Five hundred fifty children, age six to ten, attend every three weeks. A staff of three doctors and four nurses, aided by a physical education teacher and one instructor for each group of fifteen children, look after the children, teaching them special breathing exercises to enable them to control their asthma. I recalled the severe asthmatic attacks Che Guevara had suffered during his lifetime and wondered if a program like this might have changed Che's life and, thereby, the course of the Cuban Revolution.

We visited some of the dormitories and drove past the "bastistiana" mansions, now stripped of their luxurious furnishings and filled with double-decker beds for the children. A large open-air amphitheater overlooked a lake where hundreds of children were swimming, boating, and diving. Across the lake was an amusement park with all sorts of rides, including a ferris wheel and an aerial tramway. Our guide told us the camp accommodated 21,000 children.

On the way back to Havana our taxi driver said his daughter was at the camp now—her second visit—and she was very happy there. They had a problem with the Pioneers, though, he said. Previously the Pioneers stopped with the sixth grade, but recently it had been extended to children in the seventh to ninth grades. "The seventh graders feel it's too babyish an organization for them," the driver said, adding, "Fidel is always after them to be neater in their dress, too. He says they should tuck their shirttails in and their ties shouldn't clash with the color of their uniforms."

Fidel. Fidel. Everywhere we heard that name, as though Fidel were the boy next door—a popular boy next door, but not someone anyone was in awe of. The newspaper, *Granma*, also spoke of Fidel with the same easy familiarity.

In the evening we walked along Malecon Drive by the sea and watched the carnival stands going up; one of the press releases I read said, "If you haven't been to Cuba you haven't seen a carnival." The whole city was preparing for a gigantic carnival. A few amusement centers were already set up.

Several stands featured a larger-than-life figure in top hat and tails with a sign over it saying "Smash the Imperialists." A few people were already throwing hardballs at one of these figures, but they stepped aside pleasantly and smiled at us, showing no hard feelings that we were probably imperialists, too.

July 26 was the twenty-fifth anniversary of the attack on Moncado, the forerunner of the Cuban Revolution. Olban told us that the press center was running a tour to Santiago de Cuba for the celebration of the anniversary. The trip would cost one hundred dollars apiece, and we would have to sit up all night on the train, spend all day in Santiago, then take the night train back. We thought we would be too tired to enjoy it, and when Olban said we could

watch the whole thing on the television set in the lobby of the Havana Libre or on the sets in the press center we decided to stay in Havana.

The press center, a huge room on the ground floor of the Havana Libre, was well supplied with banks of typewriters for the use of correspondents, international telephone lines for calls, and information centers with piles of newspapers, press releases, magazines, and books about all phases of the festival. A special newspaper, *Festival Informa*, began publication on July 26, and there were also the regular editions of *Juventud Rebelde* and *Granma* (named after the yacht, that Fidel, Che, and other revolutionaries took from Mexico to Cuba, which now resides in a glass case in a Havana park). I gathered a pile of literature and read about Castro's attack on the army barracks at Moncado in 1953.

As We See Moncado, an attractive hardcover book with illustrations and text by children, gave a child's eye view of the revolution, beginning with the "poet, journalist, and revolutionary intellectual" José Martí (1853-95), who "planted revolutionary ideas in the minds of the Cubans." José Martí, Cuba's national hero, was a poet and essayist who died in battle, fighting for Cuba's independence from Spain. Many buildings, squares, schools, and other public places throughout Cuba bear his name.

Santiago had been in the midst of carnival as Fidel and his friends planned their attack on Moncado. Julia Castro, age seven, one of the authors of *As We See Moncado*, drew a picture of a farmhouse where the revolutionists' weapons were kept, weapons that "were going to be used to get rid of the bad rulers and the imperialist Yankees that there were in Cuba."

I continued the story in a small booklet on Abel Santa Maria. Abel's sister, Haydee, recalled her first meeting with Fidel when Abel brought him to her house. "I had just cleaned up, and he was walking around dropping ashes on the floor. I thought to myself, 'He's going to muck up the whole place, this fellow.' " Haydee was to see much more of "this fellow" because she and her brother joined the revolutionaries.

The attack on Moncado was a failure. Abel, second in command to Fidel, was captured, tortured, and killed, and Fidel was sent to prison. At his trial he made his famous "History will absolve me" speech. All of the journalists received a handsome hardcover edition of Fidel's speech, illustrated with black-and-white photographs. I looked with interest at an early picture of Fidel, his chin pressed down toward his chest so that a fold of neck seemed to give him a double chin. There was only a stubble of shadow on his chin and upper lip, where the luxurious beard would later appear.

There was a crowd around the television in the lobby of the Havana Libre when Fidel made his 1978 speech at Santiago. "This is the twenty-fifth time we have commemorated the 26th of July 1953: in prison, in exile, in the mountains, and in our homeland liberated with the weapons that began the battle anew," Fidel began to applause in Santiago and more applause in the lobby of the Havana Libre. It was a long speech. Fidel spoke of the U.S. blockade, of CIA plots to kill him, and of diseases and plagues introduced into Cuba by the "imperialists." He told of how the Soviet Union had helped Cuba and how Cuba had helped Angola. "Being internationalist is one way of paying our debt to mankind," he said. There was general cheering in the lobby as the speech ended.

On Friday, July 28, we went to our first press conference held in a big committee room of the hotel. Allen Gresh from the International Preparatory Committee gave a few statistics on the festival—18,500 delegates would attend, representing 2,000 organizations from 145 countries, and special guests, journalists, and so forth brought the total number of visitors to 25,500. Gresh told of the months of preparation, the meetings between the local preparatory committees and the international committee, the raising of funds, the face-lifting of Havana, and the cooperation of youth throughout the world. Ethiopia, Western Sahara, Timor, and Angola were among the countries attending a festival for the first time; Cambodia, which had been invited to come, did not reply to the invitation.

At the press center I picked up a brochure on the first ten youth festivals. The idea of holding regular festivals originated in 1945, at the First World Congress of Youth in London. The first festival, held in Prague in 1947, was a "manifestation of the young, progressive generation of the world for peace, peaceful coexistence, democracy, social progress, friendship, and active solidarity of young people. Therefore, they are synonymously against imperialism, colonialism and neo-colonialism, all forms of fascism, racism and oppression, and exploitation." I learned from the brochure that the largest organizers of the festival were the World Federation of Democratic Youth, based in Budapest, and the International Union of Students, based in Prague. Delegates came to the Prague festival from seventy-one countries and helped to rebuild the town of Lidice, destroyed by the Nazis.

The second festival was originally scheduled for Paris, but the French government refused permission, and the festival was held in Budapest in 1949. The third festival in Berlin in 1951, met with similar opposition, with some capitalist countries forbidding their youth to attend and blocking transit through their countries. The French sailor, Henri Martin, sent to prison because he refused to fight in the war against Vietnam, was the hero of the fourth festival in Bucharest in 1953. At the fifth festival, in Warsaw in 1955, delegates demonstrated against the atom bomb on the anniversary of the dropping of the bomb on Hiroshima. Paul Robeson was the outstanding guest at the sixth festival in Moscow in 1957, which set a record of 34,000 foreign delegates from 137 countries. The seventh festival, in Vienna in 1959, also met with opposition from the right. The eighth festival, in Helsinki in 1962, honored the first cosmonaut, Yuri Gagarin, and the ninth festival, in Sofia in 1968, welcomed cosmonauts Valentina Tereshkova and Alexei Leonov. The tenth festival, in Berlin in 1973, had 25,000 delegates from 140 countries, with the broadest representation of all types of political, philosophical, and religious views.

The Cuban festival was the first to be held in the Western hemisphere. Among the honored guests were Yassar Arafat, Harry Belafonte, and Hortense Allende, sister of the late Marxist president of Chile. There were 2,000 Cuban delegates, 1,000 from the Soviet Union, 750 from East Germany, 350 from West Germany, 650 from France, 500 from Italy, and 450 from the United States, among others.

The official opening of the festival was to take place at the Latin American Stadium in Havana on July 28, and at 3 o'clock that afternoon we set out in a fully loaded bus. We went two blocks and stopped, as bus after bus converged along the same route. The Cuban sun beat down on us in the packed bus. We would move one inch, then stop, move one more inch and stop. Finally, we did not move even the inch.

The drive to the stadium, normally a fifteen-minute ride, took us a little over an hour. We poured into the stadium with thousands of others and had just gotten settled in our grandstand seats (under cover) when torrents of rain descended. The card section of bleachers across from us had no cover and were drenched, but they shouted, "Hoo-rah! Hoo-rah!" and flashed their cards in the symbol of the festival, spelling out the words *Eleventh Festival*, and then flashed "Viva, Viva!" on yellow cards. Fifty grounds attendants in yellow slickers dragged a huge tarpaulin over the field as the rain gathered puddles and ponds in the tarp.

People were still coming in, and the stands next to us were filling up. One African delegation wore dark blue serge suits, with coats and ties and vests in the humid heat. They occasionally mopped black brows with handkerchiefs. There was constant movement in and out, with people going for drinks in paper cups and paper-wrapped sandwiches. "Wa wa wa tsunga," one group in the stands chanted, and an Angolan group next to us shouted, "Cuba! Angola! We're the best friends! Cuba! Angola! We're the best friends."

The rain stopped, and the fifty grounds attendants began squeegeeing the water off the canvas cover, though there was already a river of water around the edges of the field. They had just removed the cover, billowing it up with rhythmic movements, when another hard rain descended, and they scrambled to put it back again. At 5:30 they took up the tarpaulin again and began another mop up.

By 6 PM everyone was singing *Guantanamera*, a Cuban song we heard everywhere. The grounds attendants were smoothing down squares of artificial green grass on the field. Some of the African delegations were beating drums. At 6, twenty-six men in blue pants and white T-shirts with a red border around the neck, marched out into the field. There was a sudden rustling in the stands as the crowd stood up. "Fidel! Fidel! Fidel!" There was wild applause. The sun broke through the clouds for the first time as Fidel and his party took their places.

The National Army Band marched in with the festival flag and pictures of Fidel, followed by the groups of delegates in alphabetical order—Afghanistan, South Africa, Angola (great unanimous applause), Arelia, Argentina, Australia, Austria. Each delegation was dressed distinctively, carrying banners proclaiming various slogans. Still they came—Burundi (native dancers), Guinea (more native dancers), Canada ("Ban the Bomb"), India, Iran, Italy (raised fist salute), Jamaica, Japan, Mali (an acrobatic troupe), Oman, Palestine (steady, thunderous ovation from the crowd), Senegal, Sri Lanka, Sudan, Sweden, Switzerland, Surinam, Timor, Togo (another raised fist salute), USSR (more thunderous applause from the crowd), United States ("U.S. Solidarity with Cuba," "Just Peace in the Middle East," "National Rights of the Palestine People"), and finally Yemen, Yugoslavia, Zambia, and Zimbabwe.

Many of the African delegates wore grass skirts and carried spears as their ankle-braceleted legs gyrated in war dances. The African spectators in the stands declared their solidarity with much clapping and chanting. As each delegation finished a round of the stadium, they marched to the center of the field, their native flags waving, until all were assembled. The Cuban delegation, as host, was the last to march into the stadium. The band played the Cuban national anthem, which was sung by a 9,200-voice choir, as the card section flashed "Cuba '78" and remarkably artistic pictures of Marti, Gomez, Maceo, Mella, Camilo, and Guevara.

Eight young people from the East German site of the previous festival presented eight Cuban delegates with the festival flag, which was run up a flagpole at one side of the field while the band played the mambi Reveille. Then East German athlete Renata Stecher handed Cuban Olympic champion Albert Juantorena the torch to light the festival flame. Juantorena raced up the steps of the stadium to applause that was the equal of that accorded Fidel.

The program began with a reading of salutations from Leonid Brezhnev and other world leaders, including Erich Honecker (East Germany), Todor Zhikov

(Bulgaria), Gustav Husak (Czechoslovakia), Edward Gierek (Poland), Janos Kadar (Hungary), Yu Tsedenbal (Mongolia), and Mengistu Haile Mariam (Ethiopia). Allen Gresh, coordinating secretary of the International Preparatory Committee, gave the opening address, followed by a speech from General of the Army Raúl Castro (Fidel's brother).

Next came a remarkable gynmastic and sports display in which 10,000 gymnasts, the 4,560 members of the card section, the 2,000-voice choir, 500 musicians, and 60 guitarists took part on the theme "For Anti-Imperialist Solidarity, Peace, and Friendship."

The prologue was acted by 1,200 boys five years old and younger from day-care centers and 1,200 young men from military schools. The little ones did calisthenics and pantomime to the Granma March and sang, "I Want to Be an Athlete" and "The Children's Song."

Scene followed scene: "The Same Sun Shines on All of Us," by 1,472 women students of the schools for day-care education and the José Martí Teacher Training School; "Victory Lies in Unity," with 1,296 military school students; "Peace," with 1,470 students from the President Salvador Allende Teacher Training School; "The Future Is Peace," with 972 children from sports schools; "We're Part of the Great Family of Humankind," with 1,280 students from the Lenin Vocational School; and finally the "Song to Friendship" and "The Anthem of Youth," sung by everyone in the stadium as fireworks exploded into the night.

We got home at 11:30 PM, nine hours after we had set out. We went to bed, but the young festival delegates, who had formed a huge conga line as they danced out of the stadium, now spread out in the streets of Havana to dance the rest of the night. I think anyone, anywhere in the world, would have called it a successful day.

The official program of the festival listed over one hundred activities for Saturday, July 29, the first full day of the conference. Outside the hotel there were row after row of big buses to take the press to the activity of each correspondent's choice. We were torn among a number of the morning's events: Solidarity with the Youth of South Africa, Namibia, and Zimbabwe "for National Independence against the Maneuvers of Imperialism and for the Total Liquidation of Racist Regimes," which took place at the Andrés Lujan Plant; "Struggles of Youth in Capitalist Countries," meeting at the Central Organization of Cuban Trade Unions; talks on "Children's Rights" at the José Martí Pioneer Camp; or a tour of Havana to see the "Achievements of the Revolution."

We chose the tour of Havana and went to look for our bus. We finally settled in the right bus, after choosing two that were going to other destinations. We felt a moment of doubt when we saw only a handful of passengers on our bus; evidently we had not chosen a popular event. We reached the José Martí Plaza de Revolucion in a few minutes, but there was no connecting bus—just a large deserted square with the towering marble José Martí monument in the center and huge portraits of Martí, Marx, Engels, and Lenin on one building and portraits of Che Guevara and Fidel Castro on another. The bus driver and

Olban ran around the square trying to find our connecting bus, but after an hour of waiting and looking they decided we should return to the hotel. Back at the hotel, our little group huddled together in the lobby, still hoping for a tour, but at 11:30 Olban reported sadly that there would be no trip today. He was so apologetic that we did not complain. At lunch we saw Tom and others who said their morning had been abortive as well. Each one of us thought the other members of the press had seen something fascinating until we compared notes.

"I think Communist festivals are like American Bar Association meetings or any other large convention," my husband said. "There is a small in-group of people who attend meetings only if they are the featured speakers. They are busy deciding among themselves who the next officers will be and entertaining and being entertained by each other. Then there's a slightly larger group that is trying to get in the in-group. They don't go to convention meetings either. They watch the in-group, and some information filters down to them. Then there is a group that cares nothing about any of the convention—they came for the drinking and dancing and are bent on having a good time, which they do. The largest group consists of people like us, the well-meaning and good-intentioned, who don't know what is going on. They're never on the right bus, miss the exciting events, and feel very insignificant."

My husband's remarks gave me an idea. I had listened carefully in the lobby, in the elevators, and halls for the sound of Russian and was not long in hearing it. "Do you know where the Russian delegation is staying?" I asked one Russian speaker but got no answer. I checked at the information desk, where the attendants were extremely friendly. "Come back later," they said. When I came back later they were still friendly, but they also still didn't know the answers.

I had noticed at the opening that Soviet journalists wore bright pink shirts (later I found they alternated the pink shirts with yellow or green ones). In the hotel I heard one striking blonde woman speaking Russian with various pink-shirted men, and I decided I would follow her.

After lunch Blondinka (the Russian name for a blonde) went up to the information desk in the lobby. "Where is the Soviet delegates club?" she asked. The same woman who had told me to come back later when I asked that question was just as friendly to Blondinka. But again she replied, "Come back later."

Blondinka consulted with some of the pink-shirted journalists, and though I stood as close as possible I could not hear what they said. I followed Blondinka into the press room, then out onto the sidewalk in front of the hotel, where she approached several bus drivers. "Where is the Soviet Club?" I listened, but the answers did not seem definitive. "Come on," my husband complained. "We can't follow them around all day."

Blondinka and her friends got on a bus and I followed; my husband and Olban followed me. The bus started up with just the Soviet group and us on

board. We drove across town to Ninety-Second Street, where the bus turned in to an impressive array of buildings. In the curving driveway were a group of very, very blonde girls in Russian native costume and some boys in Russian boots and Cossack uniforms. One girl carried a large platter with a loaf of bread on it, and another had a bowl of salt—the traditional welcome of bread and salt. Blondinka began to take pictures, rearranging the entire ensemble. "Young lady," she called to one girl in costume, "stand over here where I can take your picture." She was very intent on what she was doing, very interested in everything. In a few minutes another delegation drove up, and the ceremony began. The visitors were given bread and salt; then they watched as the girls and boys danced.

After the dance we all went inside, the three of us following the crowd up a stairway and into a meeting hall. The meeting began with a standing ovation to Fidel Castro, as everyone shouted "Viva Fidel! Viva Fidel!" Then the chairman proclaimed new victories for Cuba and the Soviet Union and friendship between the youth of the two countries; the crowd roared, "*Druzhba! Amistad!*" (*friendship* in Russian and Spanish).

Olban identified the people on the platform for us: Orlando Dominquez, secretary of the Cuban Young Communist League; B. N. Pastukhov, first secretary of the Central Committee of the Komsomol (successor to Tyazhelnikov, whom we had met in Moscow); a Soviet poet; a Soviet composer; a Soviet pilot; and a man from the Soviet Academy of Sciences who said that science was a natural base for Communism.

As various speakers talked of the important role the Soviet Union played in the political world of the Cuban people, my husband slipped out of the hall to take pictures. When the meeting was over, he said, "This is a very capitalistic set-up they have here. It's really luxurious. It must have been a fashionable yacht club before the revolution."

We looked around at the swimming pools, the beautiful harbor, and the pleasant rooms and terraces, so fascinated that we did not notice that Blondinka and her friends had left. We had no transportation back to the hotel. Olban said we could walk to a bus stop, but it was very hot and we had no idea how far we might have to walk.

I noticed a Soviet jeep parked near the Club, and suggested that Olban ask the driver if he would take us back to the hotel.

Olban was horrified: "That's a Soviet soldier."

"I know it," I said. "But he doesn't seem to have anything to do, and he wouldn't shoot us just for asking."

"I couldn't ask him," Olban said, trying to make himself small, as though the Soviet soldier could hear what we were saying.

I walked over to the soldier and said, "Hello," in Russian. He immediately began to smile, and when I asked him about taking us to the hotel he said he would be delighted.

Olban and my husband got in the jeep rather timidly, but by the time we got to the hotel my husband had recovered enough to take my picture getting out of the jeep. When the first picture didn't turn out, I got back in the jeep and out again for another picture. We thanked the driver in Russian, and he waved back saying he had enjoyed it.

We never did understand the festival bus system, but the drivers were extremely friendly and accommodating and would drive several miles out of their way to show us something we wanted to see. We learned to take a taxi when we really wanted to get to a particular place. Taxis were scarce and had to be ordered far in advance. They also separated the expense account press from the non-expense account press, as the latter could not afford taxis.

Most of the meetings were late getting started, and we often felt frustrated that we had gone to a dull meeting and missed a fascinating one.

Due to jet lag, dancing all night, and the general peaceful atmosphere of the conference, many of the delegates slept soundly through the meetings, and at least one panel member did the same. "I've heard it all before," one American Communist party member told us, although he seemed fascinated with the Higher Institute of Art and attended meetings there everyday. "What's there?" I asked, and he said, "Free lunch and free beer."

Because of our interest in the Pioneers, we spent a good bit of time at the José Martí Pioneer Camp, which focused on the rights of children. The speakers said there were two basic rights of children:

1. The right to live. Sixty percent of the casualties in the Vietnam War were children. War must be stopped and the neutron bomb banned. The money the world spends on arms should be used instead to help the more than 8 million children in the world who suffer from malnutrition and poor living conditions. In some countries more than half of the children die before they are five years old.
2. The right to education. Millions of children between ages six and eleven are not in school. The speaker said that 2.5 million disadvantaged children in the United States did not attend school.

On August 4 one of the most significant events of the conference, the proclamation of the Cuban Code on Youth and Children, took place at José Martí Pioneer Camp (renamed J. M. Pioneer City in July 1978).

The code was adopted by the National Assembly of People's Power on June 28, and went into effect on August 4. It is a comprehensive document providing for the rights and responsibilities of Cuban youth in the formation of a Communist personality. Article 102 specifies that children from the first through the ninth grade may voluntarily join the José Martí Pioneer Organization, "whose basic objective is to introduce them to social tasks and activities that contribute to this Communist formation."

The children had been practicing for weeks the marches, re-enactments of Moncado and other revolutionary battles, songs, dances, and galas that took place at the ceremony. Fidel appeared, like a revolutionary Pied Piper with swarms of children clinging to each arm. "Fidel shouldn't criticize the children for not tucking their shirttails in," my husband said. "Look at his trousers."

One pants leg of the olive uniform was neatly tucked into a boot top, but the other flopped loose, giving Fidel a rakish air. There were shouts of "Fidel! Fidel!" as he passed through the crowd, and more children ran out to grasp his hand or touch his arm. There did not seem to be very much security, although one American girl told us that when Fidel popped up at another festival meeting the security had been very tight. Here he was on home ground, and the children loved him.

The renaming of the Isle of Pines to the Isle of Youth was another important youth event during the festival. Discovered by Columbus in 1494, the Isle of Pines had been inhabited by Spaniards, some of whom farmed, though many were smugglers. By the nineteenth century the Isle of Pines was used mainly as a prison, where political prisoners were indiscriminately mixed with criminals. José Martí himself was imprisoned there at age seventeen, and twentieth-century revolutionaries also spent time there.

Under Batista the Isle of Pines became a duty-free port. The island took on new life after the disastrous Hurricane Alma in 1966. Young people were asked to come to the island to "transform adversity into victory." New schools combining study and work, based on the principles of Marx and Martí, were formed for the children who came from all over Cuba and the more than two thousand students from Angola, Mozambique, and Ethiopia. The so-called model prisons were turned into "model" schools, and the "new pines" (as Martí referred to the children) were planted on this island.

Education still presented important difficulties in many countries, we found when we attended a discussion entitled "Brain Drain" at the International Students Center of the University of Havana.

Over 40 percent of students from African countries who go to Europe for higher study do not return to Africa, one student reported. Those who do return are often ill-equipped to handle local problems. Medical problems studied in capitalist countries are different from those found in underdeveloped countries, and this is also true in engineering, law, and other fields. The best minds of a country are too often drained off because capitalist countries encourage superior students to stay rather than return to their native lands. The delegate concluded that it takes great ideological commitment to give up the riches of a capitalist country and return to a poor native land.

A delegate from India said that 78 percent of the people in India were illiterate and that culture was something only the privileged class could afford. A black from Togo said that for many years religious colonists had denied that there was any native culture at all in Togo, but now the country was busy trying to revive its national traditions.

"Youth Accuses Imperialism" was a daily forum. The day we visited it, young people from Uruguay told of tortures they had endured at the hands of CIA agents. One man claimed he had been a former CIA agent in Cuba and told about attending a CIA training school to learn different forms of interrogation. The graduates of the school, called "technicians," combined sadism and science in their torture.

In spite of the accounts of torture and a realization of enormous problems to be overcome, the mood of the festival was optimistic. I was particularly surprised to find various family members of Allende, Letelier, and other Chilean exiles optimistic about the future. We found, as must have been true for the delegates as well, that the festival allowed us to talk with diverse groups of people and to see a side of the world we would not ordinarily have seen. It also gave us a perspective on the role of the Soviet Union quite different from the one we have in the United States.

13

The Media
and the Arts

The Soviet state publishes 233 Komsomol and Pioneer magazines in twenty-six languages of the Soviet people. These publications have a total circulation of over seventy-five million copies, and, along with radio programs, films, books, and theater, they are designed to instruct Soviet children as well as to entertain.

To be effective, these newspapers and magazines must be read. Therefore the first task of the Soviet teacher is to see that they are read. An article in *Nachalnaya Shkola* (Primary School) from the Academy of Pedagogical Sciences, told how one teacher succeeded in getting the children to read these publications.

At the beginning of the year, only seven students in a third-grade class of twenty-six read children's publications, despite the fact that they were all interested in joining the Pioneers. The teacher began by showing the children the different departments of various magazines and newspapers, reading them a few stories and telling them how to get information from magazines and newspapers. The next morning the children found a copy of *Pionerskaya Pravda*, the Pioneer newspaper, and a list of rules for reading it on each desk.

1. Read a newspaper every day. The newspaper helps you learn about important events in the world and the life of people in the Soviet Union and abroad.
2. Begin by reading the headlines of all the articles. This helps you choose the most important materials.
3. Read each article attentively, observing the main points you can learn.
4. Write down the words you don't understand and learn their meaning.

At least once a week, preferably on a regular day and for ten or fifteen min-minutes at a time, the children read aloud. They are asked to report on the most important political event of the week, a sports event, or some Pioneer activity in order to reinforce their reading habits.

147

When all of the children are able to read independently, they are asked to put their questions in a box, to be answered the following week. The answers are sometimes prepared collectively in the *zvezdochka,* or little star group. In a discussion on the war in Vietnam, one child may say that there was a cease-fire in Vietnam on January 23, and another will add that the war ended on January 27. The teacher feels that her campaign is a success when the children begin a project, such as collecting waste paper, because they have read an article about it in *Pionerskaya Pravda.*

Pionerskaya Pravda is one of a trio of *Pravdas* which includes *Komsomolskaya Pravda* and *Pravda* itself. *Pravda* (Truth) was founded by V. I. Lenin on May 5, 1912, and is the organ of the Central Committee of the Communist Party of the Soviet Union. A similar newspaper, *Izvestiya* (News) is the official government newspaper. The pages of *Pravda* are a little wider than those of the New York *Times* and Washington *Post*, and the paper consists of only six or eight pages of rather small type. The first page is usually devoted to speeches by Brezhnev or other high Party officials and a picture of Brezhnev greeting some foreign dignitary or a workers' delegation.

If Brezhnev has not made a speech or greeted anyone, there are pictures of various workers making hay or operating machines or pictures of Pioneers and Komsomol members at various activities. A column on the left side of the front page discusses moral or political issues, and usually the lower right-hand corner carries small news items on such topics as the price of gold, the rate of unemployment in the United States, or international film festivals under the heading "From the Teletype Tape."

Beginning in January, the arrival of spring in some part of the Soviet Union is also front-page news. Spring plowing has begun in one southern region, apricot trees are blooming in another, and so on. Until spring comes to the whole Soviet Union, there is something about spring on *Pravda*'s front page every day.

Page two has a feature called "Party Life." "Oh, that's like Betty Beale," said a friend of mine, referring to a celebrated Washington society columnist. "No, it's not like Betty Beale," I replied. "This party is the Communist Party."

Articles about the Cold War or the hostages in Iran, columns of advice to parents, articles on Communist morality, and some humorous pieces appear on the inside pages. Before the copyright agreements, Art Buchwald was a favorite columnist, and many of his columns were reprinted intact from American papers.

When I first started reading *Pravda* about fifteen years ago, I had to look up almost every other word in my dictionary. One day the paper had a very touching story about a man who was told that his old hunting dog should be put to sleep. Feeling that it was unfair to his old friend to have the vet do it, the story concerned the man's sorrow at having to shoot his dog. Tears streamed down my face as I laboriously looked up word after word. Now, I glance at the headlines, as the Pioneers are taught to do, and skip a great many articles.

Pravda's back page is probably the most widely read by Soviet readers; it contains the TV, radio, and theater schedules and sports news. Like newspapers everywhere, *Pravda* is also used to wrap things in, to make paper hats, to sit on, and to hold over one's head to ward off sun and rain.

Komsomolskaya Pravda, founded in May 1925, is the organ of the Central Committee of the Komsomol. It is the same size as *Pravda* but consists of only four pages. Its format is a little livelier than *Pravda*'s, although both papers have frequent articles proclaiming the indestructable ties between Party and people in the Soviet Union. Like *Pravda*'s, *Komsomolskaya Pravda*'s back page lists TV programs and sports news. The third page usually is titled "The World: News and Problems," and here international problems as well as Komsomol programs are discussed. *Komsomolskaya Pravda* also has features designed to appeal specifically to young people. One called "Scarlet Sails" discusses such problems as, "What kind of person am I?" and "Pocket money comes from whose pocket?"

Pionerskaya Pravda is published by the Central Committee of the Komsomol and the Central Council of the Pioneers. It comes out on Tuesdays and Fridays and is a very lively-looking newspaper of four pages, twelve inches wide and sixteen and a half inches long, using green, brown, yellow, and red type as well as black. The paper always has interesting photographs of children dancing, skiing, playing games, or doing any of the interesting things children enjoy and also has many articles and pictures featuring birds and animals.

There are reports on the various phases of current march routes, anniversaries, rallies, and future events. To call attention to an important announcement a symbol of a radio signal says, "I am a signal! I am a signal!" Future *zarnitsa* competitions are marked with the red arrow and bayonet symbol, and Timur events are marked with the steering wheel symbol, so children involved in a particular program will not miss an announcement of interest to them.

I was interested in the way the three newspapers carried the events in Afghanistan, which began in December 1979. We were in Moscow at the time, and a Soviet friend told us about it before it appeared in the press in either the United States or the Soviet Union. "When you get back to the United States your newspapers are going to be full of Afghanistan," he said as we were driving to his apartment for dinner. "Amin has been executed. Your government is going to be upset by that."

The next day, *Pravda* had a small article headed "Appeal of the Government of Afghanistan." It said that in accordance with the Afghan-Soviet Friendship Treaty of December 5, 1978, in which the Soviets promised political, moral, economic, and military aid to Afghanistan, the government of Afghanistan had asked the Soviet government for help in quelling internal disorder. Below this article was one headed "Communication from Kabul," which said that Babrak Karmal had been named the new head of the people's Democratic Party of Afghanistan and mentioned that Amin had been sentenced to death. Soviet television reported that Afghanistan had requested Soviet aid and that the Soviets had responded. No one seemed upset about what appeared to be a short-term emergency.

For some months before, the Soviet press had been carrying pictures of a nuclear bomb with a huge "X" across it along with articles about NATO missiles in Europe and reports that the United States was "playing the China card." There had been articles about the death of SALT II and angry articles criticizing President Carter's advisor Zbigniew Brzezinski for his anti-Sovietism. Clearly the Soviet government was feeling encircled by a hostile world. There had also been articles about Afghanistan and alleged CIA activities there; so the events in Afghanistan were not quite as startling to Soviet readers as they were to Western readers.

It was not until January 22 that *Pionerskaya Pravda* commented on the Afghanistan crisis, in an article headed, "Don't Leave [Them] in Trouble." What a hard fate Afghanistan had had, the article began, a colony of England until 1919, then an undeveloped country until their revolution of April 1978. At that time, only one in every fifty children had an elementary education. Surrounded by enemies who created camps of Afghan mutineers, "instructed" by Americans, Chinese, and Egyptians, Afghanistan became a spy center where a "certain Louis Dupree of the CIA, posing as a diplomat," organized a counter-revolutionary movement. The article said that Dupree had been turned out of Afghanistan but was now the head of a ring of CIA agents in Pakistan.

The same issue of *Pionerskaya Pravda* had an article on the Olympics telling of the marvelous press facilities the Olympic games would have, illustrated with a picture of workers building the Olympic complex on Peace Prospect. During the spring of 1980, *Pionerskaya Pravda* ran several short articles about Afghanistan and a number of stories on the forthcoming Olympic Games, including a countdown of the number of days until the opening of the games.

Pionerskaya Pravda has a section called The Bell, which answers questions Pioneers have about international issues. When the newspaper receives sufficient letters on a particular subject to warrant a reply, the editors ask an authority on the subject to write a short explanation.

By April 1980 the paper was receiving more and more letters asking, "What's happening in Afghanistan now? How do people in Afghanistan live?" In reply, a correspondent told of his experiences in an Afghanistan town on the border of Pakistan. One day at noon he heard an explosion and went to investigate in a patrol jeep of the People's Army of Afghanistan. He found that there had been an explosion in the midst of a group of children who were playing in the street, killing one child and injuring two others. Even as the smoke was clearing away, a doctor was on the scene, bandaging the wounded children. The doctor, said the author, was "Ours—Soviet."

The killers were not Soviet, the article explained. They were bandits, mercenaries, well paid. "Convictions? Principles? These are empty words for bandits." The article went on to say that the "bandits" were also interfering with the spring sowing, adding that Soviet soldiers were helping the Afghans in every way—even teaching them how to make Ukrainian borshch.

Although *Pionerskaya Pravda* does not put a heavy emphasis on foreign affairs, it does try to keep its readers informed of world events. A July 10 article on the U.S. presidential race told of the stormy applause that greeted each candidate every time he assured his constituents that if they elected him president, life in the United States would be greatly improved.

Who are these presidential candidates? *Pionerskaya Pravda* asks. Ronald Reagan, the Republican candidate, is a *yastreb* (hawk) who is opposed to detente. Who is Carter, the present president? The article answers it's own question. "A millionaire." Who is Kennedy? "A multi-millionaire." Only a millionaire can afford to appear on television, the writer explains, since it can cost up to a hundred thousand dollars for thirty seconds of television time.

There are two political parties in the United States, the article continues, two parties, two hands of the rich capitalist ruling class. The people of the United States are continually told that their troubles stem from the Soviet Union—"Not from the banks of the Potomac (the river on which Washington is located) but from the banks of the Moscow River." Americans are reminded that they must deal "decisively" with the Soviet Union, but still their fears for the future increase, says the article, concluding that the American people are constantly told of the "Soviet threat" and the "Afghanistan question" because this helps the president solidify his mass support.

Pionerskaya Pravda has a circulation of about nine million. The most popular Pioneer magazine, the monthly *Pioner*, has only about one and a half million subscribers, but each copy is read by a number of children. In addition there are twenty-nine other Pioneer newspapers and forty Pioneer magazines in nineteen languages of the Soviet people. These regional magazines and newspapers are produced independently, although guided by the central committee of their respective republics, and their editors meet with the editor of the Moscow *Pioner* at least once a year.

When we met with the editor of *Pioner*, Stanislav Furin, he told us his magazine could be characterized by two words, *monthly* and *children's*, and that the word *children* was the crux of the matter. "I don't call it a literary magazine or a social-political magazine, but a children's magazine with a wide range—from chess to serious politics, from politics to puzzles. The specific types change from year to year. Before 1935 there was more Communist material. After 1935, when Soviet literature was on the upswing, the magazine was thicker and paid attention to good poetry, prose, and other literature. *Pioner* addresses all sides of a child's life today."

The magazine is divided into various departments, whose heads we met— Simonova for Pioneer and school life, Sokolova for the Pioneer movement, Bliznenkova for science and technology, Khristovaya for Communist education, and writers like Fedulova and Krapivan for special articles. Every year the staff selects a general theme, which usually follows the same general theme of the march routes and each issue carries some article toward this goal. The favorite department is "Play," and the page of riddles and jokes on the inside back cover is the most widely read.

Mr. Forin showed us a room where several people were opening letters from a gigantic pile. He said that *Pioner* gets fifty to eighty thousand letters a year from its child subscribers. One letter was from a little girl who was ill who said that she had moved to another town and her former friends had forgotten to write to her. After her letter was published in *Pioner* she was flooded with mail—thousands of letters in all. Mr. Furin added that the little girl got well.

We also visited the staff of *Vozhaty* (Leader), which has a smaller circulation of about two hundred thousand. *Vozhaty* is a methodological journal concerned with Communist education, published chiefly for older Komsomol or Communist leaders who deal with Pioneers.

Since the ideal of Communist education is an all-sided development, the departments in *Vozhaty* are as varied as those in *Pioner*. The staff included Greenberg for political education, Pinkov for sports, Evgeniya Orlova for art, films, and books, Irena Zarakhovich as assistant editor, and Vladimir Matveev for psychology. I. N. Moroz and Misha Baskin also joined the group, and we laughed and joked as we drank tea and ate cookies and candy. I have never seen a group who seemed to enjoy their work and each other so much.

Although Soviet children have dozens of newspapers and magazines to choose from, *Pionerskaya Pravda* and *Pioner* (and *Murzilka* for the Octobrists) are the most popular. In addition, *Molodaya Gvardiya* (Young Guard), a children's publishing house, prints more than 7 million copies of children's books a year, including a children's encyclopedia called *Tovarishch* (Comrade), the handbook for Pioneer leaders and books on the major march routes. Major children's books from other countries are also translated into Russian and other Soviet languages, and Soviet children read *Winnie the Pooh, Tom Sawyer*, Jules Verne, Jack London, Hemingway, and Anderson's fairy tales as well as Tolstoy, Gaidar, Agnya Barto, Mayakovsky, and other Russian writers.

Science fiction is popular in the Soviet Union but is often used as an ideological tool to improve the reader's moral unbringing. Gennady Prashkevich's "The Plundered Marvel," "The World Where I Am at Home," and the "22nd Century" speak of moral problems man will face in the new world. Sergei Drugal deals with ecological problems in an Institute for the Restoration of Nature, A. Balabukhi presents short stories concerned with a perfect society of the future, and another writer worries about the way a scientist should treat a discovery that could be used for the people's detriment.

Soviet fiction includes many works of real literary value, and hack political indoctrination is subjected to a certain amount of criticism. "We tend to picture the future in the forms of the present, and when it assumes a different guise we want to reject it," writes a contributor to a literary magazine. On the other hand, some writers like to think that Soviet young people will outgrow their "affected behavior, their guitars and jeans, and become just like us."

"Each period in history has two phases—dark and light," said one Soviet writer we interviewed. As examples of these phases he mentioned the good books Soviet children read and then expressed his dislike for television, which he compared to Oscar Wilde's story of the woman who took all the gold from the heart and converted it into small change. "When the base of culture is wide, the level is lower," he said.

Soviet television and radio are controlled by Gostelradio (State Television and Radio), which produces programs by and for children. Pioneers lead exercise programs on television and are shown at meetings, parades, and festivals or just sliding down a snow-covered bank outside the Kremlin.

The Gorky Central Studio of Children's and Youth Films auditions children for parts in films, and we were invited to watch some of the tryouts. Some of the children came with their mothers, and some came alone. Some were nervous and forgot their lines, and others were completely self-assured. One of the directors told us that they did not always take the children who did best in the auditions. "We can teach them the lines," he said. "What we look for is spontaneity and personality."

In 1974 the editor-in-chief of the Gorky studio invited Soviet children to name a new series of films for children. They accepted the word *yeralash*, a Russified Tatar word which means the highest degree of disorder and chaos, and since the short children's films were full of humor this seemed a good description for them. We saw some of the films and thought they were very funny.

The films were about the length of our TV commercials. One was about a boy practicing the English phrase, "I sail down the river," while eating prunes and playing with his pet starling. Suddenly the starling says the phrase correctly. The boy calls his friend to tell his friend his starling can speak English. "That's nothing," the friend says. "My dog has spoken English for some time." He puts the dog on the phone and the dog says, "I'm sorry. I'm sorry."

Another film, *The Duel*, shows a boy sitting in the front row in a theater. He drives the actors mad as he loudly crunches candy and apples.

Longer films run about an hour and a half and cover a wide variety of subjects. Some are heroic and didactic, like *A Trying Winter*, which tells of a child with tuberculosis of the bone who fights his illness with bravery. Another, *The Secret of the Underground*, was based on a true story of some children who discovered a cache of weapons that retreating Germans had left behind in a cave. A storm closes the entrance to the cave, and the children are cut off from the world. *I Bought a Papa* is concerned with a fatherless child who finds a new father.

Films for older children, such as *The Forest That You Never Enter*, about the transition from childhood to adolescence, and *The French Lesson*, from the story by the popular writer, Rasputin, are concerned with contemporary problems.

Some films are controversial, and critics argue back and forth about their merits or demerits. A film called *Fantasy of Vesnukhin*, set in the town of Vesnukhin, portrayed characters of three types—some kind and considerate and others simply amusing, but the majority of the citizens were shown as "helpless and absurd." This film provoked considerable comment. One writer said that children's films should not be too didactic but should not go to the other extreme either.

Films for teen-agers are changing. In the newer films the ending does not present the old didactic solution but arrives at a more realistic one. *The Diary of a School Principal, Let's Wait till Monday, What If It's Love?* and *School Waltz* do not always show their main characters as invincible heroes but rather as interesting, complex human beings. A children's "Oscar" called the Red Carnation is presented annually on May 19 (Pioneer's birthday) to the best children's film of the year.

The long films, which take about a year to make, are shown to a board of the State Committee of the Film Industry for approval before being released. A board in each republic may then choose whether or not to show a particular film or have it translated into the language of that republic. One unexpected criticism came from the mother of the astronaut Gagarin, who saw a film about her son. She thought the boy in the film looked just like her son but pointed out that the story took place in summer, not winter. The film was remade to make it correct for season.

The Soviet Union also has over a hundred theaters exclusively for children, including several musical theaters. We were walking down a Moscow street with Harry Eisman in the spring of 1976 when we passed the Moscow Musical Theater for Children. "I'd like to see that," I said, and Harry suggested we go inside. Harry explained to the doorman that I had written a book about Soviet children, and presently we were led into the office of Nataliya Sats, the director of the theater, who told us enthusiastically that the greatest reward in the world was not fame or money but the feeling that you were helping put mankind on the road to a better future. She showed us around the theater and gave us tickets to two performances.

At the first performance Mrs. Sats's daughter, Roxanne, presented a ballet, "The Mosquito and the Samovar." "What is a ballet?" she asked the audience, who shouted back, "They dance."

"Correct." Miss Sats said, and as the ballet proceeded, she continued to explain various aspects to the children.

The second performance was Mrs. Sats herself doing "Peter and the Wolf," which Harry said Prokofiev had written especially for her years ago. "She's modest about her fame," Harry said. "She's a People's Artist of the USSR and

received a Laureate State Prize of the USSR, two of the highest awards any person in the arts can have."

Mrs. Sats did the best "Peter and the Wolf" I have ever seen. I could hardly believe that she could be old enough to have welcomed the first spectators to the first Soviet children's theater, which opened in 1918 on the first anniversary of the Revolution. That theater became the first State Theater for Young Spectators in 1920, and is still in operation today. In a *Pravda* article, Mrs. Sats said that the children's theaters solved the main tasks of Communist education, not by offering boring lessons but by fascinating young spectators with examples of beauty.

14

First Love

At one children's theater performance, my husband and I were the only adults in the audience. The cashier at the box office thought we wanted the ticket office for the Bolshoi, which was next door, and called the manager to explain to us in English that this was a children's play. When we said we wanted to see children attending a theater just for children, the manager shook his head in disbelief, but he gave us two good seats.

Almost the entire audience was composed of children between ages twelve and fourteen—old enough to go to the theater by themselves but still young enough to hang over the velvet-covered rail of the orchestra pit and race up and down the aisles, pushing each other and giggling.

One boy about twelve years old was pulling at the long braids of a girl who looked slightly older. The boy pulled her braids furtively at first, barely touching them, then ran his fingers down the shiny hair. The girl, who was carrying the schoolchild's customary briefcase, pretended not to notice until the boy gave a sudden jerk to her braid. At that point she swung around and hit the boy on the shoulder with the briefcase, her whirling giving extra impetus to the blow. The boy's shoulder gave a sharp crack, as though broken, and the girl stopped in mid-air with a look of alarm.

The boy rubbed his shoulder involuntarily, but his face reflected indescribable ecstasy. "She notices me. Maybe she even likes me," his eyes seemed to say. The girl, assessing the damage she had done, noticed the boy's expression, and flirtatiously ran away, her braids provocatively brushing the boy's face as she ran past him.

In the row in front of us another boy and girl sat together sedately, discussing the play *Konki* (Skates) like adults, though they were the same age as the hair-pulling boy. They seemed more like a devoted, but long married, couple than twelve year olds.

157

We also had a chance to observe children at two different "balls" during the New Year's holiday season. One ball was for younger children, and these danced together unself-consciously. This dance was more an exercise or a sport than a romantic occasion, as ten-year-old boys and girls whirled each other around energetically, hardly seeming to notice a distinction between the sexes.

The second ball was for teen-agers, and the director of the Moscow Pioneer Palace told us we would notice a definite difference in the behavior of the two groups.

Little children are not shy with each other. But somewhere in the early teens, everything changes. It's as though boys and girls suddenly discover that the opposite sex is different, and it comes as quite a

surprise to them. It makes them shy with each other. At a ball like
this, the girls stand against one wall, and the boys stand against the
other wall.

Since the balls were New Year's affairs, Grandfather Frost and the Snow
Maiden attended them. Grandfather Frost dresses in a red coat and has white
whiskers like Santa Claus, but Santa Claus has nothing to equal the Snow Maiden,
who is a beautiful blonde dressed like a princess. On television, one Grandfather
Frost, asked about his home at the North Pole, said in view of his age and a
little arthritis, he preferred to spend his winters in Spain where it was warmer.

Grandfather Frost and the Snow Maiden help get the balls started and also
distribute presents. At the teen-age ball they made a dramatic entrance as the

orchestra played a lively tune. The director was right. The girls were lined up on one side, the boys on the opposite, and all looked as though they wanted to crawl into the walls, they pressed so hard against them. The dance floor was completely empty, and I was sure the party was going to be a flop. Very tentatively, two girls started to dance with each other. They were joined by two more, then two other girls joined in, and the six did a folk dance in a circle. They danced sedately at first, then with more abandon. Finally one boy advanced from the opposite wall and watched the girls. They held out their hands to him, and he joined the group. Another boy approached, and one girl detached herself from the group and started to dance with him.

There was a roll of drums from the orchestra, and Grandfather Frost suggested a John Paul Jones type of dance, in which everyone joined hands and marched around the room. At first the circle was small, but many girls joined, then boys. Various figures were called to the music, and soon all of the girls and most of the boys had left the walls and were dancing. Grandfather Frost was dancing with the Snow Maiden.

When does love begin? When does friendship turn to love? *Izvestiya* reported that, after a lecture on love and friendship, a fifteen-year-old girl sent up a question: "What is this 'love'? Give a complete answer."

Soviet educators believe that through television and cinema today's children have seen and heard more than their parents had at that age. Through a process called "acceleration" they hurry to taste joys they are too inexperienced to appreciate. In response, Soviet youth cite Romeo and Juliet and Natasha from *War and Peace*, and Soviet educators reply, "Yes, but they are examples from books. In real life. . . ."

In real life, Soviet educators and leaders try to prepare Soviet youth for real life. In his book, *Adolescent Psychology*, I. S. Kon says that the changes that take place during puberty are too fast for the parental eye to see. While the child has grown up and changed, his parents' image of him is several years behind actuality. Kon also observes that most parents and children have positive attitudes toward each other but each expects a negative reaction from the other.

The Soviets want each citizen to be a thinking, feeling person. To find out what kind of empathy is shown by children of different ages, a study was made to test responses to the experimenter's unfinished stories. Two kinds of empathy were identified—feeling with somebody and feeling about somebody. In the first case the child identified himself with the person in the story; in the second he felt for the person. Feeling with was more characteristic of younger schoolchildren, and feeling about was characteristic of adolescents.

An article in the magazine *Family and School* points out that the teen-ager is beginning to recognize himself as a separate personality. In his early school years his opinion of himself came from external factors, but now he is beginning to internalize his feelings. The desire to be like his friends, to do "what every-one is doing," is becoming balanced by the desire to be himself as he looks for answers to questions such as "Who am I?" "What kind of person am I?" "What can I be?"

The teen-ager compares himself with his friends, but Soviets say he is usually far better able to evaluate his friends' strengths and weaknesses than his own. What attributes does an adolescent value in his friends? Soviet teens name varied characteristics in response to this question: a good comrade who will always help and never refuse a request, never betray a friend, doesn't complain or argue over trifles, is a willing worker, never does a bad turn, and gives intelligent advice.

Educator L. S. Vygotsky thinks that, although the educational system must respond to changes in a child's personality as he grows into adolescence, if the child has learned self-control from kindergarten age he will not have trouble as a teen-ager.

The two most widely read and quoted of Soviet educators are A. S. Makarenko (1883-1939) and V. A. Sukhomlinsky (1918-70), although Sukhomlinsky is often criticized. Some readers feel that Sukhomlinsky and Makarenko are opposed to each other, with Sukhomlinsky favoring the individual and Makarenko the collective, but others think they complement each other.

Sukhomlinsky developed a sense of responsibility by giving each first grader in his school a baby lamb to care for. He taught moral responsibility by using what he called the "algebra of ethics," including such strictures as not wasting a piece of bread, saying something nice to one's mother, caring for a sick friend, and protecting a bird or a branch of a tree. To Sukhomlinsky, these were building blocks for dealing with the more complex challenges of adulthood.

Makarenko worked with the homeless children who roamed throughout the Soviet Union following the disruptive days of Revolution and Civil War. These children often ravaged the countryside like packs of wild dogs. When Makarenko gathered them together in his first school, he faced an entirely different task from that of Sukhomlinsky.

Makarenko believed in having his students do work for the collective and stressed the value of certain rituals such as raising the flag and duty posts. He make exacting demands on the pupils but treated them with the utmost respect. Makarenko felt that educational goals were not immutable but that they changed as society changes. In the early 1930s the goal of education was the development of character traits necessary for the Soviet state in the era of proletarian dictatorship.

On the other hand, Sukhomlinsky was opposed to what he considered to be mindless tasks with no moral purpose. "To be a truly educated person," he wrote, one must love his native land but also "take to heart the anguish and troubles of our Fatherland—for we do have them, in our economy, in scientific and technical development, and in interpersonal relationships." In "The Wise Authority of the Collective," he criticized some Young Pioneers whose only aim was to take first prize. His book, *I Give My Heart to Children*, ranks with Makarenko's *Road to Life* as a classic of Soviet education.

Sukhomlinsky believed that one of the most important tasks of the teacher was to lead the child through the complicated world of human relations. The child cannot live without joy, he wrote, but this joy must not be careless; it must involve the child's conscience so that he shares his happiness with others. To this end, the child's ability to love must be nurtured by teachers who understand the complexities of his personality.

To help nurture desired character traits, *Pionerskaya Pravda* has a club, *Zerkalo* (Looking Glass) which answers questions from subscribers. The looking glass, defined as a shining surface of glass or metal, known from the third century, which gives an exact reflection of the object in front of it, reflects the images of the Pioneer.

In addition to the page in *Pionerskaya Pravda* and a book by I. Zemskaya on *The Looking Glass* there is a television program called *Telezerkalo.* All of these are designed to help teen-agers answer such questions as: How well do you know yourself? What kind of person are you? Do you know your own strengths and weaknesses? Do you like yourself? Can you correctly evaluate your conduct and actions and, without taking offence, listen to just criticism? Can you look at yourself from all sides?"

The editors pose the questions, and the Pioneers themselves compose the answers. The three most important features in life, says one correspondent, are "enthusiasm, a dream, and faith in yourself." Most agree with Soviet leaders that a successful life must have one major goal, in addition to the dozens of small goals for each day.

Looking Glass helps with the small goals as well as the large ones, offering advice on dress, manners, and behavior. To girls who are not beautiful, Looking Glass gives advice on how to improve their looks and dress but emphasizes that real beauty is internal and a girl must be true to her own style and not follow fads slavishly. Looking Glass's concrete advice is based on the general admonition "Know yourself": if a girl's face is round, short hair drawn back over the ears will lengthen the face; if a forehead is too high, bangs will help hide it, and so on.

Many children dislike their noses. Looking Glass comforts them by asking, "Whose nose is best?" Then it answers, "Yours! Only *your* nose suits *your* face."

On the other hand, should manners be considered unimportant? No, says Looking Glass. Your manners show your cultural background, and if you happen to be a Pioneer in a visiting delegation abroad, they show the cultural background of your country as well. Instructions are specific: Do not eat with loud, smacking noises or talk with your mouth full. If you bite into something unpalatable, like a piece of gristle, do not spit it out on your plate, but remove it onto your fork or spoon behind your napkin. Do not wipe your mouth with your hand; use a napkin and, when through with the napkin, place it neatly to the left of your plate. And never, never, in jest, put your napkin on someone's head.

A table knife has two functions: to cut and to help the fork gather food. When eating fish, if there is no fish knife on the table, another fork may be used as a pusher. If there is only one fork, it is used in the right hand. Otherwise the knife is held in the right hand and the fork in the left. Cutlets, beef Stroganoff, salad, macaroni, and other listed foods are eaten with a fork; sausage, ham, and cheese are put onto your plate with a fork (never your own). Meat, chicken, and sandwiches may be eaten with knife and fork, but if you want to make your own sandwich never hold the piece of bread you are buttering in the palm of your hand. Lay it on your plate and add cheese, ham, and so forth.

Soup is eaten with a spoon, but if the soup contains a large piece of meat it may be cut with a knife and eaten with a fork. Bread and *pirozhki* (turnovers) are eaten with the hand, but bread is eaten in small pieces broken off from the main piece. Tangerines are peeled by hand, but oranges must be peeled with a knife. Grapes are pulled from the cluster with the fingers, and the seeds must not be spit onto the plate but carefully arranged on it.

There were many more rules, but one I was told by a Russian who had often been in the United States surprised me. He said that Russians considered it rude for a hostess to ask her guests to help themselves from a buffet when there is no maid. Instead, the hostess herself should serve each guest to show her concern for them.

The Soviets' interest in etiquette has been evolving slowly. Just after the Revolution having good manners indicated that a person was a member of the "White" Russian aristocracy and, therefore, opposed to the Revolution. Now that the Revolution is no longer in danger, people may have good manners without their politics being suspect, and even *Pravda* has advocated a Russian Emily Post for the Soviet people.

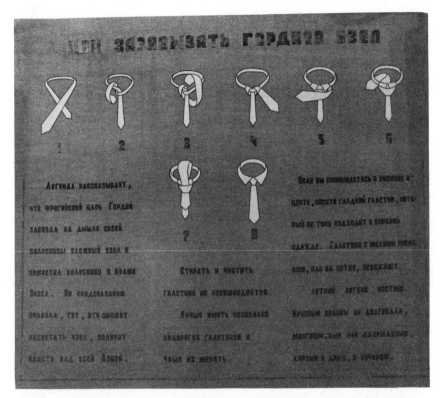

We have noticed a great improvement in manners from our first trip in 1963. On that trip, if my husband opened a door for me, ten husky Russians would push through ahead of me. An American friend with us always stood back politely, and our guide said, in surprise, "Mr. Chandler is so polite, yet he is successful in your country." Today Soviets have discovered they can be both polite and successful. I hope other American tourists in the Soviet Union can follow Mr. Chandler's example for our country, too.

Manners help smooth the way for romance, and both meet with challenges when the child becomes a teen-ager. "Looking Glass, Looking Glass, help! What am I to do? I'm fourteen years old. I have now changed completely. I'm in a bad humor, want to be alone, don't like noise. Sometimes I lie on the sofa for several hours without moving. Mama is upset. Some people say that I am at an age of transition. What is that? What's wrong with me?" says one letter. Others say:

"Looking Glass, friend, tell me please, can this be real love at thirteen?"

"When my girl friends go out to school evenings or to skate, I sit at home and envy them. Sometimes I don't even want to go to school. I'm too tall."

The age of transition is a difficult, complicated period, says the author of Looking Glass. The child's whole organism is growing, arms and legs lengthening, the circulatory system expanding, which in turn affects the work of the heart, often leading to sudden tiredness and headaches. Girls have an even more complicated time with the onset of menstruation and the beginning of sexual maturity, which will not be complete until the girl is age twenty or twenty-two. At age twelve or fourteen most girls also consider themselves "in love" says the author.

Love does not reduce the need for friendship, says Professor Kon; in fact, it intensifies the need to confide in a third person. Boys need another boy confidant and girls need girl friends. Boys, beginning with the sixth grade, will explain that a friend is someone of the same sex who thinks as he does and shares common interests and that understanding a person means knowing him well. Girls, beginning with the seventh grade, tend to share their feelings with a girl friend they have known since the third grade. Girl friends are more apt to discuss their intimate life with each other than are two boys. Boys are more drawn to a collective, and girls are more inclined to keep to themselves. Girls are also more likely to keep intimate diaries.

When asked from which sex they would choose their best friend, 84 percent of Leningrad tenth graders chose a boy, and only 16 percent chose a girl; most girls said they would chose a boy as their best friend.

There is much discussion in the press about today's girls and boys. In an article on the contemporary girl, *Family and School* asked the girls themselves, the boys who knew them, and the adults associated with them what they considered "contemporary girls" to be like. The girls described themselves as social, tender, feminine, independent, work-loving, modest, intellectual, energetic, and multifaceted.

Some boys described the girls as being proud, honest, and demanding of self, knowing their own value, able to be a pal as well as maternal and sympathetic, and other boys said they were sly, took all the best command posts in school, and were pretty dolls who didn't know how to do anything or talk about anything except equal rights.

The adults thought the contemporary girl was well educated and well dressed but added, "at my age I wasn't like that." Some adults felt the girls were stubborn, capricious, impatient, tactless, in conflict with their parents (especially mama), egotistical, sly, and didn't want to get their "lily white" hands dirty.

The girls said they admired Natasha in *War and Peace*, Anna Karenina, and Juliet from *Romeo and Juliet*. The Soviet girl is a "Juliet in jeans," said one contemporary, though he added that each girl was different. Some girls said they wanted to be like movie actresses and start smoking and dress fashionably; however, 58 percent said their ideal was to be like a real-life friend.

The Soviet teen-age boy is often pictured unfavorably in Soviet cartoons, which show him wearing long hair, jeans, and fringed jackets and always accompanied by a guitar or a transistor radio. One cartoon on the cover of *Krokodil*, the humor newspaper, showed three such lads lolling on trolley-bus seats, as offended older women stood in the aisles. "Sleeping beauties," was the caption.

We did see young people with guitars everywhere. They organize into "beat groups" with names like "The Best Years," "The Time Machine," "Champions," and "The Sandal Salesman." *Pravda* says some of these musicians have become interested in amateur art groups and have gone on to better music so that these "Beatles" do have some positive aspects, although Soviet leaders as a whole deplore most of the guitar players.

Soviet films and plays depict the life of teen-agers sympathetically in such films as *One Hundred Days After Childhood, Blue Portrait*, and *School Waltz*. *School Waltz* was a particularly controversial film since it seemed that the "bad" girl, who had had a baby out of wedlock, was happy, and the "good" girl was not. We asked young people, teachers, and parents what they thought of the film and found that the young people generally approved and the adults generally disapproved.

"I consider such films necessary to prepare young people for life," said one high school boy about *School Waltz*. A teacher said, "The girls in the film are very independent. The behavior of the one is hard to understand. It is a very difficult problem."

The "difficult problem" is sex, which is handled as a moral problem in the Soviet Union. "Do you like to discuss moral problems?" I asked one tenth-grade class. "Yes—immoral ones as well," was the answer.

Sex education is not overemphasized. In the early 1970s the Academy of Pedagogy's Institute of General Education Problems opened a sex education laboratory, which conducts surveys of schoolchildren. It was found that 70 percent of the girls questioned learned about the physical changes of puberty not from their mothers but from friends or acquaintances. (In contrast, 82 percent of another group questioned had had their first *drink* at home during family celebrations.)

For one of its programs, the sex education laboratory conducted adult education classes at Moscow School No. 628. Parents were found to be poorly informed about sex but anxious to learn. The parents felt that children should first learn about sex in the home, but there was also some sentiment that sex education courses should be made compulsory in schools.

In 1980 an experimental course was being tested in Moscow schools. The program runs from the first through the tenth grades and deals with such matters as family relations and economics, sexual hygiene, and physiological processes, and in the tenth grade childbirth and child care. Many of the lectures are given to boys and girls separately.

Teen-agers receive little advice about birth control, although abortions are legal if performed in a hospital. In one article on adolescent mothers, *Kom-*

somolskaya Pravda said that the unmarried teen-age girl who has had an abortion leaves the hospital spiritually devastated. "Without having loved, she has already survived love; without having given birth, she has already buried."

Eighth graders believe absolutely in love, one Soviet survey showed, ninth graders showed some doubt, and tenth graders' belief in love dropped sharply. Still, of the 15,000 people studied by a Perm sociologist, 70 to 80 percent said they married for love (emotional and sexual attraction being included in the category of love); 15 to 20 percent married because "everybody was doing it"; and 3 to 10 percent out of rational calculation. Surprisingly, of the group who married for love ten to eleven couples considered the marriage unsuccessful for every ten who said it was successful. For the "everyone is doing it" group, the ratio was four or five to ten, and in the rational calculation group, seven to ten.

The Civil Registry Office, where marriages and divorces are registered, has a young people's club where lectures are given on the moral, legal, aesthetic, psychological, pedagogical, and medical aspects of married life. When young people file their applications for marriage, they are invited separately into a "bride's room" or a "groom's room," where officials hold frank discussions about family life.

Most weddings are held in "wedding palaces" and have become quite elaborate, with piped-in music and traditional bridal gowns, including long or short white veils. From our windows in the National Hotel we could watch a procession of brides as they came directly from the wedding palace to Red Square to lay a wreath on Lenin's tomb and then walk to the Tomb of the Unknown Soldier, where they put the remainder of their wedding flowers. The newlyweds then drive off in a car or taxi decorated with ribbons and balloons and usually a doll on the radiator as well.

At the wedding a Soviet official has told the young couple that the Soviet state hopes they will have children who bring them happiness, but they must remember that children are also a responsibility.

The Soviet state fully agrees with Makarenko's statement in the *Book for Parents*: "In molding their children modern parents mold the future history of our country and, consequently, the history of the world as well." The young couple may say, as Makarenko did, "Can I shoulder the burden of so tremendous a subject?"

15

Family, School, and the Street

"You interfere with everything I do, you're always telling me what to do, trying to control me. I'm fed up. Leave me alone."

"Lena, you didn't used to be so rude."

"And I'm not rude now. You just regard any independence as rudeness. You have to have obedience: 'Yes *Mamochka* [Mother dear] right this minute, *Mamochka*! I can't be like that. I have my own thoughts."

"You often act thoughtlessly."

"That's just the way it seems to you. It's my business."

"And mine. You remember when Chapaev asked Furmanov, 'Who is commander here, you or I?' Furmanov answered 'You,' and then added 'and I.' "

"Mama, why are you always finding fault? Have you forgotten that you, yourself, were young once? You've changed completely, completely."

The door slammed, and Lena's mother was left alone, thinking that compared to her own childhood Lena was having a holiday. This story in *Family and School* says that most family conflicts are over a question of "rights." The child has a "right" to go to the movies with her friend. The mother has a "right" to have her daughter stay home and help with the housework. The children say the parents are dealing from a "position of strength," whereas the parents say they are acting from a "position of love."

Relationships between children and adults are rich but complicated, say Soviet educators. All the connections between children and adults are expressed in numerous nuances of sympathy or antipathy. The parent says, "I certainly know my own child," yet cannot understand when that child suddenly turns into a different person at age eleven or twelve.

Educators caution parents that their idea of a "good girl" being polite, neat, and obedient, or a "bad boy" being one who is rude and won't listen, is often too simplistic. As a Russian proverb says, "To raise children is to raise trouble."

After a lecture, the psychologist Shershakov was approached by a Soviet mother who said that her son, who had always been a "normal" child, was now impossible to handle.

Shershakov, after some questioning, discovered that the boy had been a *kaprizny* (capricious) child as a preschooler, which his mother considered natural for that age, but lately he had become much worse. The Russians use the word *kaprizny* to describe a child who throws himself on the floor, beats with his arms and legs, cries to the point of hysteria, and will not listen to an adult's entreaties, commands, or admonitions. Shershakov says that caprice is a manifestation of weakness on the part of the child. If he cannot, for some reason, attain his wish, say to have his mother buy him a new toy, he makes a "scene," knowing that his mother will then agree to buy the toy.

This boy's mother considered caprice normal for a preschooler, but when the boy continued his actions into his teens she considered him a "difficult" child. Shershakov said that "teen-ager" was almost a synonym for "difficult" but it should not be so. Instead "teen-ager" should be an indicator of all previous education. Tolerating caprice in a preschooler sets a bad precedent and can easily produce a difficult teen-ager.

Soviet parents are told that, when a doctor treats a patient, he must first get a complete picture of that patient. So the parent must see the child not just from one point of view, but from the viewpoint of his major influences. *Literature Gazeta*, in an article on "Teen-agers: Lessons of a Dangerous Age," says the child himself may not know why he acts the way he does. When criticized for bad behavior he may say he doesn't know why he acted that way. He may shrug his shoulders and look out the window as though the conversation about his behavior is boring him. The article said the three main influences on the child were family, school and the street, and I thought this a good outline to follow.

"Difficult" children come from difficult "almost normal" families, says another article in *Family and School*. There is the distrustful family, which mistrusts neighbors, co-workers, and all those with whom they have dealings. This family considers itself always right and all outsiders always wrong. Its members are in conflict with everyone around them, and when their teenager is in trouble with his teacher or his Pioneer leader the family makes this conflict a great cause for indignation.

Another type is the thoughtless family, which lives for the pleasure of today without preparation for tomorrow. Members of this family have no plans for the future. "That's how it is," they say, with no effort to change even the things they dislike about their lives. In their free time they sit, inert, before the television set. Watching TV is their main activity, though they also quarrel with each other over trifles. Faced with family problems they "throw up their hands" and do not try to cope. Their teen-agers are weak-willed, disorganized, and want only to be entertained.

Members of a scheming family are always looking for shortcuts to success, which require a minimum of effort on their part. They know how to make a good impression on the right people and have great plans for their children's futures, plans that involve making contacts useful to the children, as the family uses everyone around it for its own ends.

The pugnacious family loves a fight, and members build up their physical strength because they believe that "might makes right." They pride themselves on their bravery, their uncompromising attitudes, and their rude language. Although they often beat their children and fight with each other, they will always back their own children in a fight with other children.

The author of the article says there are many other types of families, but he hopes his readers will see themselves in some of these characteristics. He encourages readers to ask themselves, "What am I teaching my children every day from observations from the life of our family?" and concludes that to cure the child in the family, the family must first cure itself.

In 1979 a group of experts met in Moscow to discuss the problems of family life. One of the major problems discussed was housing. Since much housing in the Soviet Union was destroyed during World War II, housing has been scarce and still is, despite many huge new building projects. A family with three or four children may obtain a larger apartment in *two to four years*, while parents of twins may get an apartment within one year.

At best the apartments are not large, and most Soviet children must share a room with a sibling. Students who marry while in college must often continue to live in separate dormitory rooms.

To get an apartment they want, or simply to get an apartment at all, Soviet citizens often resort to a monthly magazine, which lists apartments people want to swap for one in another section. One Soviet couple we know, living in Moscow, made an eight-way swap, including an apartment in Leningrad (where a couple was getting a divorce) and an apartment in Kiev (where the wife's grandmother lived), as well as six apartments in Moscow. The grandmother died two days after the swap was consummated. If she had died two days earlier, or if the couple in Leningrad had decided to reconcile, all eight swaps would have fallen through and months of negotiating would have been lost. Swaps are usually confined to one city, but those with apartments in Moscow are allowed to swap with tenants in Kiev and Leningrad, among others.

Rent is very low: fourteen kopeks a month per square meter of housing (excluding kitchen, bath, closets, and balcony, for which there is no charge). People living in nine- to sixteen-story blocks of apartments are charged an additional two kopeks per square meter.

The rates for utilities are fixed: sixteen kopeks per month per family member for gas, four kopeks per kilowatt of electricity (half this rate if cooking is done by electricity), fifty kopeks per family member for hot water, and six to eight kopeks per square meter of floor space for heating and waste disposal.

For an average forty-eight-square-meter apartment for a family of four, the rent is six rubles and sixty kopeks a month and with utilities the total cost of housing comes to about twenty rubles a month. (This "typical" family has two wage earners but pays only about four or five percent of the family's monthly income for rent and utilities, and families who lost someone in World War II pay only half the standard charges for those items.)

While not luxurious in either space or construction, the apartments must be considered a bargain. In each building, a committee called the *Zhek* (Living Quarters Operation Office) takes care of maintenance and repairs of the building and mediates relations between the tenants. The committee is headed by the building's superintendent.

Most accounts by American journalists say Soviet apartments are guarded by suspicious superintendents who carefully screen visitors, but we have never seen any such person. In fact, we have often looked for a superintendent to ask where a certain apartment is. Unable to find a superintendent, we have knocked on doors to ask directions which were cheerfully (and not suspiciously) given.

Harry and his wife live in an apartment with a large, high-ceilinged living room, a bedroom, a kitchen large enough to eat in, and a small hall and bath. Their windows look out over a pleasant vista of trees. Other apartments we have visited have oriental rugs on floors and walls, and in several we saw beautiful antique furniture, paintings, and Faberge ornaments.

Many of our Soviet friends also have a *dacha* (country cottage) where they spend weekends. People who do not have a dacha of their own may visit a friend or go to a country hotel for an inexpensive weekend. People are permitted to own their own apartments (co-ops), as well as their country houses,

and the government makes this easy with low down payments and easy monthly installments.

Quality of construction has been a problem in the past. Some of the buildings erected in Stalin's time have protective metal nets around them, placed there to catch falling bricks or stones. Some years ago, an American friend of ours asked a Soviet engineer why the Soviets didn't seem to be able to make decent mortar. "That's what Khrushchev wants to know," the Soviet engineer answered. The newer buildings are improving, though, and are getting better looking as well.

Every apartment complex includes stores, nursery schools, kindergartens, and grade schools, and usually a cinema or recreation hall and a sports complex or playground. Theoretically apartment houses are built around a factory or shop so that workers will not have to go far from home, but with two wage earners in almost every family someone usually has to travel some distance to work. Compared to the United States there are few privately owned automobiles; so transportation is by trolley bus, bus, or subway, which are efficient and cheap.

After World War II, in which 20 million Soviets were killed, the state encouraged Soviet families to have many children. Medals were given for motherhood, and a woman who had a great many children received the title Mother Heroine. Today, with the exception of some Central Asian Soviet republics, the average Soviet family consists of a mother and father and one or two children.

There are also many single-parent families, due largely to a greatly increasing divorce rate since the mid-1960s. In a study of divorces in Kiev, 61 percent of the divorce proceedings were instituted by wives, and in 47 percent of these cases drunkenness or alcoholism were given as the main reason for divorce. V. Perevedentsev, a writer in *Literaturnaya Gazeta* questioned this finding, pointing out that statistics often cited in prerevolutionary Russia said that in a year of poor harvests there was an increase in the number of fires in villages. Conversely, a good harvest was associated with few fires. These facts actually had no correlation with each other, but they were brought about by a common cause—the amount of rainfall. A rainy summer brought few fires and a big crop; drought brought many fires and crop failure.

Perevedentsev thought the fire-harvest analogy could be applied to divorce. He said statisticians were looking for causes of divorce within the family when the cause might be shortcomings in living conditions. Perevedentsev also noted that the Soviet family was in transition, from a patriarchal structure, with the husband as the supreme head, to a biarchal family in which husband and wife are equal.

Another researcher compared the family to a barrel held together by a number of bands—legal, moral and religious, economic, and so on, many of which have been severed by socialism. Today's Soviet woman often claims to be head of the household. In a letter to *Komsomolskaya Pravda* a writer said that ninety out of one hundred women polled claimed to be heads of their families, and their husbands agreed. Of the ten husbands who said they were the family heads, one wife agreed, and when this man was offered a choice of prizes he turned to his wife and asked her which he should choose.

Due to the war there are still more women than men in the Soviet Union, though the present birth rate of 105 boys to every 100 girls is narrowing the gap. But the death rate for those in the group twenty to forty-five aged is three times greater for men than for women, with injuries and alcohol as major factors.

In 1975, 54 percent of the students in specialized secondary institutions and one-half of the students in higher schools were women; 92 percent of all working-age Soviet women are either working or studying. In industry the largest number of women work in machine building, with light industry in second place. Forty percent of all scientific workers and 70 percent of all teachers and physicians were women.

On one occasion, we were being shown through a university in a Central Asian republic when we passed a classroom marked "philosophy." I asked if I could go in and was met with the permissive "Why not?" The class was about equally divided between girls and boys. The girls looked very old-fashioned in the long figured dresses typical of old Central Asia. They wore their hair in long, dark braids down their backs and reminded me of the brides who, before the Revolution, were "sold" to their husbands. But the discussion was about equal rights and women's liberation, and these old-fashioned girls were up to the minute in their arguments. Seventy percent of physicians were women, they said, so why was there still a disproportionately large number of men who were

heads of hospitals? Why did women come home to cooking and housework after a day in the work force? The boys were looking very browbeaten. "*We* agree with you," they said, but the girls kept hammering home their arguments.

Kharchov and Golod, in a study of *Women's Work and the Family*, created a chart of household responsibilities and the member of the family who performed them. Their chart shows the percentage of families in which given work is done by the wife, husband, wife and husband together, or other family members:

Task	Wife	Husband	Wife and Husband	Other Family Members
Shopping	61	3	19	17
Preparing breakfast	58	10	18	14
Preparing dinner	64	4	16	16
Washing dishes	10	17	39	34
Small repairs	22	67	1	10
Doing laundry	64	2	21	13
General cleaning	32	12	39	17
Paying bills	45	31	12	12

At the Sixtieth Session of the International Labor Conference in 1975, it was noted that women make up 49.3 percent of the labor force in the Soviet Union, as opposed to 35 percent in North America and 19.6 percent in Latin America. When housework is included, the Soviet woman usually works longer hours than the Soviet man.

Soviet women are rebelling against this inequality, as the current Soviet movies show. In the film *Young Wife*, the wife leaves her chauvinistic husband, although the film ends with the husband coming home to find his returned wife washing the floor. But in *The Wife Left* the wife leaves at the beginning of the film and does not return, and in *Scenes from Family Life* the husband carries his wife in his arms, washes the floor himself, and prepares dinner, but his wife leaves him anyhow.

When children are involved, it is still the wife who is most likely to be the parent in a one-parent situation. She is often aided by the parent's committee of the school her child attends.

The parent's committee is the school's link with the family, "a miniature university of pedagogical knowledge, a farm of propaganda for Communist education," as one school director expresses it.

It is important that meetings of the parent's committee be interesting so that the parents will want to attend. The teacher is advised to wear a becoming dress to the meeting, to call the parents by their first name and patronymic, and to enlist the help of her pupils in preparing interesting exhibits of schoolwork

and engaging programs. Teachers are warned that if they devote the period to telling the parents all the bad things their children have done the parents will soon become bored and stop coming. If the teacher really needs to discuss a child's misbehavior with a parent, the parent should be invited to an individual consultation on a Saturday.

By working with the committee that runs the affairs of an apartment block, the parent's committee may organize activities for the children's free time, such as setting up playrooms in the apartment house or organizing dramatic circles, and it often helps run various Pioneer activities as well, since the Pioneers are based in the school system.

Soviet psychologists say that children are faced with two conflicting desires—the striving to be independent and the striving to be part of a group. If that group is the Pioneers everything is fine, but children are also attracted by the influence of the street.

Teen-agers are fascinated with the street, and a favorite activity is strolling up and down in the evening, meeting old friends and making new ones. "There are great guys here. It's cheerful. It's interesting and there are lots of girls. We like it here," *Komsomolskaya Pravda* quoted one young man as saying about the "hundred-meter strip," as Kirov Street in Astrakhan is affectionately called.

That same evening, the police reported fifteen cases of public drunkenness, five fights, seven arrests for petty hooliganism, disciplinary action against seventeen people, and warnings for twenty, out of the 1,000 people between ages fifteen and twenty-four who paraded down the Kirov Street strip.

On our Soviet trips during the past few years we have been waylaid around the Rossiya Hotel by boys asking for chewing gum, for which they are willing to trade Pioneer pins if an outright gift is not forthcoming. "Are you a Pioneer?" I ask, and when the boy says "Yes," I ask if he enjoys the Pioneers. "Of course," is the immediate answer. When I persist, asking if he thinks the Pioneers approve of begging on street corners, I am met with silence.

Older boys on other streets in the Soviet Union ask the tourist to change money or offer to buy cameras, transister radios, or articles of clothing. This illegal practice is distinctly frowned on by the authorities, and, when caught, these black marketers receive stiff fines or prison sentences, though the practice continues despite these penalties.

Pionerskaya Pravda warns its readers against trading with tourists: "Your dignity is linked with the dignity of the Motherland, your honor with its honor." The article goes on to describe with great disapproval a Soviet youth wearing Wrangler jeans who wanted to sell the Led Zeppelin record *Black Dog* for "thirteen-zero" (130 rubles).

All of the Soviet press deplores the passion for possessions—tape recorders, watches, motorcycles, blue jeans. It campaigns against radio "hooligans" who broadcast illegal hard rock, interfering with official shortwave clubs of the Voluntary Society for Assistance to the Army, Aviation and Navy, which answers calls for help and relays urgent information. Amateurs who tape foreign broadcasts and replay them on official channels may be prosecuted under the law, which bans all forms of anti-Soviet agitation and propaganda.

Mopeds are another item popular with Soviet youth. I read about a Moped in a Soviet magazine and didn't know what it was. The word *moped* was not in my Russian dictionary, and it wasn't until I sat next to a prominent Washington lawyer at a dinner party that I discovered what they were. He explained,

> Mo for motor and ped for pedal. Add a pint or so of gas and you have transportation. Mopeds have been in Europe since the end of World War II. They are specially built units, stronger and heavier than a bicycle, with one or two horsepower. They can be pedaled like bicycles, and most of them have to be pedaled before the motor can be started. They cost between $300 and $700 and get from 150 to 300 miles per gallon.

I could see why Soviet youth wanted Mopeds but agreed with a Soviet writer who said: "Big dreams and childish means, that is a teen-ager."

In 1978 there was general alarm in the Soviet papers when American singer Dean Reed was arrested in Minnesota, charged with trespassing on the right-of-way of a 427-mile high voltage power line. TASS sent a man to cover Dean

Reed's trial, as wrath and indignation at the arbitrary rule of the U.S. authorities was pouring in. (An article in *Pionerskaya Pravda* cited John Harris and Dr. Spock as examples of ridiculous arrests made in the United States.)

"Who is Dean Read?" I asked, and soon *Time* magazine answered my question, in an article titled "Who is Dean Read and Why is the Kremlin Making Such a Fuss About Him?" *Time* said that Dean Read was a forty-year-old Denver-born country and western singer, more popular than Frank Sinatra in the Soviet Union. One of his big hits was "War Goes on." *Time* said that Read refused to post $300 bail and went on a hunger strike. "I consider myself a political prisioner," he said. Soviet protesters petitioned President Carter to ask for his intervention in Read's release. The jury acquitted Read, and the Soviet press quoted this and said that the singer hailed his acquittal as a courageous and unpopular decision.

Soviet youth also like Elvis Presley and Bob Dylan, and their parents approved of Dylan's songs of protest during the 1960s. "He praised love, damned war, and ridiculed the money grubbers," said *Literaturnaya Gazeta* of September 7, 1977, but added sadly that Bob seemed to have sold out to the capitalists.

In 1979 the British rock star Elton John "rocked" Leningrad. Fans shouted "Elton! Elton! Elton!" under his hotel windows, and in the theater they danced on their seats and in the aisles as Elton sang "Daniel," "Goodbye Yellow Brick Road," "I Heard it Through the Grapevine," and "Back in the USSR." Most of the nearly 4,000 in the audience were young and wore blue jeans.

Jeans are probably the most wanted item for a Soviet teenager. Almost every Russian visitor to the U.S. goes shopping for jeans to take back to children and friends, and in Moscow and other Soviet cities foreigners are waylaid by teenagers wanting to buy or trade something for the jeans they are wearing. Black marketers sell Wrangler or Levi jeans for 170 to 250 rubles a pair—about half of an average family's monthly income. (Sunglasses may go for 30 rubles on the black market.)

In 1973 plans were made for Soviet production of jeans, following a round-table discussion headed "Devil Skin." The Soviet jeans did not satisfy Soviet teen-agers. One critic writing in *Nedelya* (The Week) said, "If you walk down the street on a summer day, you will notice that by no means do everyone's jeans fit as though the wearer had been poured into them. One sometimes gets the impression that the garment exists independently of the person."

Many Soviet young people feel they must have American-made jeans, no matter how they get them. If they are unable to acquire them legitimately, they may resort to what the Soviet police call "jeans crimes." The Soviet press recounts incidents of young people, girls as well as boys, attacking youths who are wearing jeans, stripping them of their jeans, and even knifing them if they resist.

One case reported in a Soviet paper told of some boarding school students who went out hunting for somebody wearing jeans. They spotted a young Soviet who was wearing a denim suit and demanded that he give it to them, but he shed the jacket and started to run. The boys caught him and beat him up, removed his jeans, and dressed him in trousers belonging to one of them. Then they left their victim, badly wounded, with no thought for anyone but themselves.

In another case, two girls wearing jeans were attacked by other girls who slashed their faces with a razor in the course of expropriating their jeans. It was found in this case that the attackers had been raised without fathers and that the mother of one of the girls was a mental patient, but the article mentioned that statistics from Soviet Georgia show that two-thirds of juvenile crimes were committed by youths from two-parent, relatively well-off families.

The moral poverty of these young criminals stemmed not "from a deficit but a surplus of material goods provided by their parents," concluded the author, and he attributed "jeans crimes" to the fact that parents buy too many material things for their children, misplacing their sense of values. He also added that the Soviet Union should try to improve the quality of Soviet jeans. I read later in an American newspaper that the Blue Bell jeans company was going to open a factory in the Soviet Union; so the future supply of jeans may deter jeans crimes.

16

The Children's Room

"Jeans crimes" and other youthful violations of the law are handled by the Children's Room of the *Militsiya* (police), which deals with children from ages eleven to eighteen. The Children's Room is as much concerned with prevention of crime as it is with punishment. A young Soviet lawyer who had spent a year at the Harvard Law School volunteered to take us to a Children's Room in a Moscow police station so we could see firsthand what it was like.

On our way to the station this young lawyer told us a little about the structure of the Soviet legal system. The Supreme Court, elected by the Supreme Soviet (also called the Soviet of People's Deputies) is the highest court in the Soviet Union. In addition, there are supreme courts of the fifteen union republics, supreme courts of autonomous republics, territorial, regional, and city courts, district people's courts, and military tribunals of the armed forces.

Judges are elected for a five-year term, and people's assessors for a term of two and one-half years, by the citizens of the district. Power of supervision over the laws is vested in the procurator general of the USSR, who is appointed by the Supreme Soviet for a term of five years. The procurator general, in turn, appoints the procurators of the union and autonomous republics.

On a local level there are informal collective bodies, called comrades' courts, which are set up in factories, collective farms, housing developments, and so on. Members of the comrades' courts are elected by general meetings of the organization, and their task is to promote the education of citizens in the socialist way of life as well as to apply censure to offenders. Usually the members of these courts know the offender personally, and he knows them, so offenders often prefer to stand trial in a court of law and be judged by strangers rather than having to face their comrades.

Comrades' courts examine breaches of labor discipline, such as breakage of equipment, absenteeism, and poor workmanship, as well as cases of drunken-

183

ness and misbehavior in public, maltreatment of women or children, and some civil cases involving property valued under fifty rubles. The comrades' court may administer a comradely warning or public censure, with or without publication in the press, and impose a fine of up to ten rubles or damages of up to fifty rubles. The comrades' court may also demand a public apology to either the injured party, the collective, or both. An offender may be evicted from an apartment house where he has made a nuisance of himself; or management, at the offender's place of work, may be advised to assign him to unskilled, manual work for a period of fifteen days.

All cases are examined in public with at least three members of the comrades' court present. The accused has the right to demand additional documentation or to summon witnesses. Decisions of the comrades' courts are made by a majority of the members hearing a given case. The court's decisions are final, with the exception that the trade union or executive committee of the local soviet of working people's deputies has the right to ask the comrades' court to reexamine a case if the legality or validity of the decision is questioned. Collective censure is the most powerful weapon of the comrades' court, since the offender must live with these people who judged him and all his neighbors know about his disgrace.

The police works with the courts and the procurator's office. It sees that laws and public ordinances are observed, maintains order in public places, protects state, public, and personal property, and the security of its citizens, sees that traffic rules are obeyed, issues car and driver's licenses, investigates crimes before they are brought to court, and arrests criminals. There are special schools and colleges for police personnel.

The police is assisted by members of voluntary citizens' groups, called citizens' *druzhinniki* (patrols), who patrol streets, parks, and stadiums once a month in their free time. These squads are not vested with administrative functions or powers, but use persuasion, admonition, and advice as their main instruments. The *druzhinniki* may report the offender to his school or place of work or take him to the police.

There are also voluntary traffic inspectors who have special badges entitling them to stop traffic violators or those driving while intoxicated.

To help forestall potential problems, the police sponsors clubs to promote interest in law and civics, and the Soviet Army has a club for future soldiers. In the schools, eighth graders have a course in principles of Soviet state law, and the Pioneers have a club called Young Friends of the Police to help them become acquainted with the police and their work and problems.

"Patriot" clubs for younger children meet in local movie theaters to see movies showing "rules of the road" for seven to nine year olds and special general interest films for older children. There is also a "university for parents" with courses in how to bring up children. In the winter various industries in the region organize winter camps for children, and in the summer the children go to Pioneer camps or day camps.

The Academy for Difficult Children, under the Ministry of Internal Affairs, has special camps outside of Moscow where problem children work on farms and have lectures on character building and Soviet law while continuing their education. A people's information office counsels parents of difficult children and follows up to see if parents have followed their advice. The goal of all of these organizations is to reduce the number of teen-agers with which the police have to deal.

The police station we visited had eleven officers working in its Children's Room. These served a region of 340,000 people, of whom 75,000 were teen-agers. Each region has an inspector under the Ministry of Internal Affairs. The inspector for this Children's Room was an attractive woman who said her main task was to try to prevent offenses. She said she received a great deal of help from the Komsomol, regional committees, the district office of education, teachers from a vocational training school, members from the aviation institute located in her district, the citizens' patrol, and the commission for juvenile cases of her district. The inspector's job also included organizing councils in schools and investigating cases of problem children from ages eleven to eighteen.

The inspector invited us into a board room at the police station where we had cakes and tea and met some of the other officers, some Komsomol leaders, and other people interested in helping the police.

A member of the citizens' patrol of the Komsomol told us about the two thousand Komsomol members in that area who were in the citizens' patrol, 80 percent of whom were in the "Big Brother" program, each assigned to a particular problem child. Each difficult child is given an individual supervisor from the Komsomol. This counselor, called a *nastavnik*, studies in the same school or works in the same plant or office as his charge but is usually a little older. He helps teach his problem youth skills, takes him to the theater, and advises him on any matter that comes up.

Together with the inspector, the counselors help organize clubs for special interests, encourage sports activities, and work with the operating committee of the housing development where the problem child lives.

The citizens' patrol watches to see if children under fourteen are on the streets after nine in the evening. A Komsomol or policeman may question a child as to why he is out late, but they are not allowed to take him into the police station unless he is lost. If they notice the same child repeatedly out after curfew, the child's parents are contacted and warned.

The curfew is imposed first for health reasons, since a youngster needs his sleep, and second because there seem to be more chances for getting into trouble at night. Everyone agreed that age fifteen to sixteen was the most difficult. "They are changing from children to adults, and find the transition hard to handle," one Komsomol said.

If a teen-ager commits a criminal offense, the case goes to the procurator after a preliminary investigation by the inspector. If the procurator decides the case should go to trial, it is heard in a people's court. Although age eighteen is the dividing line between children's and adults' offenses, teen-agers who become eighteen while confined to a correctional institution are not transferred to an adult prison.

According to some studies carried out by the All-Union Institute for Study of the Causes of Crime and for Development of Crime Prevention Measures, one out of every five persons who breaks a law escapes punishment. The Kharkov Law Institute studies particularly those criminal cases involving minors and the role of punishment. One-half of the minors studied were put on probation, one-third were sentenced to corrective labor, and one-fifth were sentenced to short terms of deprivation of freedom. One form of punishment is to assign a minor to an enterprise collective for rehabilitation. The effectiveness of this measure depends to a large extent on the responsibility the enterprise assumes. Probation and corrective labor produce excellent results if there is active participation at the place of work and if the courts oversee the carrying out of the sentence.

The citizens' patrol program is geared more to prevention than punishment, everyone repeated. The troubles it dealt with most often were fighting, petty vandalism, and hooliganism. Alcoholism is also a problem, but when I asked about drug abuse I was told, "There may be some cases, but narcotics are usually impossible for teen-agers to get, since they are sold only in drugstores."

On the way home the Soviet lawyer stopped by a bookstore with us and helped me buy some of the books I had seen in the offices of the Children's Room. I bought a lovely big book with pictures called *Moya Militsiya*, a smaller book about teen-age problems called *The Cup, Drop by Drop*, and two other small pamphlets the lawyer recommended, *Pedagogy of Counseling*, and the statutes for work with minors.

We got back to the hotel just as a Soviet friend and his twenty-year-old daughter stopped by to take us to dinner. The daughter was amused at my books. "I, myself, am a *nastavnik*," she said, and on the way to dinner she told me something about her "problem child," Sasha. He was assigned to her because he got into a fight that brought him into his first contact with the police. Sasha's father had never been a part of the family. His unmarried mother was in a mental institution, and he lived with his sister, an erratic girl with intermittent jobs. Now seventeen, Sasha has a job, and our friend's daughter visits him at his place of work once or twice a week, as well as going to his apartment house, where she talks to his sister and his neighbors. The woman who lives next door to Sasha says he helps her carry her baby carriage upstairs, which our friend considers a good sign. She has been working with Sasha for about six months, and he has not had another fight since then. He wants her to take him to the theater, but she says, "Wait until you can take me."

There are more than two million counselors in the Soviet Union. Many of those who worked with young workers had considerable lengths of service in the same organizations as their charges and could help the younger worker professionally as well as personally. The book on counseling gave many suggestions for dealing with actual problems, stressing particularly the importance of the first meeting. Before the first meeting, the counselor should learn as much about the person as possible—likes, dislikes, family life, job performance, and so forth. At the first meeting he should be sure to shake hands with his charge. Shaking hands is a sign of respect and trust, and if the counselor is mistrustful the charge will be too. At first the "problem youth" is often openly hostile, and the counselor must overcome this feeling. From the very first meeting he must try to inculcate better work habits in his charge as well as a desire to improve his behavior. Often the problem youth can be involved in helping others, which, in turn, helps himself.

General responsibility for Soviet children and youth belongs to the Commission for Work with Minors, whose regulations are drawn up by the Presidium of the Supreme Soviet under the Council of Ministers. The commission organizes work with minors in sanitarium schools, boarding schools, vocational-technical schools, children's homes and dwellings, as well as in the regular schools. For instance, expulsion of a child from school must be done with the consent of the Commission for Work with Minors.

The commission consists of a chairman, vice chairman, executive secretary, and six to twelve members, the number depending on the volume of work of the executive committee of the Supreme Soviet or Council of Ministers under which the commission works. Members are drawn from among Soviet deputies, professional, Komsomol, and other social organizations, organs of the Ministry of Internal Affairs, health organizations, and other institutions. Decrees of the commission are enforced through the executive secretary and the inspector for work with children. The commission works with factory and office committees, Komsomol and parents' committees, citizens' patrols, house committees, and other social organizations, all of whose work with minors is coordinated by the commission.

Erring minors between ages eleven and fourteen may be sent to special schools, and those from fourteen to eighteen may be sent to special vocational-technical schools. The commission may also advise the local courts to reprimand parents of neglected children and recommend that certain parents be deprived of parental rights.

The offense most often mentioned in the Children's Room is "hooliganism." The July 26, 1966, decree "On Increased Liability for Hooliganism" defines petty hooliganism as "insulting annoyance of citizens and other activities that infringe upon public order and the tranquility of citizens."

Hooliganism is often caused by one of the problems most baffling to Soviet society—alcoholism. Soviet surveys show that 70 to 80 percent of all juvenile offenders use alcoholic beverages, and almost 50 percent of all juvenile crimes are committed while under the influence of alcohol.

Excessive drinking is not a new problem for the Russians. As far back as the tenth century, when Vladimir was choosing a state religion for Russia, he is said to have rejected alcohol-forbidding Islam in favor of Greek Orthodox Christianity because "the Russians can't live without drinking."

A 1980 report by the All-Union Knowledge Society's Committee for

Anti-Alcohol Propaganda at the USSR Academy of Internal Affairs showed alcoholism up and the drinking age down. The authors of the report said that the percentage of people who began drinking prior to age eighteen jumped from 16.6 percent in 1925 to 90 to 95 percent at present. One survey of twenty-seven preschoolers found twenty who had already tried beer, seven who had tried wine, and one who had drunk vodka with his father. Ninety percent of all alcoholics started drinking before age fifteen, and one-third of them began before they were ten.

More and more teen-agers throughout the Soviet Union are being taken to drying-out stations. There is one youth under sixteen for every 450 adults brought in, but for sixteen and seventeen-year-olds the figure is one per forty-four adults.

The law forbids the sale of liquor to minors, but one liquor store operator explained his predicament to *Komsomolskaya Pravda*:

> Do you know what inventory equivalent is? This means that for every ruble of the plan I should also have a ruble's worth of merchandise. If I don't get twelve bottles of milk delivered to me but one bottle of vodka instead it's considered that I have the inventory equivalent, and I'm supposed to fulfill the plan. If I don't fulfill it, the whole store will go without a bonus.

The store manager suggested that his plan not include vodka. "Then we'll observe all the rules."

The same article tells of boys drinking "stunner" (*bormotukha*, the nickname for strong, red vermouth) with no police, Komsomol, or citizens' patrol around to prevent them. *Uchitelskaya Gazeta* (Teacher's Newspaper) of October 3, 1979, reported that it was becoming a tradition for tenth graders to "wash down" every exam they passed. The newspaper said that students should be reminded of Catherine the Great's remark, "A drunken people is easier to rule."

"Drunkenness is incompatible with the principles of socialist morality," *Pravda* and other Soviet publications repeat. Every department of the Soviet government is opposed to alcoholism, and parents too say they deplore drinking among their children. Yet surveys show that most children had their first taste of liquor at home.

Why do they drink? Very few liked the taste. Most said they drank "because everyone else is doing it." They drank at home in the afternoon when their parents were both working and they and their friends were without adult supervision. They drank at night, on the streets and in dance clubs and cafes. They drank because they were bored or because permissive parents gave them too much money.

"Alcohol is a perfidious, cunning, and resourceful foe," says an article in *Sovetskaya Kultura* (Soviet Culture). For those who advocate moderate drinking as an alternative to alcoholism the authors refute the idea of opening a bottle only on a suitable occasion. "But when one adds up funerals, anniversaries, birthdays, holidays, visits of special guests, etc., it turns out the average adult

may have forty-five to fifty such 'suitable' occasions in a year."

Soviets are also concerned that drinking parents may bear retarded children. Mentally retarded persons who were conceived by intoxicated parents exhibit the same uninhibited behavior as drunkards, other Soviet scientists say. These retarded children must then be sent to special schools, where teachers help them develop self-control and perhaps teach them a trade until they graduate at age fifteen to eighteen, quite likely to commit more crimes.

The anti-alcohol policy is not wholly consistent, however. In 1973, the Soviet state offered its first course in bartending. In addition to the standard drinks, students in the course learn to mix a sobering-up cocktail for a bar patron who has had too much: eighty grams of milk, twenty grams of cognac, ten grams of fruit syrup, and an egg; shake well.

On our first visit to the Soviet Union, I took a tennis lesson from a Soviet tennis pro in a resort town. He continued to write to us over the years, at first in Russian and then in English, which he said he had learned from reading *World Tennis*, to which we sent him a subscription. "How many tennis teachers are there in your village? How much do they make?" one of his earlier letters said. The last letter said, "Could you send me a bartender's manual?"

17

What Is Good and What Is Bad

Even before the Soviet child can read, he has heard Mayakovsky's poem, "What is Good and What Is Bad." Like most Russian poetry, it is hard to translate into English, but in Russian it has a jolly rhyme and the unusual form characteristic of Mayakovsky. Bad children get their clothes dirty and are afraid of crows, but good children are brave and clean. When first graders read part of this poem for themselves, they are asked to tell in their own words what is good and what is bad.

In the first grade what is good and what is bad is clear cut, but by the second grade a new element is added—complex morality. This topic is introduced with a story called *Chestnoe Slovo*, which is a typically Russian expression meaning your word given in good faith, honesty—the Russian equivalent of "Cross my heart and hope to die."

The author of the story saw a little boy crying in a park. When he asked the child what was wrong, the child said, "Nothing."

"Then let's go. The park is about to close."

"I can't leave," the boy said. Then he explained that an older child had appointed him sergeant in a war game and told him to stay at his post until relieved. The older boy had said, "Give me your word of honor that you won't leave your post."

"*Chestnoe Slovo*, I won't leave," said the boy.

The older boy had gone off, and now the younger child was left guarding a post he believed he could not leave because he had given his word. The author wanted to help the child and offered to guard the post for him, but the boy said he could not turn his post over to a "civilian."

"Wait here a minute," the author said, rushing across the street to where he saw an army officer about to get on a bus. Catching the officer by the arm, he yelled, "The boy has to stay on duty. He can't leave because he gave his word. He's very little. He's crying."

The officer was startled, but when the author explained more fully, he, too, wanted to help. "Let's go. Let's go. Of course! Why didn't you tell me right away?"

When the officer told the boy he was relieving him of his duty, the boy asked, "What is your rank?" It wasn't until the officer proved he was a major that the boy would relinquish his post. "I gave my word," he said.

The author offered to walk home with the boy, but the child said he wasn't afraid. The story concludes with the author's observation the boy would grow up to be a "real man."

"Why did the author think the boy would grow up to be a real man?" the exercise in the reader asks. A few pages on, after another story, there are some Russian proverbs. One, "Don't give your word lightly, but when it is given, keep it," appears under the caption "Which story does this proverb remind you of?"

Most Soviet educators believe that morality always shows a class character. They point to the television program Sesame Street as an example of subtle capitalist propaganda, which is beamed to Third World countries with the object of popularizing the ideas of the American middle class. The main characters in "Sesame Street" are private shop owners, and private ownership is made "to appear natural and never the root of contradictions." Since Communism is based on state ownership of the means of production, "Sesame Street" is considered anti-Communist propaganda, or "cultural colonialism," as an article in *Sovetskaya Kultura* calls it.

Classic Marxism-Leninism teaches that morality is one of the basic forms of social consciousness and that man cannot exist outside of the social conditions of his life. When these social and economic conditions change, man's idea of morality changes with them.

Morality comes from the Latin word *moralis*, which means custom, says a Soviet article on Marxist-Leninist ethics. Morality changes from century to century and from country to country; what is considered bad in one time and place may be considered good in another. Each class in society has its own system of morality, which expresses and defends its class interests.

Engels said that men consciously or unconsciously derive their moral ideas from the practical relations on which their class is based, the economic relations in which they carry on production and exchange. Engels divided the morality of his day into three types—Christian (further divided into Catholic and Protestant with various subgroups under each), bourgeois, and proletarian. He considered Christian morality a representative of the past, bourgeois morality of the present, and proletarian the morality of the future.

Proletarian morality, now usually called "Communist morality," is of great concern to Soviet educators, since their job is to mold the new Soviet man in the spirit of the Communist world outlook. This requires that each person develop a harmoniously balanced well-rounded personality capable of under-

standing the beauties of life and art in the real world without reliance on a supernatural power. The Communist world outlook does not include God.

The separation of church and state was declared soon after the Revolution, and in 1921 a new decree banned the teaching of religion to anyone under age eighteen. This rule was changed in 1923 to prohibit giving private religious instruction to children in groups of more than three.

In 1925 the League of Militant Atheists encouraged Pioneers to wreck churches, destroy icons, and make fun of anyone with religious tendencies. Today the attitude is much more lenient, with some churches being restored as tourist attractions. "As far as the destruction of some churches in the first years of Soviet power is concerned," writes a commentator in *Science and Religion*, "let us recall Marx's remark concerning identical charges made against the Paris Commune: 'If the workers of Paris behaved like vandals, it was a vandalism of desperate defense not the vandalism of triumphant conquerors.'"

In 1964 the Institute of Scientific Atheism was created in the Central Committee's Academy of Social Sciences to deal with urgent problems in the scientific atheistic upbringing of Soviet children. The institute helps the Party set up centers to study the best methods of overcoming religious beliefs and replacing these beliefs with a scientific materialist world outlook.

When increased atheistic work with children was suggested, some Moscow parents' committee members asked, "What for? The children are overloaded with work now."

Soviet educators respond with the warning that God may seem very attractive to children. They note that childhood is an important stage in human development, and the dangers of religious beliefs at this stage are very real. The child not only swallows information, he evaluates it. He is looking for answers to questions such as: Why is snow white? Where does wind come from and why does it blow? Why do leaves turn yellow?

To answer children's questions in a realistic way, there is a three-volume encyclopedia, *What's What, Who's Who,* as well as many other books with titles like "Why Does This Happen?" and "Miracles Without a Miracle." Older schoolchildren are given the *Book for Young Atheists, Is There a Place for God? Great Heretics, Argument with Yourself,* and *When the Specter Appears.* Atheism, like any other science, has its problems, say Soviet educators.

When Pioneers are confronted with believers they often appeal to *Pionerskaya Pravda* for answers. How do you show a believer that God does not exist? The newspaper replies that this is a complicated question. Proving the non-existence of God is not as easy as "two times two." The article says it is necessary to know why the believer believes in God. Does he love God, fear him, or want something from him?

Believers say people have souls, which you can't see, hear, or touch, and that God exists in the same way. The Pioneer leaders reply that souls exist, but only in living people. "The dead do not think, feel, or have a will to act." Religious people say prayer works miracles, and the Pioneers respond that when the Pope died in 1958 all the prayers of Catholics in the whole world couldn't keep him alive.

Can Communism and religion cooperate? Soviet leaders say this is another complicated question. There are religious people who are anti-capitalist, and there are religious people who use religion for reactionary purposes, such as the Moslem Brothers, whom the Soviets say are stirring up trouble in Afghanistan. Soviet leaders think it is important for believers and nonbelievers to unite for the common goal of peace in the world, and they cite the fact that the Soviet Union has more than 20,000 Orthodox churches, Polish Catholic churches, synagogues, Lutheran churches, Old Believer churches, mosques, Buddhist temples, and meeting houses for Evangelical Christian Baptists, Seventh Day Adventists, and other groups, as well as about twenty monasteries and convents.

An article in *Science and Religion* says some Moslem leaders have relaxed the five traditional pillars of faith (reciting the confession of faith, five daily prayers, observance of the month-long Ramadan fast, payment of the purification tax, and pilgrimage to Mecca) and have become more friendly with Communism. An "Appeal to All Moslems of Dagestan and the Northern Caucasus," adopted at a congress of Moslem clergy in the northern Caucasus on October 16, 1975, called the building of Communism the great earthly "ideal of the prophet Mohammed," according to the article.

It is a few Baptist sects who give the Pioneers the most trouble because members of these sects often refuse to allow their children to participate in Pioneer activities. At a trial of four adults for "breaking the laws of separation of church and state, church and school, and disseminating anti-Soviet fabrications," the eighth-grade son of one of the defendants testified that his mother had dragged him to illegal gatherings every Sunday, where he was forced to spend hours in a stuffy room singing hymns and reciting religious verses until he sometimes fainted. He was not allowed to become an Octobrist or Pioneer, and when his mother was at work he had to make tape recordings of foreign religious broadcasts. The boy was taken away from his mother and sent to a boarding school, but she continually called him asking, "Do you pray?" Finally she kidnapped him from the school and hid him with Baptist dissenters. The court again rescued the boy, and his mother was deprived of her parental rights.

Pioneer and Komsomol organizations are cautioned to continue their anti-religious propaganda, even though current official interest in newly repaired churches, restored icon paintings, and some religious literature may lead children to think religion is good. The Soviet Constitution actually guarantees freedom of religious belief, but it also guarantees freedom of anti-religious propaganda, and the Soviet child today is less likely to be religious than his parents or their parents were. A writer on atheistic subjects jokingly told us that it was sometimes necessary to explain who God was in order to explain atheism.

One of the foundations of Communist morality is education for work and the giving of one's strength and work for the common good. Soviet leaders try to implant this idea deep in the child's consciousness in order to make him want to be a responsible citizen aware of his personal responsibility toward building Communism.

Socially useful labor is good, the Soviet child is told over and over. Such repetition is necessary because the Soviet worker is not characteristically inclined to serious work. *Krokodil*, the Soviet humor weekly, constantly pictures workers assiduously smuggling sausages out of a sausage factory or going through a magnetic door, which draws stolen metal out of the pockets of workers in a metal factory. Pictures of offices show workers playing cards, drinking, socializing (the social part of socially useful labor is very popular), or doing crossword puzzles instead of working. Bribes are solicited in cartoons of large outstretched palms or desk drawers conveniently open for dropping in rubles in return for bureaucratic favors.

A waiter, looking over my shoulder as I was reading *Krokodil* one day in a Moscow restaurant, went through the entire issue with me, explaining each cartoon. He laughed particularly at a picture of a restaurant where all the waiters were congenially leaning against a refrigerator in a room full of empty tables while a horde of angry would-be customers pounded on a door hung with the sign, *Mest net* (No tables).

I liked the picture of the inspector at a collective farm who was checking on a sheep herd. There were only one or two woolly sheep in the picture. The inspector asked where the rest of the herd was, and the farmer replied with a straight face, "The moths ate them."

Various Soviet surveys show that the social status of a child's parents has a definite effect on the child's vocational preferences. Most children of collective farmers and agricultural workers want to become industrial workers. Most children of workers want to be office employees or members of the intelligentsia. Most children of the intelligentsia want to remain in that group. The social position of the parents can also interfere with romance, as a letter from a young man to *Soviet Culture* attested. The young man had been in love with a girl, but during his two-year army service she had enrolled in an institute. When he returned from the army she said he too must enter an institute to ensure his "future position in society." Bothered by this intellectual snobbery, the young man eventually married another girl.

In the Soviet system, the goal of social homogeneity often conflicts with the equally important need for promoting the most efficient use of the country's intellectual potential. According to an article in *Izvestiya*, the correct choice of an occupation requires that at least three conditions be met: the person should have a certain inclination toward the job, his health and psychological and physiological characteristics should suit the vocation, and both these factors should combine with the real needs of the economy.

One survey attempted to match people's job aspirations with their actual employment opportunities. Jobs were ranked according to desirability, from most attractive (cosmonaut) to least attractive (unskilled laborer). Job opportunities showed a graph that reversed the desirability pattern.

Ideally, tasks required for particular types of work should be matched with a psychological profile defining the worker's personality. For example, workers responsible for automated control systems in which breakdowns are likely to occur, involving stressful situations threatening people's health and life, require strong, even-tempered personalities. Motor vehicle drivers also needed strong nervous systems.

To prepare workers to choose an appropriate job, vocational guidance is being used more and more in Soviet schools. The school is asked to study the children's inclinations and develop these into future vocational interests.

Such characteristics as perception, memory, reasoning, attention, agility, as well as specialized abilities in math, music, art, technical, and organizational skills are matched to various professions.

Beginning in the first grade the child has "work" lessons for two hours each week. These lessons introduce the child to people from various professions and stress the idea that all sorts of socially useful work are good.

In the upper grades the child may spend the "third semester" (summer vacation) at a labor and recreation camp. Here the day begins with gymnastics. After breakfast the campers work in a neighboring collective farm until dinner time, which is in the middle of the day. The afternoon is for sports, swimming, competitions, or rest, and after supper there are games, amateur theatricals, or stories around a campfire.

The Communist Party would like to make more active use of summer vacations for the labor and ideological upbringing of Soviet youth. Young

Pioneers often form agricultural brigades, school repair and forestry sections, or detachments for gathering medicinal herbs, seeds, mushrooms, and berries.

The Kharkov Tractor Plant was one of the first enterprises to set up a production-training center for young people, grounded in a broad base of polytechnical labor training. The young people were able to become acquainted with about ten specialties ranging from motor vehicle construction to work with calculators. In Moscow, the Bauman district, consisting of eleven enterprises, offered young people an opportunity to learn such diverse specialties as the operation of machine tools, milling machines, and electronic equipment, as well as how to do hand embroidery. There was psychophysiological testing of students and vocational adaptation directly through production work.

Eventually the state plans to set up production training centers in every district in Moscow. These centers are thought to be better than vocational classes in individual schools because the centers have superior equipment and can offer a broader range of training. In one center the student could learn to be a welder, furrier, secretary, telegraph operator, postal clerk, tailor, or cabinet-maker. The children find it more exciting to go to the training center, often for the whole day and away from school, to learn "social maturity." Students in a training center receive the usual eight- or ten-year academic education but also learn a trade.

In the Kharkov Tractor Plant, ninth graders visit the center and choose a particular type of training. For the first six months they are free to change their original decision; after that they are expected to make a final choice. Since many of these students go into the labor force after completing their course at the center, they have been stabilized by the time they are ready to enter the permanent labor force. The Soviets have found that this stability is a factor in both reducing labor turnover and increasing job satisfaction.

The Soviet press is often critical of lags in building vocational schools and the quality of the construction on them. The Institute for Research on Vocational Training and Guidance of the USSR Academy of Pedagogical Sciences has been asked to increase its work in this field and also to create textbooks and visual aids for the courses it develops.

To work out some of the problems, the Armenian State Committee joined with the rector's office of the Armenian Pedagogical Institute to organize a special problem laboratory for occupational psychology and vocational and technical education. Yerevan's Secondary-Vocational Technical School No. 10 was designated as the experimental teaching center, and here special attention was paid to the ideological, political, moral, ethical, aesthetic, and physical upbringing of the students.

We visited Vocational-Technical School No. 120, in Moscow with Harry. This was a day school drawing its 460 students from the area of Moscow near the school. (Some schools take boarders, and many have up to 1,000 pupils.) School No. 120 was connected to a dress and hat factory located nearby. The school schedule had been worked out jointly between the factory and the school. The course lasted three years, covering the eighth, ninth, and tenth grades, with lessons in academic subjects and three in technical specialties each year. Each student receives a stipend of from thirty-eight to forty-nine rubles a month, and students are paid regular factory wages for their work in addition to the stipend. In July of their third year they must pass an exam to receive their diploma, which proclaims them qualified workers.

At the school we met a pleasant woman who was teaching the children to make hats. She was a retired worker who was volunteering her time, and there were many other volunteers who came regularly to the school to help, including graduates of the school and a number of retired factory workers.

In addition to the teaching staff, all of whom have a higher education, there is a foreman who has a middle technical education. The principal told us that in years past vocational schools had been looked on as places for dumb children but that the image had now changed so much that there were more applicants for the school than places. She said the school recently had begun to offer post-graduate work for students who had graduated from the tenth grade (the equivalent of our graduation from high school). The school's main

task is to prepare qualified workers for skilled labor while giving them the well-rounded development of a regular secondary school education.

The dress and hat factory works closely with the school, paying for all the equipment used and making contributions for sports complexes, assembly halls, and uniforms. The school principal presents her needs for the school to the factory, arguing with them to secure the greatest possible level of support.

We went through classrooms where children were designing and making children's dresses and women's hats. These products are sold in Moscow stores just as any other factory product would be. There was a whispered conversation between several of the teachers and pupils, and I could tell they were planning to give me something. I thought it would be one of the flowery hats and was wondering how I could take it home when they brought out a small teddy bear with Eddie Cantor eyes. "This is Mishka, the mascot of our Olympic games," they said, handing me the little plush body, which I instinctively hugged.

Vladislav Krapivin, the author of many children's books, says that each new generation solves the old problems in its own way. "The child lives through a whole epoch in the years from seven to fourteen—a short span but extraordinarily important for the future." A courageous character begins in childhood, but whether or not the child retains this character depends on the adults around him. Do the adults nourish the courageous beginnings, or do they push the child into compromises, asks Krapivin.

18

The Last Bell

We had discovered our favorite Soviet School quite by accident in the early 1970s. An Intourist guide asked if we would like to visit an English-language school, explaining that many Soviet schools offered intensified instruction in a particular foreign language beginning in the second grade.

The director of the school was a large, friendly man who led us through a hall filled with good-natured pandemonium. Children darted out from behind doors to pounce unexpectedly on a friend. They did cartwheels. They were in constant, sometimes violent, motion. The principal walked along calmly, chatting amiably. From time to time he would intercept some child's raised arm, and once he cupped a small head in his hand and turned it away from another argumentative child.

A bell rang, and one group surged into a classroom where I heard a teacher say, "Tone down a little. Collect yourselves."

The children were sitting at their desks when we entered the room. They stood up politely when they saw us, and the director introduced us. "We are discussing some aspects of American life," the teacher said. "The class is conducted entirely in English because that is the specialty of our school."

She showed us a place to sit at one of the school desks, then turned to the class. "Make your answers brief and to the point. Victor, do you want to begin?"

A light-haired, blue-eyed boy of thirteen or fourteen stood up. "Well, well, on the 4th of July, thirteen American colonies went together and produced the Declaration of Independence, and, well," his voice trailed off.

"We hold these truths to be self-evident," the teacher prompted.

"Yes," Victor said. "We hold these truths to be self-evident that all men are created equal. Then the Declaration of Independence goes on to say that everyone is entitled to life, liberty, and the pursuit of happiness. That whenever any form of government becomes destructive of these ends, it is the right of the people to alter or abolish it."

"Very good, Victor. We all know that the American Revolution was and is a great inspiration for revolutionaries all over the world."

There were a few more comments on the American Revolution from other members of the class. Then the teacher asked, "Can anyone name some American holidays?"

"Christmas," said a plump girl in the first row.

"A fine holiday, but not entirely American. How about the 4th of July, Independence Day?"

The class moved on to American literature. "The literature of the United States reflects the history of the country, and it is essential for us to know the history of the United States," the teacher said. "The first American writing took the form of political pamphlets—Franklin, Jefferson, and Paine. Romantic literature developed later in America than in Europe. It had its own features, somewhat modified by American realism. Fenimore Cooper, Longfellow, Edgar Allen Poe."

Victor stood up again: "Mark Twain was one of the early realists. His writings are also colored by a romantic vision of life. *Tom Sawyer* is called the poetry of childhood."

"The poetry of childhood," the teacher savored the words. "Tom Sawyer and Huckleberry Finn were not exactly babies and not exactly youth. What is the poetry of childhood?" She nodded to a girl in the second row. "Natasha, you may look upon yourself as a volunteer."

"Tom Sawyer was not a model boy," Natasha said, and the class laughed. "His life was full of jokes and funny scenes. Tom was a mischievous boy. He was a challenge to the repressive atmosphere of his village."

Another bell rang and the class was over. We shook hands with the teacher and went back to the principal's office to get our coats and hats. As we were leaving the building we passed a fourth-grade English class and heard a concerted chorus of "Come with me to the zoo, zoo, zoo, to see the kangaroo, roo, roo."

My husband had taken a number of pictures at the school, and when we got home he made up an album which we thought we would take to the principal on our next trip to the Soviet Union. Two years later we took the album with us to Moscow but could not find the school.

I asked at the Intourist office, but the guide who had taken us to the school had left Intourist, and no one else had any idea which school it might be. "We have many, many schools in Moscow," they said. I thought I remembered the general area where the school was located so we set out on foot to canvas the neighborhood.

On many Moscow streets are small kiosks, called information bureaus, where one may inquire about theater tickets or general information. I took the album to several of these bureaus and asked the attendant if she recognized any of the people in the pictures or could tell us where the school might be. The attendant always looked at the pictures with great interest and usually had some suggestion as to where we should inquire next, but we still could not find the school.

Harry thought he might be able to locate it for us, but even he failed, and sadly we took the album back to the United States with us. At home, looking at some other slides we had of the school, we discovered the number of the school on one of them. Again we took the album to Moscow with us, and this time, having the number of the school, had no trouble locating it. Harry offered to go with us, but we said it was not necessary. We simply walked in the front door of the school and made our way to the principal's office.

We were shown in to the office of a nice-looking woman who told us she was the acting principal. Looking through our album, she came to a picture of the genial principal we had known. "Ivan Ivanovich," the woman said. "He was such a nice man. He died last year of lung cancer. He is greatly missed." As she thumbed through the pages she identified by name each person in the pictures—Lena, a girl Pioneer leader, Victor, Natasha, had all graduated. The Russian woman who taught English in the class we watched had emigrated to Philadelphia. "Perhaps you could give her my regards if you are ever in Philadelphia. She doesn't write now."

Our pages of pictures already represented the past, we thought a little sadly, and yet we could hear the same boisterous childish noises in the halls outside the acting principal's office. "Come visit us any time," the woman said. "We are happy to have you. Perhaps you might like to come to our graduation ceremonies on May 25, too. It's quite a festive occasion."

We went back often, dropping in without previous notice. We got to know some of the students and sometimes were greeted at the theater or on the street by a boy or or girl we had seen at the school. Harry said we certainly should attend a graduation exercise at the school. "We call the ceremony 'The Last Bell,' " he said. "It's a very beautiful ceremony—the end of childhood and the beginning of youth."

We attended the graduation exercises several times, the last time on May 25, 1976. The school was a sturdy, prerevolutionary building with decorative moldings around the front door, which opened directly from the street. Two boys were kicking a pebble around the sidewalk, on which was written in big chalk letters "Good Luck Class 10-A." Inside another boy was sliding down the bannisters of the stairs. Outside the principal's office stood a row of first graders, the girls wearing crisp white pinafores over their dark dresses, and white tarleton hair ribbons, the boys in short dark blue pants and long-sleeved white shirts. They clutched small bouquets of lilacs and tulips and looked a little apprehensive.

Upstairs rows of Pioneers lined the halls, the girls in dark blue skirts with long-sleeved white shirts and the boys in long dark blue pants and long-sleeved white shirts. All wore the red Pioneer necktie. Some had on white caps, some

red, and some blue, apparently differentiating separate grades in the school.

Two of the older Pioneer boys greeted us and showed us into an assembly hall where we were given seats in the front row. The room was large and had floor-to-ceiling French windows, some of them open to the May air. On the stage a long table covered with red velvet fringed with gold stood behind great baskets of blue and white hydrangeas. The school's teachers sat in rows of chairs arranged behind the table, and on the wall behind them was a huge profile of Lenin. A number of parents were already seated in the back of the hall and were greeted by new arrivals from time to time.

The acting principal, who had invited us and who was now the official principal, took her place at the speakers' table on the stage, and other teachers followed. I noticed that two of the women wore the identical dress—a dark blue background with circles of various colors printed on it.

"Attention! Comrades!" said a man in a brown suit who had come forward on the stage. There was a moment's silence, then a bugle blast outside. The tenth grade marched in carrying balloons and flowers. Some of the boys wore dark suits, white dress shirts, and dark ties. Most of the girls wore white pinafores over dark dresses as did the first-grade girls. There was great applause from the parents and the teachers and an air of excitement from the tenth graders which communicated itself to the room.

Another blast from the bugle and class 9-A came in, also carrying balloons and flowers. Another blast, 9-B. The rows were filling up in the auditorium. Some seated children called to late-coming parents. "Mama! Mama! I'm over here." The rest of the school filed in and everyone settled down. The principal addressed the group: "Today in our country is a festive day. Millions of children

are finishing school. It is a day of joy but a sad one, too. The Last Bell is an occurrence in life which will always be remembered. Ten years ago you were first graders; now you have finished your exams and we have this festive last meeting." The principal presented a grey-haired woman who had been the graduates' first-grade teacher.

"It's hard for me, the oldest, to tell you how I feel," the grey-haired woman began. "When you heard your first bell you said to yourself, 'I can, I can.' Now you hear your last bell. A new life begins. You are the pride of our school, our minds, and our hearts. I wish you success in your new life. I wish you happiness."

A tenth-grade girl called on next, said, "I will try to tell you about the last day of our school." She read a class prophecy and gave humorous biographies of the teachers as another girl showed caricatures of the teachers. The audience laughed and applauded, with some teachers getting such an ovation that it brought tears to my eyes. Then students presented the teachers with balloons and flowers.

A Pioneer leader sang a song, becoming so sentimental that she sobbed in the middle of the song. As a Pioneer from the audience gave her flowers, a balloon burst, and the mamas wiped away their tears and laughed. The Pioneer leader kissed the boy who gave her flowers.

There were awards for Pioneers and certificates for graduates, much applause, and great joy.

A man in an army uniform was introduced. "It has been ten years since you came here," he said. "Ten years is a short time, though it seems long to you.

When I grew up there were no atomic bombs or TV. In 1941 I saw some of the children from this school go to war. Take some of your flowers to the memorial for the dead from our school. Don't forget them."

The head of the English department gave the main address. "Ours is a specialized English school, I am found with a rather complicated problem. In my English class I have little practice speaking English because my pupils do all the talking. It's next to impossible to stop them, and I can hardly get in a word," she apologized, then continued. "Why is this a happy day? You are on the threshold of a new life, but what about us, your teachers? We are happy and sad because in each of you is a part of ourselves.

"What do we wish for you? We want you to be original thinkers, modest about your own successes, workers for peace, not war, but most of all we want you to remember one thing: never be indifferent. Indifference is the main source of evil in the world. Indifferent people are the real evil people in our world. You must care about your country and your world."

After some songs and recitations, the girl from 10-A spoke again. "We are now grown-ups. Remember our school and this street, but most of all remember *us*. Each of us thanks you, our first teachers. Thanks to everyone for these ten years. Success in your personal life and for the school. All the happiness in the world."

A Komsomol committee handed out pots of forget-me-nots to the graduating class, then the first graders rushed in with flowers for the graduates, who hugged and kissed the children in return. A little girl from the first grade made a speech, but forgot the poem she was reciting in the middle of it. The Soviet poet Agnya Barto once told us that at a similar loss of memory another little girl had said, "I'm sorry, but half of my poem has fallen ill."

The little first-grade speaker was lifted off the stage by a tenth-grade boy, and the two went out into the hall together. The song "The Last Bell" was played on the loud speaker, and the audience quieted down for a minute as the last bell rang outside. Then with a roar, the audience shouted, "I wish you success." Everyone got up. There were hugs and kisses, laughter and tears. Autograph books were passed around for signatures as everyone began to leave the school.

That night, as is traditional, there was a ball for the tenth graders, with dinner parties beforehand. The girls wear expensive white dresses to these balls, and the boys wear dark suits and frilly white shirts. When the party was over, everyone went to Red Square to watch the sunrise and toast the ringing of the Last Bell.

What were the graduates doing a year later? I did not know what happened to the young people we saw graduate, but the magazine *Soviet Life* told about another class a year after graduation. On graduation day, thirty out of a class of thirty-two said they wanted to go on to an institute, but only twenty-four of these graduates actually applied for admission to one. Of the twenty-four who applied, ten passed the entrance exams and submitted applications to one of the seventy-eight higher educational institutions of Moscow. Five of these survived the competition for admission. One was admitted to Bauman Higher Technical School, two to a medical institute, and two to a military engineering school.

Those who failed to get into an institute blamed themselves: "I didn't take school seriously enough." "Too lazy and not enough ambition." "Failing the exams is really a plus. I didn't get where I wanted to go but I think that it's a good lesson for the future." These were some of the comments reported in *Soviet Life*.

What kind of jobs did the young people get when they were rejected by the institute? Two who had reached the draft age of eighteen were inducted into the army. Nine got jobs in factories as electrical fitters, radio assemblers, or controllers. Nine went to research institutes as laboratory assistants or draftsmen. One girl became a librarian at the Lenin Library, one boy a printer at *Izvestiya*, one a clerk at the Supreme Court, one a teacher's assistant in a kindergarten, and one a computer operator at the Central Telephone Station.

During the next two years my husband and I traveled to Israel, China, Cuba, Morocco, and other places around the world. "When are you coming back to Moscow?" wrote Harry.

Then one day we had a telephone call from him. He was in Detroit; could he spend a few days with us? Harry was beaming as we met him at the airport in Washington. "I thought I might not get here at all," he said. "I went to the American Embassy in Moscow to get my visa and one of the questions on the visa application was, 'Are you a Communist?' I thought if I said yes they wouldn't give me a visa. If I said no they would find out somehow that I was and there'd be the devil to pay. Anyhow, I got in."

Harry had visited the reform school in Hawthorne where he had been so many years before. He asked to be allowed to address the student body, but his request was refused. "It looked like a very good school, though," he said. "Better than when I was there." He had looked up some of his comrades from his American Pioneer days. All of them were glad to see him, but most had left the Party.

We had several days strenuous sightseeing. At Harry's request, my husband photographed him in front of the Lincoln Memorial, Mt. Vernon, Kennedy's grave, the Capitol, the Library of Congress, the Washington Monument, the Kennedy Center, and the Supreme Court. At Mt. Vernon, Harry told a very plump guide that he was Russian and that he considered her a fine figure of a woman. The guide laughed and said, "If that's detente, I like it."

As we passed Padaruski's grave at Arlington Cemetery, another guide said, "As soon as Poland is freed from the Communist yoke, Paderuski's body will be taken back to Poland where it can be buried on free soil." Harry nudged me. "You have your propaganda too." he said. He enjoyed himself immensely in the United States but was glad to be going back to Moscow, his suitcases brimming with bargains from J.C. Penny's.

In 1979 we were invited to a conference on the International Year of the Child to be held in Moscow. Harry urged us to attend, and said it was an honor to be invited as there would be famous people from all over the world. We accepted the invitation, and on March 21 left Washington on the Concorde for London.

After a night in Brown's Hotel, we were at the airport for our BOAC flight to Moscow early the next morning. But Sheremetyevo Airport in Moscow was fogged in, and we watched the departure board flash one delay after another on the Moscow flight. By three in the afternoon BOAC had decided to put us all up at an airport motel and try again the next day. The next morning the flight was scheduled, canceled, then reinstated. We took off at about 1:30 PM London time and arrived in Moscow at about seven the same evening, Moscow time.

"You're late," said the lady at the airport Intourist office. "You should have come yesterday."

"We wanted to come yesterday. We tried to come yesterday. Your airport was closed," I said indignantly.

"I have to telex Moscow. You wait." Fortunately the wait was short and we were soon in our private limousine noticing the many new high-rise buildings that had been built on the outskirts of Moscow since our last trip.

"You're late. You must pay a fine for being late," the desk clerk at the National Hotel greeted us, when we came in with our bags. I was about to be indignant again when a pleasant-looking Intourist woman said firmly to the desk clerk, "No fine." Then she turned to us and said, in English, "You have a nice room looking over the front yard."

Our "front yard" turned out to be the broad Square of the Fiftieth Anniversary of the October Revolution on Karl Marx Prospect with a glimpse of Red Square beyond the Historical Museum, the walls of the Kremlin, and the Tomb of the Unknown Soldier across from us, the huge yellow Central Exhibition Hall on the right and the Moskva Hotel on the left of the square. The red stars on the Kremlin towers shone through the dark night.

We had an immense living room furnished in prerevolutionary French antiques, a large bedroom, and a large bathroom with a tub so high that it was necessary to step on a slatted wooden platform to get in it. Among the oil paintings, cut crystal glassware, and marble ornaments which decorated the living room were two incongruous but welcome objects—a large white, modern refrigerator and a color television set.

I called Harry. His wife Faiya, answered. "Harry is sick. Very sick," she said in Russian, but Harry took the receiver from her and said, "I had the flu at Christmas time and don't seem to be able to shake it." He dismissed his own health and asked about us and when we could come to their apartment. "How about supper tomorrow?"

When we arrived for supper, Harry did not look well, but his conversation was as ebullient as ever. From time to time he would get up and pace up and down the room with a hand against his back. "Does your back hurt?" I asked.

"Something hurts," he said. "The doctors thought it might be my lungs. They took X-rays but there was no sign of any trouble. My lungs were clean. I'm going to have some more tests next week."

We talked about the Pioneers, and Harry showed us some articles he had written about the United States for *Pionerskaya Pravda*. After one article appeared, he received six thousand letters from children. Harry showed us the pile of letters, most written in careful, childish Russian. "I've had a good life," he said. "These letters mean more to me than a million dollars. In fact if I had a million dollars I'd live just the way I do now."

We told Harry about our plans for a trip to Siberia before the conference began. "There was a time when no one went to Siberia of his own free will," Harry joked. "You were *sent* there."

He seemed to think a minute, then said, "Like any average citizen of the Soviet Union, I spent my time in Siberia."

"Under Stalin?" I asked.

Harry nodded. "The funny thing is that I was sentenced to Siberia because I knew a certain person. Actually, although I knew her, I couldn't stand her."

"Don't you feel bitter?"

"No. Those were bad years, but we Russians are through apologizing for Stalin. We're too busy. We put Stalin in his proper place and go on building socialism. I didn't waste my three years in Siberia. I had three years with the Siberian people, who are building socialism, too. Several years ago I went to the opening of a Pioneer camp in that little Siberian town. The people remembered me and had a big party in the town square for me. So you see, Kitty, I didn't waste those three years. I gained three years. The Soviet Union will always have enemies, but we know how to deal with them."

On our way back to the hotel we talked about Harry and his ability to get along in any situation. "What are *we* going to do with all these suitcases?" I said, as we packed for our trip to Siberia.

Local Soviet airlines did not allow as large a luggage weight allowance as intercontinental flights, so to avoid paying excess baggage charges we left some of our luggage at Harry's while we went to Bratsk. We were surprised to find Siberia dazzlingly bright after the grey, rainy fogs of Moscow. The weather was cold but not unbearably so. Frozen Lake Bratsk with its blue ice sparkling against snow-covered banks was beautiful. We visited schools, Pioneer palaces, and camps and had a good trip.

When we stopped to pick up our bags on our way back from Siberia, we found that Harry was worse. He had had more tests but the doctors could not discover anything wrong. "My sister lives in California," Harry said. "I thought maybe if I got away from this grey, wet weather and into some sunshine I might get well, but I couldn't afford the doctors in California. Here all my medical care is free."

"How about Sochi on the Black Sea?" I asked.

"I've thought of that. I could go there and the Soviet government would pay all my expenses. Maybe that's what I should do. They have good sanitariums there."

Harry didn't want to talk about himself any more. He thought I should go to see Fedulova again and said he would come along to help me. I wasn't sure he was up to it, but he insisted. Several days later we picked him up in our car (he wanted to go on the subway and meet us, but we insisted he was better in a car), and we had a nice visit with Fedulova. Harry seemed more like his old self as he talked animatedly about the Pioneers.

After the conference began I let two days go by without calling Harry. When I called I was going to tell him what one of the conferees had said about children's ideas of time. "The child does not understand time. 'Sometime ago,' 'tomorrow,' and 'too long' are the only things he knows."

But Faiya answered the telephone. "Harry is in the hospital," she said. Visiting hours were after five in the afternoon, so we arranged to pick her up and take her to the hospital, which was on the opposite side of Moscow from their apartment.

"Harry has cancer of the pancreas," his wife told us on the way to the hospital. "The doctors say he has no more than a month to live. Harry doesn't know."

The hospital was a huge building. Harry was in a room with four other men, who were sitting at a table by the window, playing cards dressed in their hospital pajamas. Harry was sitting in bed propped up against the pillows, talking with a nice-looking man who was sitting in a straight chair next to the bed. A small night table held a glass with a knife and fork in it.

Harry smiled and introduced us to the man. "This is Bovka. You remember I told you about Bovka? He's the boy who spoke against me long ago at the Komsomol meeting when I needed to be straightened out, but then after he spoke against me he patted me on the shoulder and said he was still my friend. That pat on the shoulder meant a lot to me. I'll never forget it."

"Harry's a good friend," Bovka said. Harry smiled again.

"Harry, you have your usual smile," I said.

"That smile is part of me. I'll die with that smile on my face."

Faiya told us that Harry was in constant pain. "He gets two shots a day and each one helps, but only for about an hour and a half."

"Couldn't they give you more shots?" my husband asked. "I don't tell the doctors what to do," Harry said. "That's their business."

An attendant came in with some trays of food, and one of the men who was playing cards came over to the table next to Harry and reached for the knife and fork that were in the glass. "Are we in the way?" I asked, but the man shook his head, taking his knife and fork over to the card table to eat his dinner. Harry's dinner would come later.

We talked about various things. When we got back to the United States Harry wanted us to call a friend in New Jersey who was planning a trip to Moscow. "I won't be able to help him with his sightseeing as I promised. Maybe he won't want to come if I can't help him."

"Should we tell your sister you're sick?"

"No use alarming her," Harry said. "I'll be all right soon." Later he said, apropros of nothing, "I'll be buried in my Pioneer tie. I've lived with it and I'll die with it."

As we were leaving, Faiya whispered to us to get Harry's sister's telephone number from the American friend he had asked us to call. "Harry has his sister's address and telephone number in his address book, which he keeps under his pillow in the hospital. If I ask him for it he'll know something is wrong, but I do want his sister to know that he hasn't very long."

We called his friend the minute our plane landed in New York, and he called Harry's sister, Eda Beck, who flew to Moscow at once. Harry's daughter and grandson met her at the airport. "Things are bad. We must go to the hospital right now."

Harry sat up when his sister came in. *"Molodets"* (well done), he said,

kissing and hugging her. He asked about Eda's family and his American friends, then he bragged a little. "How do you like my hospital? See, little Harry has a room for himself, and nurses. Did you see our beautiful young nurses? This is the hospital for old Bolsheviks. I don't consider myself old, but I'm honored. I *am* a Bolshevik, you know, and let's not forget it."

Eda said that Harry suddenly looked as though transfixed. He lay back in the bed, his eyes closed. "He will sleep." The nurse said, and Eda and the others left the hospital.

At Harry's funeral, on May 9 at the Moscow Crematorium, there were hundreds of mourners—representatives of the Komsomol, the Young Pioneers, the Party, and the Writer's Union. Harry's friends walked around the flower-bedecked bier where Harry lay, dressed in his Pioneer uniform, like a little boy sleeping.

Eda Beck gave one of the eulogies: "I bid you goodbye, our little brother. Yours was a unique life—brave, giving, and idealistic. Always your understanding sustained you. Always you stood firm for what you believed."

"You had a childlike capacity for fun and laughter. The joy and excitement of living was yours. The great ability of giving and loving and of maintaining old and new friendships was the stuff of your makeup. To us and the great circle of your comrades you will always remain a symbol of heroism and giving."

In the park around the Old Palace, which is now the Moscow Crematorium, there is a monument put up by the Young Pioneers. On the monument a few words are engraved:

Harry Eisman
Forever Young Pioneer

Bibliography

IN RUSSIAN

Periodicals

Istoriya SSSR (History of the USSR). Academy of Sciences History Institute monthly.

Izvestiya. Central government daily.

Kommunist. Communist Party central organ, eighteen issues yearly.

Komsomolskaya pravda. Young Communist League daily.

Krokodil (Crocodile). Humor magazine, three times monthly.

Literaturnaya gazeta (Literary Gazette), Soviet Writers' Union weekly.

Molodoi kommunist (Young Communist). Young Communist League monthly.

Nachalnaya shkola (Elementary School). Minister of Education RSFSR monthly.

Nauka i religiya (Science and Religion). Knowledge Society atheist monthly.

Novy mir (New World). Literary monthly.

Pioner. Central Young Communist League and Central Council of Pioneers monthly.

Pionerskaya pravda. Twice weekly.

Pravda. Central Communist Party daily.

Uchitelskaya gazeta (Teachers' Gazette). Three times weekly.

Voprosy filosofii (Problems of Philosophy). Academy of Sciences Philosophy Institute monthly.

Vozhaty (Leader). Young Communist League and Pioneers monthly.

Yunost (Youth). Literary monthly.

Books

Pioneers

Artek. Simferopol: Krym, 1970.

Bud gotov! (Be ready!). Moscow: Molodaya gvardiya, 1972.

Estafeta pionerskikh pokolenii (Relay Race of the Pioneer Generation). Moscow: Molodaya gvardiya, 1972.

Istoriya VLKSM i vsesoyuznoi organizatsii imeni V. I. Lenina (History of the Komsomol and the All-Union Lenin Organization). Moscow: Prosveshchenie, 1978.

Kniga vozhatogo (The Leader Book). Moscow: Molodaya gvardiya, 1968.

Kniga vozhatogo (The Leader Book). Moscow: Molodaya gvardiya, 1972.

Krupskaya, Nadezhda. *O yunykh pionerakh* (About the Young Pioneers). Moscow: Akademiya pedagogicheskikh nauk, 1957.

Kungurtsev, I. *Pionerskii shtab*. Moscow: Molodaya gvardiya, 1974.

_____. *Sovet druzhiny*. Moscow: Molodaya gvardiya, 1977.

Pionerskaya Pravda. Moscow: Molodaya gvardiya, 1976.

Priglashaem v oktyabryatsk (We invite you to the Octobrists). Moscow: Molodaya gvardiya, 1975.

Pust vsegda budet solntse (May There Always be Sunshine). Moscow: Molodaya gvardiya, 1979.

S imenem Lenina (With the name of Lenin). Moscow: Molodaya gvardiya, 1974.

Solntse, more i my (The sun, the sea and us). Moscow: Molodaya gvardiya, 1963.

Sputnik pionerskogo vozhatogo (Companion to the Pioneer Leader). Moscow: TsK Komsomol, 1972.

Zori sovetskogo pionera (Dawn of the Soviet Pioneer). Moscow: Prosveshchenie, 1972.

Komsomol

Dokumenty TsK VLKSM 1968 (Documents of the Komsomol Central Committee). Moscow: Molodaya gvardiya, 1969.

Istoriya VLKSM (History of the Komsomol). 3 vols. Moscow: Molodaya gvardiya, 1967.

Khrestomatiya po istorii KPSS (Reader in the history of the CPSU). 3 vols. Moscow: Gosizdat politicheskoi literatury, 1962.

Leninskii Komsomol (Lenin's Komsomol). Moscow: Molodaya gvardiya, 1969.

My molodye (We Are the Young). Moscow: Molodaya gvardiya, 1971.

Nachalnyi kurs nauchnogo kommunizma (Beginning Course in Scientific Communism). Moscow: Politicheskaya literatura, 1975.

Orlyata (Eaglet). Leningrad: Detskaya literatura, 1972.

Osnovy politicheskikh znanii (Foundations of Political Knowledge). Moscow: Gosizdat politicheskoi literatury, 1962.

Programma shkoly: Osnov Marksizma-Leninizma (School Program: The basis of Marxism-Leninism). Moscow: Politcheskaya literatura, 1975.

Slavnyi put leninskogo komsomola (Glorious Path of Lenin's Komsomol). Moscow: Molodaya gvardiya, 1978.

Slovo o komsomolskom bilete (A Word About the Komsomol Card). Moscow: Znanie, 1978.

Stroitelstvo kommunizma (Building Communism). Moscow: Nauka, 1966.

Tovarishch Komsomol (Comrade Komsomol). 2 vols. Moscow: Molodaya gvardiya, 1969.

Textbooks

Bibliografiya detskoi literatury (Bibliography of Children's Literature). Moscow: Kniga, 1969.

Istoriya SSSR (History of the USSR). 2 vols. Moscow: Prosveshchenie, 1967.

Nasha rodina (Our Motherland). Moscow: Prosveshchenie, 1971.

Rasskasy po istorii SSSR (Stories in the History of the USSR). Moscow: Pros-veshchenie, 1965.
Rodnaya rech (Native Speech). Moscow: Prosveshchenie, 1965.
Rodnoe slovo (Native Speech). Vols. 2-3. Moscow: Prosveshchenie, 1970-71.
Vneklassnoe chtenie (Afterschool Reading). Moscow: Gosudarstvennoe uchebno-pedagogicheskoe izdatelstvo ministerstva prosveshcheniya RSFSR, 1960.
Vospitanie yunykh internatsionalistov (Education of Young Internationalists). Moscow: Prosveshchenie, 1974.
Zvezdochka (Little Star). Moscow: Prosveshchenie, 1971.

Law and Order

Deistvitelno harodhaya. Moscow: Yuridicheskaya literatura, 1977.
Moya militsiya (My Militia). Moscow: Planeta, 1976.
Polozhenie o komissiyakh po delam nesovershennoletnikh

IN ENGLISH

Periodicals

Current Digest of the Soviet Press. Published weekly by the American Associa-tion for the Advancement of Slavic Studies, 1314 Kinnear Road, Ohio State University, Columbus, Ohio 43212. Excellent translations and summaries of articles from the Soviet press covering a wide variety of subjects.
Problems of the Contemporary World. Social Sciences Today editorial board, USSR Academy of Sciences. The October Revolution and the Youth (1978) From the Historical Experience of the Leninist Komsomol (1978) Youth in the Modern Society
Socialism: Theory and Practice. Bi-monthly, 13/5 Podkolokolny pereulok, 109028, Moscow, USSR.
Social Sciences. USSR Academy of Sciences Vol. 9, No. 2, 1978.
Soviet Life. Published by the Embassy of the USSR.
Soviet Woman.
Sputnik. Digest of the Soviet press by the Novosti Press Agency.
Studies in Soviet Thought. D. Reidel Publishing Company, Dordrecht-Holland.

Books

Amalrik, Andrei. *Will the Soviet Union Survive Until 1984?* New York: Harper & Row, 1970.
Brezhnev, Leonid. *Little Land*. Moscow: Novosti Press Agency, 1978.
_____. *Peace, Detente and Soviet American Relations*. New York: Harcourt Brace Jovanovich, 1979.
_____. *Rebirth*. Moscow: Novosti Press Agency, 1978.
_____. *Report of the CPSU Central Committee and the Immediate Tasks of the Party*. Moscow: Novosti Press Agency, 1976.
_____. *Speech at the 18th Congress of the All Union Leninist Young Communist League*. Moscow. Novosti Press Agency, 1978.

_____. *The Virgin Lands*. Moscow: Progress, 1978.

Bronfenbrenner, Urie. *Two Worlds of Childhood*. New York: Russell Sage Foundation, 1970.

Carr, Edward Hallett. *The Bolshevik Revolution*. New York: Macmillan, 1961.

_____. *The Interregnum 1923-1924*. New York: Macmillan, 1954.

_____. *Socialism in One Country*. 4 vols. New York: Macmillan, 1958.

Castro, Fidel. *About Youth*. Havana, Cuba: Organizing Committee of the Eleventh World Festival of Youth and Students, 1978.

Constitution of the Union of Soviet Socialist Republics. Moscow: Novosti Press Agency, 1978.

Current Soviet Policies; Documentary Records of Communist Party Congresses. I: 19th Congress, New York: Praeger, 1953. II: 20th Congress, New York: Praeger, 1957. III: 21st Congress, New York : Columbia University Press, 1960. IV: 22nd Congress, Columbia University Press, 1962. V: 23rd Congress, Columbus, Ohio: American Association for the Advancement of Slavic Studies, 1973. VI: 24th Congress, Columbus, Ohio: AAASS, 1973. VII: 25th Congress, Columbus, Ohio: AAASS, 1976.

Engels, Frederick. *Anti-Duhring*. New York: International, 1972.

Five Goals of U.S. Foreign Policy. Department of State Publication, no. 7432, Washington, D.C.

Florinsky, Michael T. *Russia*. 2 vols. New York: Macmillan, 1961.

Gromyko, Andrei. *On Practical Ways to End the Arms Race*. Moscow: Novosti Press Agency, 1978.

Kapp, Yvonne. *Eleanor Marx*. 2 vols. New York: Pantheon Books, 1976.

Lenin, Vladimir I. *Collected Works*. 44 vols. Moscow: Progress, 1970.

_____. *On Youth*. Moscow: Progress, 1977.

_____. *Youth and the Future*. Moscow: Progress, 1977.

McNeal, Robert H., ed. *Lenin, Stalin, Khrushchev: Voices of Bolshevism*. Englewood Cliffs, N.J.: Prentice-Hall, 1963.

Makarenko, A. S. *The Road to Life*. 3 vols. Moscow: Foreign Languages Publishing House.

Marx, Karl. Collected Works. Progress Publishing.

Medvedev, Roy. *On Soviet Dissent*. New York: Columbia University Press, 1980.

Morton, Miriam. *A Harvest of Russian Children's Literature*. Berkeley: University of California Press, 1967.

Novosti Press Agency Yearbook. 1977-79, yearly.

Philby, Kim. *My Silent War*. New York: Grove Press, 1968.

Programmatic Platform of the Communist Party of Cuba. Havana: Department of Revolutionary Orientation of the Central Committee of the Communist Party of Cuba, 1976.

Rauch, Georg Von. *A History of Soviet Russia*. New York: Praeger, 1957.

Reed, John. *Ten Days That Shook the World*. New York: Vintage Books, 1960.

The Soviet State and Law. Edited by V. M. Chkhikvadze. Moscow: Progress, 1969.

Soviet Union: A Geographical Survey. Moscow: Progress, 1976.

Trotsky, Leon. *The Young Lenin*. Garden City, N.Y.: Doubleday, 1972.

Vernadsky, George. *A History of Russia*. New Haven: Yale University Press.

List of Photographs

Name Index

Subject Index

Acknowledgments

W arm acknowledgment for their help with this book must go to my Soviet friends at the Embassy in Washington and the House of Friendship in Moscow, as well as to Fedulova and her associates in the Young Pioneers. I would also like to thank James Kraft, who introduced me to Praeger Publishers, Patrick Bernuth, publisher of Praeger, Marina Psaltoudis and Susan Yount, project editors, Deborah England, art director, Sharon Gartin, who helped with the final typing of the manuscript, and a special thanks to my editor, Lynda Sharp.

About the Author

KITTY WEAVER lives in Virginia with her husband, Henry Weaver. The Weavers have traveled extensively, including ten trips to the Soviet Union. In addition to an A.B. from William and Mary, an M.A. in English Literature from George Washington University, and a B.S. in Agriculture from the University of Maryland, Mrs. Weaver spent four years in graduate study of Russian Area Studies at Georgetown University, George Washington University, and the University of Pennsylvania. In 1971 Simon and Schuster published Mrs. Weaver's book, LENIN'S GRANDCHILDREN, a study of Soviet pre-school education. That book was also translated into Spanish, Italian, and German for worldwide sales.

HENRY WEAVER is a Washington, D.C., lawyer and freelance photographer who holds degrees from the College of William and Mary (B.A.) and the University of Virginia (LL.B.). In addition to illustrating his wife's books on the Soviet Union, his pictures have appeared in such publications as SMITHSONIAN MAGAZINE, U. S. NEWS AND WORLD REPORT, VIRGINIA SPUR, and NETA Documentary on Ethiopia.